PEOPLE IN CORPORATIONS

Issues in Business Ethics

VOLUME 1

Series Editors:

BRIAN HARVEY

University of Nottingham, U.K.

PATRICIA WERHANE

Loyola University of Chicago, U.S.A.

People in Corporations

Ethical Responsibilities
and Corporate Effectiveness

edited by

GEORGES ENDERLE
University of St. Gallen, Switzerland

BRENDA ALMOND
University of Hull, United Kingdom

and

ANTONIO ARGANDOÑA
University of Navarra, Spain

KLUWER ACADEMIC PUBLISHERS
DORDRECHT / BOSTON / LONDON

in cooperation with
The European Business Ethics Network

Library of Congress Cataloging in Publication Data

```
People in corporations : ethical responsibilities and corporate
  effectivenss / edited by Georges Enderle, Brenda Almond, Antonio
  Argandoña.
      p.   cm. -- (Issues in business ethics ; 1)
  Includes index.
  ISBN 0-7923-0829-8 (alk. paper)
  1. Industry--Social aspects.  2. Business ethics.  3. Industrial
management.   I. Enderle, Georges.   II. Almond, Brenda.
III. Argandoña Rámiz, Antonio.   IV. Series.
HD60.P38   1990
174'.4--dc20                                          90-37771
```

ISBN 0-7923-0829-8

Published by Kluwer Academic Publishers,
P.O. Box 17, 3300 AA Dordrecht, The Netherlands.

Kluwer Academic Publishers incorporates
the publishing programmes of
D. Reidel, Martinus Nijhoff, Dr W. Junk and MTP Press.

Sold and distributed in the U.S.A. and Canada
by Kluwer Academic Publishers,
101 Philip Drive, Norwell, MA 02061, U.S.A.

In all other countries, sold and distributed
by Kluwer Academic Publishers Group,
P.O. Box 322, 3300 AH Dordrecht, The Netherlands.

Printed on acid-free paper

Printed in the Netherlands

CONTENTS

INTRODUCTION

Georges Enderle

Before presenting some introductory remarks on the topic of this volume I should like to outline briefly the context from which this selection of articles originates. (It seems to me necessary to emphasise these circumstances in order to make clearer the contours of what is said *and* what is not said and to understand it better.) This context involves, firstly, a general evaluation of the state of the business ethics debate today and, secondly, considerations of the question of what attitude and strategy should be chosen in order to promote business ethics most effectively.

On the present state of affairs of the business ethics debate

Today, it is extremely difficult, if not impossible, to gain even a rough overview of the business ethics debate in the different countries of Europe and North America. Many activities take place in informal circles and on a local and regional level; linguistic and other barriers impede the spread of information about them and, often, they are not even labelled "business ethics". At the same time, so many other things sail under the flag of "business ethics" that one sometimes wonders if it should not be replaced by another flag, for instance new methods of public-relations or better motivation of company's employees. Yet, in spite of these difficulties in defining business ethics activities, one statement at least can be made with certainty. For the present there is *an enormous plurality and heterogeneity* of approaches, dogmas, theses and results in the field of business ethics. In my opinion, this situation is linked to the ambitious expectation that a serious and comprehensive business ethics should take account of two fields of tensions.

First of all, *business ethics as an interdisciplinary, academic approach involving both "ethics" and "economics"* requires sufficient knowledge in the disciplines concerned: specifically, in economics and business administration, and in philosophical and theological ethics. And yet there is not even a minimal consensus in the respective scientific communities on the status, methods and contents of their disciplines. Rather, even within them, there are deep-rooted differences and contrary positions. Therefore, those who want to do business ethics, must choose among different theoretical approaches and must justify their choice. The situation is even more complex, if, in addition, one tackles the interdisciplinary problems themselves. How is one to determine the relationship between economics and business administration? How are the links between philosophical and theological ethics to be conceived? How is one to understand the relation between economic and ethical theory? After 200 years of advance in the division of labour in academia, we have now arrived at a point where we should reconsider this division of scientific labour fundamentally and try to invent new ways of co-operation. These difficulties and challenges affect business ethics particularly, because it has to deal with both positive and normative aspects.

The second field of tensions in business ethics is *the relationship between theory and practice*. If business ethics could remain a merely theoretical, scientific matter, it could comfortably install itself in the famous ivory tower and take all the time needed for basic research work. Later on, if at all, it could also turn to practical problems. Yet, in my opinion, business ethics must not apply such an ivory tower policy, for two main reasons. First, today we are faced - on a national and international level - with fundamental and extremely complex and urgent problems of economic and ethical relevance, the tackling of which will fundamentally determine the way in which human beings will live together in the twenty-first century. For this reason, the ethos of responsibility demands that business ethics resolutely faces these practical challenges and assists in their solutions.

Secondly, the analysis and solution of these problems cannot consist in academics alone devising blueprint solutions to be executed by practitioners. Apart from the fact that such a request would be entirely impractical, the competences of the practitioners would not be taken seriously and would be wasted in a way that would make true and sustainable solutions impossible. Admittedly, just as amongst academics, so there are amongst practitioners very different and contrary opinions: some expect business ethics to provide detailed advice for their day-to-day decision-making: others would like it to provide very general and broad perspectives on the world, mankind and God. Here again there exists a plurality and heterogeneity of opposing views.

Considering all the difficulties with these two aspects of business ethics, it might seem unlikely that, within the present century, we will find any kind of systematic approach or synthesis in business ethics. (Without doubt, a genius able to overcome this prevailing heterogeneity is not in sight.) Hence the evaluation of the present state of affairs in business ethics made by Oswald von Nell-Breuning, the 100-years-old German scholar of Catholic social teaching, may make us sober, but also confident. A few years ago, he wrote that, when he was young, meetings and co-operation of economists, philosophers and theologians were entirely unthinkable, let alone any institutionalisation of business ethics; that, now in the eighties, it does happen; but that we will have to work hard to ensure that the next generation at least, at the beginning of the twenty-first century, will see a more or less clear and systematic profile of business ethics.

EBEN faced with the heterogeneity in the present debate on business ethics

It seems to me of paramount importance to be fully aware of these difficulties arising from the heterogeneity of standpoints and the long-term context. For, without this awareness, the goals and tasks of business ethics cannot be discerned realistically and also the purpose of the *European Business Ethics Network* (EBEN) cannot be understood. It is the *raison d'être* of EBEN - and of the worldwide *International Society of Business, Economics and Ethics* (ISBEE), which is in the making - to promote debate and the exchange of experiences and insights in the field of business ethics and to take the double field of tensions between the various disciplines and between theory and practice as far as possible into account. Admittedly, this purpose is very ambitious and demanding, and the danger exists that we may fall between all stools - between ethics and economics, theory and practice, and so on.

Nevertheless the experience of recent years has brought some important guiding principles for EBEN's self-understanding which can be summarised as follows:

1. *Not defeatism, but commitment to the promotion of business ethics on the European level:* In view of the above difficulties in the debate on business ethics one could be tempted to give up the project before it has even properly started and abandon it in resignation. However, such an attitude does not eliminate the numerous urgent problems of business ethics today, but only suppresses them so that, sooner or later, they will come back in even more complex and threatening forms. Furthermore, such a defeatist attitude would be incompatible with the ethos of responsibility of academics and practitioners who want to render service to society.
2. *Recognition of the equal importance of the diverse competences of practitioners and academics:* From EBEN's perspective, the challenges for business ethics at the end of the twentieth century are so demanding that we cannot do without the competences of either group. Moreover, the dialogue in business ethics requires that both partners are recognised as essential and treated as equals. Therefore, no discipline - ethics included - and no group of practitioners is allowed to claim a superior position.
3. *Recognition of a plurality of views of ethics:* Because value conflicts, today, are very deep-rooted and no existing view of ethics is able to create a new consensus, we must accept a plurality of views of ethics. However, this does not mean that ethics should content itself with any arbitrary answers. On the contrary, pluralism demands the kind of ethical discussion that does not consist in simply advancing postulates and requirements, but that needs careful arguing. If we enter into this demanding business ethics dialogue, the plurality of views of ethics can become a chance for a solid intercultural foundation for business.

A "problem-oriented" approach in business ethics

Important as the three guiding principles are, they do not suffice to indicate a promising and practical way out of the difficulties mentioned above. Therefore, I would like to plead for *a "problem-oriented" approach in business ethics,* which has already been advocated by various writers and has essentially influenced this volume too.

The problem-oriented approach is based on the conviction that it is practice, combined with "refractory" experiences and controversial ethical judgements that should provide the "agenda" for business ethics. Examples are the complex of technological innovations, ecological corporate management, problems of poverty, the international debt crisis, and also the main topics of the EBEN-Conferences "People in Corporations" (1989 in Barcelona) and "Business Ethics and Company Size" (Milan, 1990).

The problem-oriented approach assumes a preconception of the "problem", which, *in a first phenomenological analysis,* contains in embryonic form all its essential aspects, and for the choice of which good reasons or at least plausible arguments can be given. Hence it is, for example, not enough for the understanding of innovations to see only their technical-organisational, economic, political and societal dimensions and to take no account of the ethical dimension until the phase of problem-*solving.* On the contrary, it is necessary to embrace *all* dimensions of the problem - the ethical one included - in the phases of its *preconception* and *analysis,* and to treat them *on equal grounds.*

Because the problem-oriented approach takes the complexity of practice into consideration, it demands, as a second step, *a serious theoretical and interdisciplinary analysis* of the problem. Multifarious aspects, contradictions and conflicts should not be harmonised precipitately from the standpoint of a pre-established theory. In this phase, the elaboration of the ethical dimension means both the *descriptive* elucidation and the *normative* discussion. Both presuppose that human decision-making and acting are not just value-neutral functioning or crude overt behaviour because and inasmuch as they are interpreted as subject to ethical responsibility. Descriptive ethics makes explicit the values and norms which, in fact, guide our decision-making and actions, whereas normative ethics deals with the complex questions of "determining and justifying what is right".

Finally, interdisciplinary problem-analysis again refers to practice. Because the agents in business are unavoidably exposed to the pressure of being forced to act, business ethics should not content itself with the analytical task but *should elaborate guiding perspectives for decision-making and acting and make a valuable contribution to solving crucial problems*.

As this outline of the problem-oriented approach in business ethics shows, all three steps are essential. Of course, the outlined *linear* procedure is intrinsically connected with *circular* movements which must also be taken into consideration. Without doubt, the project of business ethics is extraordinarily demanding in both practical and theoretical respects. Nevertheless the chances of its realisation are, to my mind, significantly higher than an approach that primarily engages in pure basic research, the results of which have to be "applied" to concrete problems afterwards.

Briefly, then, I should like to point to *three presuppositions* of the problem-oriented approach and simultaneously discuss *three common objections to business ethics*.

The first presupposition is that ethics as reason-guided and methodological reflection on morals and ethos (Hermann Krings) *can be approached scientifically*. So the basic assumption holds that reason-guided and methodological arguing about the goals of human action is possible. Yet one cannot deny that this scientific endeavour can involve extremely difficult problems which cannot be solved once and for all. However, among economists, this basic assumption is widely rejected and it is this, in my opinion, that constitutes a main reason for resistance to business ethics in universities.

The second presupposition is that ethics as reason-guided and methodological reflection on morals and ethos *can be relevant to practice*. This thesis is rejected by those who maintain a strict dichotomy between theory and practice and, consequently, postulate the irrelevance of theory to practice. In contrast to this, I think that such a dichotomy renders a problem-oriented business ethics impossible and has to be rejected because, in the long run, it is detrimental to both the theory and practice.

And *the third presupposition: the need for team-work in business ethics*. From the characterisation outlined above, it becomes clear that the problem-oriented approach is extremely demanding and beyond the competence of a single person, either academic or practitioner. The complexity of the problems to be solved requires a multitude of competences that can only be co-ordinated and productive in team-work.

On "People in Corporations"

Having outlined the wider context of this volume, I should like to make some introductory remarks on its contents. It grew out of the *Second European Conference on Business Ethics held on 27th to 29th September 1989 in Barcelona and hosted by the Instituto de Estudios Superiores de la Empresa (IESE)*. It contains the contributions to its main topic "People in Corporations: Ethical Responsibilities and Corporate Effectiveness" that were presented in plenary sessions, in a roundtable discussion and in workshops. (Numerous other contributions to the conference are not included in this volume because they treat other topics.) With this selection of articles, an attempt is made to realise a kind of "problem-oriented business ethics" by structuring the topic in four parts and approaching it from the perspectives of both practitioners and academics. (Of course, it must be admitted that this selection constitutes only a loose ensemble that, in addition, includes only some aspects of this topic, some more relevant than others.) Moreover, the reader will soon notice that the current heterogeneity of approaches and the plurality of business ethics conceptions mentioned above are also reflected in this volume.

The main theme "People in Corporations" is fairly concrete. We do not need a long introduction to show that in this field we are faced with a number of ethical problems. At stake, on the one hand, are *people* - that means creatures of flesh and blood, men and women, managers and subordinates, a multifarious richness of competences generating highly complex problems, individuals with human dignity and consciences of differing degrees of sensitivity - and, on the other hand, *corporations, companies,* economic organisations with a plurality of independent activities, entities with traditions and structures that must yield profit, defend and enlarge their positions in the market, and face numerous challenges in society.

This complex of problems is to be explored from the economic as well as the ethical point of view. Ethical responsibilities can concern the individual, the corporation as a whole, or society in general, and they may be related to corporate effectiveness very differently: by a loose juxtaposition, as an exclusive alternative, as an end-means-relationship in either sense, or as a critical and co-operative "joint-venture". Considering these relationships, it is of paramount importance to be fully conscious of whether we are looking at them from a descriptive-ethical or a normative-ethical perspective.

Part I "Personal Convictions and Corporate Claims: Ethical Conflicts and Solutions" focuses on the corporation as a goal-oriented, productive entity composed of human beings. Only if we take seriously this entity with its various aspects and partially deep-rooted tensions and conflicts, is there any chance at all to find, on a realistic base, convincing and sustainable solutions. The first two contributions are presented by two top managers, one of a private and one of a state-owned company, *Wisse Dekker* and *François Ailleret*. They make clear - the first in more general terms and the second by means of actual decision-making cases - the indispensable and increasing importance of ethical reflection in corporate practice. *Richard T. De George* confirms this from the philosopher's point of view and emphasises that business ethics should deal not only but, of course, also with questions of "doing what is right" and "motivating others to do so as well". Rather, at stake today in business, are many complex and delicate questions to do with "determining what is right". They require serious ethical research and analysis - particularly in the three following areas: the resolution of true ethical dilemmas faced by individuals and corporations; the development of ethical guidelines for firms that operate in an ethically corrupt environment; and the establishment of criteria to make up for the absence of restraining background institutions at the international level of business.

The other five contributions in Part I treat various aspects of its theme from the point of view of business administration, economics and philosophy. *Jonathan L. Gorman* shows that, under certain theoretical presuppositions (of neo-classical economics and desire-independent ethical values), "ethical responsibilities" and "corporate effectiveness" are not compatible. For *Juan Cruz Cruz*, it is crucial to conceive the corporation as an "open organisation", if it is to be understood as an organisation of human beings and as accessible to ethical reflection. *Raymond A. Konopka,* too, investigates conceptual questions and elaborates criteria for management control systems that do not hinder but promote the innovation of organisations, and simultaneously help to develop the intellectual and moral virtues of employees. A further, not less important aspect of corporate management - interpersonal trust - is discussed by *Patrick Maclagan* who proposes an analytical framework in order to reconcile competing moral claims - respect for the individual and utility for the corporation - on the judgement of those in corporations who have to decide whether or not to trust others. Finally, *John Donaldson* and *John Sheldrake* recall the fact that private and state-owned companies - like individuals - are subject to many external constraints and consequently limited in their capacity for ethical decision-making. Nevertheless they argue that personal and organisational autonomy continue to be of paramount importance and carry with them the burden of acting responsibly.

Part II "'Empowering' People: End or Means?" directs attention to the people who operate in corporations and asks for more personal autonomy and responsibility for individuals in companies. This pertinent and challenging issue is a heritage of the Enlightenment, in particular of the philosopher Immanuel Kant, and assumes its modern expression in the Universal Declaration of Human Rights. The present literature on management frequently talks of "empowering people". What does that mean? To take the employees as human subjects seriously and to give them more autonomy and responsibility, in spite of the risk that this policy will not necessarily operate in favour of the company? Or to apply this policy as a mere means, *i. e.* ultimately to instrumentalise the employees, in order to achieve more corporate effectiveness? Or is there a third possibility?

Philippe de Woot makes unmistakably clear that the corporations in their specific function of economic and technical creativity are faced with deep ethical challenges that essentially concern also the development and responsibility of the individual in the firm. *Francisco López Frías* and *Domènec Melé* explore conceptual questions: the relevance of authentic individuality (not of egotistical individualism) as a necessary condition for the integration of individuals into the corporation, and the relevance of the "image" of the corporation as an organisation that can promote the human development of its employees, but can also render it more difficult or even impossible. The next two contributions treat a question which is central for all people in corporations, *i. e.* the question of meaningful work, from different standpoints. On the one hand, *Norman E. Bowie* argues that the primary purpose of business is to provide meaningful work for employees and that if managers focus on this goal, business will produce quality goods and services for consumers, and also profits as beneficial by-products. On the other hand, *Joanne B. Ciulla* argues that the corporation cannot, properly speaking, provide meaningful work, but that it needs to take the moral view that people have a right to seek meaning in their lives and hence to provide workers with a workplace that makes this quest possible. The topic of work, more precisely of labour contracts, is also approached by *Antonio Argandoña*, this time from an economic (*i. e.* neoclassical) point of view. He concludes that, taking for granted the morality of the market economy and its institutions - including implicit labour contracts - ethical problems reappear in every specific situation, although the solutions in terms of efficiency may be ethical on average or in the aggregate.

If one takes the individual dimension of the corporation seriously, one also has to take into account the possibility of corporate whistle-blowing, *i. e.* accusations by corporate insiders that the firm has committed breaches of ethical or legal obligations. *Thomas W. Dunfee* distinguishes between internal and external whistle-blowing and, in spite of the traditional corporate resistance to both, encourages internal whistle-blowing. What can happen when individuals do not assume their responsibilities is illustrated by the case study of *Colin Boyd* on "The Zeebrugge Car Ferry Disaster" where the British vessel *Herald of Free Enterprise* sank with the loss of 188 lives. A number of important ethical issues arising from the disaster are outlined, especially in relation to the roles and responsibilities of boards of directors. This finding of the Report of the Court of Investigation is also referred to in Part IV on "The Ethical Role of Top Managers".

Part III "Men and Women in Corporations: Repression, Competition or Co-operation?" continues and concretises the theme "People in Corporations". Without doubt, today this is a subject of great importance and high priority and it should be a main topic of business ethics from both a practical and a theoretical perspective.

After some introductory remarks by *Georges Enderle*, *Brenda Almond* raises the basic question whether there exist both a male and a female ethics. She answers it in the affirmative and indicates some female ethical perspectives which are of great relevance for the modern corporation. *José Aguilá's* contribution starts by analysing major gender problems and attitudes in the Spanish context. For decisive change in the present situation he puts much hope in demographic evolution. It should, he argues, be supported and continued by corporate ethical policy and practice which, in contrast to Brenda Almond's standpoint, he takes as based on a gender-neutral anthropology. *Monique R. Siegel* takes up the policy orientation and asks more concretely how to include women in corporate decision-making. For this purpose she makes a wide range of practical suggestions concerning the personal, corporate and societal level of action.

So far the positions and tasks of people, of women and men, in corporations have been explored generally. Now, *Part IV* concentrates on one particular, important group and considers *"The Ethical Role of Top Managers"*. Based on her experiences as a top manager *Sara Morrison* pleads for authority without unacceptable, indeed unworkable, authoritarianism. Considering the ethics of operating inside a company, she argues that top management has the duty to lead, first, in the support of managers who carry the prime operational responsibility for the company's reputation and, secondly, in the company's treatment of its employees in the businesses and places in which it requires them to work. *Juan A. Pérez López* analyses the logical structure of ethical decision-making, *i. e.* of those decisions made to achieve a final purpose, and argues that it is not identical with any other kind of decisions made to achieve specific purposes. He answers the question of the decision-maker "Why be ethical?" by saying: "Just in order to learn how to develop really satisfying relations with other people. Being ethical means learning to evaluate persons as persons." Unlike these formal, decision-theoretical considerations, *Miquel Bastons* focuses on the question of the contents of corporate goals. He shows that neither the game-theoretical approach nor management techniques can answer this question and that, therefore, the business manager as a leader and "creator of goals" needs ethical reflection and ethical arguments. *Ceferí Soler* discusses the relevance of values and ethics for decision-making processes and the organisational culture of the corporation and points to the fact that the values of the decision-maker may conflict with the values of the organisations. This is a theme that was also touched upon in Part I. After these conceptual considerations, *Erwin Fröhlich* reports on a comprehensive empirical study on small business in eight European countries that put considerable emphasis on the values of entrepreneurs. These were translated into concrete business objectives and strategies, and ethical principles in management such as, for example, loyalty - for many, perhaps surprisingly - turned out to correlate positively with success in performance. A second empirical study carried out by *John H. Barnett* and *Marvin J. Karson* examines the decision-making of 513 executives in situations involving ethics, relationships and results. On the basis of decisions in ten scenarios, they analyse personal values, organisation role and level, career stage, gender and sex role; and they produce conclusions about the role of gender, subjective values, and other variables.

At the end of the volume, three statements give an *outlook* on the business ethics debate. *Jack Mahoney* explores some fundamental ethical aspects of the corporation and argues that the spheres and also the limits of ethical responsibility should be taken clearly into consideration.*Vicente Mortes Alfonso* as a professional manager offers some philosophical reflections on the foundations of ethics and points to the ethical challenge of the present European situation. In his contribution *Mario Unnia* illustrates by the example of Italy how much business ethics is shaped by the cultural context and how many initiatives have been recently developed in his country.

This short overview explains the various aspects of this volume sequentially. But readers who prefer to consider matters in a different order, can do so with the help of the subject index.

Part I

Personal Convictions
and Corporate Claims:
Ethical Conflicts and Solutions

THE RESPONSIBLE CORPORATION AND THE SUBVERSIVE SIDE OF ETHICS

Wisse Dekker

In recent years the business climate in the Netherlands and other European countries has changed considerably - and I must add, this has often been a change for the better. In the sixties and seventies large companies may have been considered nothing more than wolves in sheep's clothing, but today they are regarded more as the motor of prosperity and the outside world has high expectations of them - sometimes even too high.

We notice that the interrelationship of private enterprise and society has changed, but you may ask whether companies now operate more according to the norms and values of society or whether society itself has changed and has different and more realistic expectations of private enterprise.

You won't be expecting a heavy theoretical moral treatment from me - and you certainly won't get it. But I would like to make a few personal comments about corporate responsibilities and business ethics based on practical experience, which I think might interest you.

In making these comments I will discuss in particular the special ethical problems facing companies which operate on an international level. Also I will deal with a central issue within ethics, namely to what extent ethical principles are applicable in actual situations. From time to time I shall use concrete practical examples as an illustration.

The good citizen in a multiform society

An important aspect of the company/society relationship is that of *social dynamics* and *multiformity*. Industrial companies and society today are currently undergoing a process of rapid change.

The changes in society are to a considerable extent socio-cultural changes, such as the emancipation of women and underprivileged groups, increasing individualism, a change in the employment situation and a more "holistic" or integrated approach to the world. These developments affect the relationship between industry and society considerably. Now, society is also characterised by increasing multiformity. This often means that there is a lack of consensus on the aims of society, on the problems in society or on the best strategies for solving them. Multiformity in society means that companies are viewed from various angles and that their activities are judged according to different criteria. The different demands which are made on companies are not always consistent. The changeability of society also means that over time the yardstick used to measure them is not always the same.

In addition to the inconsistency and changeability of demands and expectations made by society on companies, there is often also a contradiction between the aim and the means, in the sense that people want to reap the benefits of industry - the goods and services that it supplies - but are not prepared to pay the price for them. Thus some groups whose aim it is to improve the environment adopt the slogan "those who pollute should pay", without accepting that if industry were to make its production processes cleaner, this additional cost would have to be passed on to the customer in the price of the finished product.

In this sometimes inconsistent and unstable field of social demands and expectations the industrialist nevertheless has to act as a "good citizen" and to realise his company's aims.

In addition to the change in standards and values, the multinational company is also confronted with the fact that standards and values can vary greatly in different countries. Was it not the philosopher Montaigne who said that what is good and true on one side of the Pyrenees is evil and untrue on the other side?

Different standards and values often pose major problems for the multinational company. On the one hand many company executives uphold the idea that one should behave as a "good citizen" in the host country and respect the standards and laws in force there, but on the other hand, they have grown up with a set of standards and values which it is not easy to disregard. But can we and should we simply transfer a social policy which works in the Netherlands to a Third World country? Or would this be "moral imperialism", raising our own standards to the status of a world standard? With our employee promotion policy in India, for example, should we disregard the caste system? Should a company transfer an employee even if this would adversely affect his or her social relationships? There are numerous dilemmas here to which there is no simple answer.

Recognition of the great diversity in standards and values should not make us blind to the transcultural values which also exist, such as those which are laid down in the Declaration of Human Rights. Here, however, we must realise that there are numerous countries that have not signed this "universal" declaration or are not really in a position to put it into practice. In this context it is perhaps worthwhile remembering that in the Netherlands too the basic social rights were first included in Dutch law with the revision of the Constitution in 1983 and that we are still not able to implement various parts of it fully, for example the right to work. For the time being civil rights will remain a Utopian prospect. Nevertheless, they form a basis for the government's obligations to the public and guide companies in their efforts to act responsibly.

The corporate aim

What is the aim of the company? The statement made in the United States by the economist Milton Friedman, that the only social responsibility of a company is to create maximum profit for its shareholders, is mostly considered to be too limited in Europe (and also in the United States outside the Chicago School of Friedman).

We see the principal task of the company as providing goods and services which society wants, whilst at the same time taking into account the social priorities. A company has to make profit in order to ensure that it will be able to create wealth in the longer term. The profit made allows the company to attract new capital and to finance extra research activities or acquisitions, for example.

According to this reasoning, profit is rather more a means to an end than an end in itself. Furthermore, when a company makes a profit, this is a good indication that its products are meeting a real need in society. Critics of the marketing methods of large companies will claim here that the company is fulfilling "false" needs which it has created itself. I do not agree with this. Although there can sometimes be a demand which has clearly been initiated and which until that point in time had only been latent, this does not mean that a company can in general manipulate consumer demand for its own profits.

Towards new social priorities

The early medieval Christian philosopher Thomas Aquinas said: "There is only hope for virtue once hunger has been satisfied". Accordingly, in our current society where the basic living requirements are satisfied, it is to be expected that other issues will be given a higher priority. This gives rise to new problems - of a different type, but nevertheless often just as pressing. As I mentioned before, it is not always clear what is considered a problem in a multiform society. For one group it will be social isolation, alienation at work and anonymity among the masses; another group may consider the main problems to be falling economic growth, the rise in crime or the threat from the East. Obviously, the question of what responsible corporate behaviour is will be answered differently by different groups.

Nevertheless, I will try to define what responsible corporate behaviour is. In our opinion acting responsibly means acting in accordance with the letter and spirit of the law or social standard. This can mean that the norms adopted by companies can be ahead of the standards in society. This can be problematic if the company operates in areas where different standards apply.

For example, should a company adhere to strict environmental standards in countries where environmental concern is not a main priority, but income, foreign currency or employment is? Should it transfer the generally accepted norms of the Netherlands to African countries? Time and time again the company has to choose between various systems of norms or between different interest groups. In our opinion, acting responsibly in business means weighing up the short-term interests against the long-term interest, the interests of those directly involved as well as of those indirectly involved. In order to weigh up these interests there must be an open dialogue, in which the company's own objectives are also put forward as necessary preconditions for maintaining the company's ability to create wealth and to manufacture products.

Responsible entrepreneurship involves constantly seeking a new way to optimise the balance between the company's objectives and potential and the different social aims which, as we have already stated, are sometimes conflicting and inconsistent. The responsible company should try to be responsive to the new social priorities.

A definition of business ethics

I would now like to make some comments about what ethics is and in particular about what is currently often referred to as "business ethics".

I shall start by saying that in my opinion the criteria "ethical" or "unethical" are not applicable to much of our daily activities. The same is true for the terms "moral" and "immoral". I believe there is a large, neutral amoral or non-ethical middle area in daily life.

Here there are a host of practical values and social conventions which do apply, but I would not call this ethical behaviour. Whether I go to work by bicycle or by car is purely a private matter and it is a practical standard that makes me drive on the right-hand side of the road. However, whether I try to make up the time I have wasted in getting up too late by driving at 100 km through a built-up area is of course an ethical decision.

I should like to reserve the terms "ethical" and "moral" for behaviour which involves an important moral or ethical standard or where a considerable interest of another is at stake. Of course it is not always easy to make a distinction between what is non-ethical and what is ethical or unethical. We must always be careful not to allot certain issues too easily into the non-ethical category. Proof of a mature and ethical consciousness is in my opinion shown by the ability to make this distinction clearly. Exchange of ideas with others can help to develop this ethical consciousness - I will return to this later.

Ethical behaviour not only involves making a choice between good and evil, but (perhaps more often) between two in themselves desirable values. However, there is no absolute, universal hierarchy of values. Some values are instrumental or preconditional for the creation of other values. Thus we can say that "freedom" or "democracy" are higher values than "food", nevertheless we will first have to eat before we can call for freedom. Bertolt Brecht put this in a nutshell: "Erst kommt das Fressen, dann die Moral" (First food, then morality). This often means the company is faced with a dilemma or is put in the less attractive situation of having to realize the "lower" value.

A closer look at business ethics

An important point of discussion in companies (but I can assure you certainly not only there) is why one should allow one's behaviour to be influenced at all by ethical considerations. I believe that we can distinguish different *levels of motivations* for ethical behaviour:

On the lowest level, people behave "ethically" because they are obliged to by law, because it avoids punishment or because they derive direct benefit from behaving in this way. On the second level, people are motivated to behave in a certain manner by the expectations of others and because by behaving in this way they fulfil social obligations and contribute to the preservation of the social system they are part of. On the third and highest level, people accept that there are ethical principles which must be obeyed for their own sake, irrespective of advantages or disadvantages. These ethical principles are considered to be self-evident or obvious.

A consequent and important point of discussion is whether it is meaningful to refer to *"business ethics"* as a special part of ethics.

According to some students, ethics relates to the individual and by referring to "business ethics" we run the risk of individuals within an organisation shifting responsibility for their actions onto the organisation. Although I believe that ultimately there are the individuals who are ethically responsible, I do believe that it can be useful to refer to "business ethics" as a separate category. The company does after all have an impact on society which individuals do not have and it therefore also has a responsibility all of its own. In addition to this, social demands are often made on the company which are not made on individuals (for example, in connection with employment, discrimination, investment).

I would describe business ethics as that part of ethics which involves the evaluation of the ethical consequences of a company's activities. Various aspects of business behaviour can be examined, for example, product safety and manufacturer's liability.

Here the question arises not only of whether it is ethical to make a given product, such as defence equipment, but also of whether as a producer you are responsible for abuse of the product (for example, if someone uses a hammer to hit someone else on the head) or for unintended side-effects. (Is a television manufacturer responsible for child aggression as a result of violent films seen on TV, for example?)

Another aspect of business ethics is the way a company treats its own employees. Do they receive a fair salary? Are their dignity and integrity respected? Even behaviour towards suppliers and customers can be evaluated on its ethical merits. Have there been honest negotiations or has pressure been used or bribes paid? Was the information given to the customer true and were no false expectations aroused? A completely different question is whether there has been damage to the environment which could have been avoided.

These are some example of situations in which the company has a responsibility and in which it is worthwhile questioning the ethical aspects.

It is not possible to draw up an exhaustive list of values which should govern business behaviour in all situations. Nevertheless, I shall venture to mention a number of values which should guide the company, both internally and externally.

1. A first value is that of truthfulness - the provision of incorrect or misleading information is fundamentally wrong.
2. A second value is that of reliability - agreements made have to be adhered to; you must do what you have promised or what can reasonably be expected of you.
3. Justice is a third value and I include here also treating another fairly, granting the other party things to which he has a right.
4. Willingness to prevent abuse of power is another value.
5. A fifth value is rectification, the obligation to put right any injustice and to repair or compensate for any damage caused.
6. I view solidarity as a sixth value - this concerns the use of the potential of the organisation to the benefit of society at large.
7. The last value I shall mention is that of respect for the integrity of others.

I am not claiming that these values are always applied to the full. They do however form a guideline for activities and are a reference framework which we can use to assess our own actions and those of others.

The use of codes of conduct

In some companies the values which ought to control the activities of the company have been laid down in *"codes of conduct"*. A study carried out by the Advisory Board in the United States has shown that three-quarters of large companies have a company code of conduct. A variety of reasons are given for drawing up a code of this kind.

First af all, by drawing up a code of conduct the company is seeking to win the trust of the public. For some categories of activities, such as in management consultancy, it is often vital that such a code be drawn up.

Codes are also drawn up to prevent the incorrect behaviour of employees or to lay down standards with regard to new issues, such as the use of drugs or privacy. Another reason given for drawing up a code of conduct is that it can help reinforce the corporate culture. Finally, the personal interest of the president is often of great importance. This does not however mean that a code of conduct can function if it is not supported by the majority of the company employees.

An important function of the code of conduct in my opinion is that the employees in an organisation - and other interested parties as well - can hold each other responsible on the basis of the code. Sometimes the outside world will also be able to benefit by pointing to the code of conduct, although this is not legally binding. I have mentioned that many American companies have a code of conduct. I think that sometimes the external legal liability of companies is also a factor in this. The management distances itself beforehand from any reprehensible behaviour of the employees.

At Philips we have no explicit code of conduct, although in 1975 a number of basic principles regarding the aims and the functioning of Philips were formulated in a document entitled "Some fundamental principles of company policy". These however are less extensive and less detailed than many American codes of conduct. Although the basic principles do not directly prescribe how one should behave in a given situation, the individual manager, who in theory has the freedom and responsibility to act as he thinks fit, can derive some guidance from these.

The relativity of responsibility

I should like to make two final comments about the *relativity* of norms and values and about how far the responsibility of the company extends. The relativity of standards not only relates to the fact that standards vary according to the culture and period, but also to the practical experience that a given standard cannot be absolute and sometimes has to be made subordinate to another standard which is more important at that moment. Should a doctor tell the truth to a patient even if this would adversely affect the healing process? Is it fair to pay bribes in order to win an order and thus to secure employment?

Often a breach of a norm is justified because it permits a higher value to be secured. For example, killing out of self-defence. Sometimes it is said that a standard should not be disgregarded for your own benefit, but if necessary it can be disregarded for the common good. However, we must be careful here: unselfish but overzealous civil servants or employees can do a lot of harm ...

Nevertheless, the question here is whether all possible alternatives were examined adequately, whether this situation in which a choice had to be made could have been prevented and whether a lesser measure would not have sufficed. To me, acting responsibly means choosing the correct alternative.

Responsibility is always limited by the restricted possibilities of the person or company in question. A person acts responsibly if he or she acts according to the best of his or her knowledge and ability. In a dynamic environment with political revolutions and technological changes there is much uncertainty about the effects of their acts. Entrepreneurship involves always acting on incomplete knowledge and this influences the responsibility of the entrepreneur. It also makes things more difficult for the responsive entrepreneur.

A subversive ethic?

So far I have made some remarks about the responsible corporation, but what about the "subversive side of ethics" I mentioned in the title of my introduction? In fact, using the term "subversive" in connection with ethics was not my idea. It was the famous American economist Friedman who spoke about the subversive effect of corporate ethics on free society. In his opinion, the business of business is only business. The main and only objective of business should be to make a profit for the shareholders. The market decides *where* a profit can be made, the law dictates *how* it can be made.

From what I told you before you may have gathered that I do not fully agree with Mr. Friedman. I agree with him that the first task of the industrial corporation is to make products and services and to generate a profit. To me, however, this profit is not so much an aim in itself as a necessary condition for the continuation of the corporation. In our socio-economic system the perpetuation of the productive potential of the corporation is a value in itself. It is the responsibility of the management and those involved in the enterprise to sustain this potential. To use the resources of the enterprise so that it would run great risks would be irresponsible - but this does not mean that profit maximization is the only objective.

I agree with Mr. Friedman that the corporation has to function within the limits set by law. And indeed the increasing network of social and economic regulations has changed what was originally an autonomous responsibility into a legal obligation - think of the employment of children or the limitation of working hours. However, there is still a large area in which the entrepreneur is free to set his aims, to choose his strategy and to develop his tactics in order to realise this strategy. If this were not so, there would be no entrepreneurship but a bureaucratic production system.

In fact, in my opinion, entrepreneurs should assume their responsibilities and look further than profit maximization in order to prevent the political and legal system deeming it necessary to regulate everything in detail. Thus, taking a broad responsibility and acting on high ethical standards is not against our system of a free society - on the contrary, it is a prerequisite for its survival. If an enterprise were to confine itself to strictly following the rules, more rules would be made and in the end our free society would turn into a totalitarian bureaucracy.

Free enterprise and ethics belong together, it is as simple as that. But this does not mean that ethics is always very simple, that it does not cause problems for the entrepreneur. The entrepreneur has to make compromises, to make the best choice between various norms and values. Operating internationally, he or she is confronted with various value systems, as I have already mentioned. It is not only legal systems but also severe competition which limits a company's freedom to act.

Let me say a few more words about ethics and competition.

Ethics, competition and the perverse domino argument

A complaint often heard is that limits are set to ethical behaviour by the unethical behaviour of the bad guys outside. "We have to pay bribes, because the others do the same", "I don't like to cheat my superior and present him with inflated sales figures, but if I do not, my colleague - the imposter - will get the job", "How can I be open and honest to the trade unions if they will use the information against me"... etc., etc. You can easily find more of these arguments.

To me, they always sound somewhat cynical. In social research carried out in the United States among a few hundred managers, this attitude was shown to be widespread. The majority of the managers thought that their colleagues were not as scrupulous as they ought to be and were at least less ethical than themselves. This is a sad but important sociological fact, that lies at the base of what I call the *"perverse domino argument"* and the *"ethics degeneration law"*. Let me illustrate what I mean by this.

First the "perverse domino argument". One has a great proficiency to justify one's actions or to rationalize them and to belittle or negate immoral aspects of this behaviour.

The "perverse domino argument" goes as follows:

1. "It is not true what you say", "we would never do such things".
2. "Well, we have done it now and then, but not as much as our competitors",

"moreover it is not that bad", "it is not against the law, is it?", "we pay for the damage if it comes out".

3.   "You know, these things are quite common practice in our business", "such is life and please be realistic, old chap".

The "ethics degeneration law" is an analogy of the well known law of Gresham which states that bad money drives good money out of circulation. In the same way there is a risk that bad entrepreneurs with bad practices will drive away the honest entrepreneurs. I think this is a real problem, and I do not yet have an answer to it, but it should be discussed in depth in business ethics.

Toward the ethical corporation

There has been much criticism of the ethical practices of corporations - sometimes this was wrong, but sometimes it was justified. Perhaps some of you will say there is nothing new under the sun, but this is an answer that wouldn't satisfy me. I think that corporations should - and can! - live up to the highest ethical standards. There may still be a long way to go, but we should continue on our way.

A first step toward improving the ethical norms is to discuss with business people what ethics is all about. As the psychologist Kohlberg has shown, the level of morality in the organisation can be increased by debating about what is to be considered as egocentric, what as social and what as ethical behaviour.

Interest in business ethics in nowadays increasing, but there is still a lack of understanding of the complexity and the working of ethical principles. There should be a greater consensus about what is ethical and what is not. The formulation of a code of conduct can be instrumental in achieving a consensus. In fact, a code of conduct has several positive aspects. It sets the mood in the corporation itself and influences the corporate culture. It can motivate the employees. It makes clear - inside and outside the corporation - what behaviour is or can be expected. It functions as an attestation.

Thus there are many advantages of a code of conduct. However, there are also some problems. First the value of a code depends much on whether there are sanctions against breaches of the rules - often this is not the case. And if there are sanctions, they can only be enforced by the management, not by the subordinates or outsiders. A second problem is that a code can only formulate principles of a high level of abstraction. The translation to or application in practical and sometimes unique situations remains difficult.

There is much more to say about ethics and business and what I have said so far is perhaps not new. Ethical deliberations on what should and what should not be done are millenia old! The debate may be old, it should however be repeated again and again. What is new is that businessmen are trying to contribute to the debate - and I am very grateful that I have the opportunity to do this. The debate itself may not give any final answers, but I am sure it will enhance our moral consciousness.

ETHICAL DECISION-MAKING IN A NATIONAL UTILITY: THE ELECTRICITY INDUSTRY IN FRANCE

François Ailleret

Like so many company managers with no special theoretical or practical training in the subject, I am entirely self-taught in the world of "business ethics". So the only contribution I can make is to present the ideas I have arrived at from practical experience in the forefront. I have been working in a state-owned industry, *Electricité de France* (E.D.F.), for ten years now and as Deputy Director General for two years. It is obvious that this background will deeply influence my considerations.

The business context

E.D.F. has to supply France with electricity at optimum conditions of cost and quality. The task it has to fulfill is therefore long-term, and is based upon its status as a monopoly, along with its stability as a state-owned industry. E.D.F. has the same objectives as any business: quality, growth, and efficiency. I say efficiency and not profit. E.D.F. does not have to show a return on its shareholders' capital; its resources are its customers' money - the money of French people - what has to be used in their best interests and to serve their needs.

E.D.F. does not have to struggle for its short-term survival, nor is it under pressure of pure profit. Faced with the ethical problems which are nonetheless present, *this situation, in my opinion, leads to more stringent demands*.

Since its creation in 1946, E.D.F. has experienced three successive eras:

- the period immediately after the war, reconstruction, the pioneer age;
- the "golden age" of E.D.F.: thirty years of constant growth and great technological challenges;
- the present day, with its slowing up of growth and its preoccupations with the environment.

Tomorrow E.D.F. will see the European Age. Growth may be extremely weak, with the consequent risks usual for any company, and competition between the various forms of energy will be intensified.

Each period is marked by its particular ethical problems. Therefore the company's ethics must evolve in harmony with the company itself.

The ethical frame of reference

When a manager makes a decision, he or she has to do so from the basis of an ethical frame of reference that should include three perspectives:

(a)   of the manager as an individual,
(b)   of the company,
(c)   of the nation, of French society.

(a) Despite the obvious difficulties, I try to express in a few sentences the cornerstones of my own ethical convictions:

-   the respect of the human person, whoever that person might be: citizen, customer, competitor, company employee, capital-owner, trade-unionist, politician;
-   the obligation to fight against all narrow self-interests and selfishness: in ourselves primarily, of course, but also the selfishness of other individuals, of social groupings or corporate interests, etc.;
-   the acceptance of full responsibility for fulfilling our duties; in other words, to strive for the advancement of our work, while being entirely aware that no single person can have total control over his or her activities, nor escape the complex, turbulent and contradictory system of political, financial, social and legal constraints in our world - knowing, however, that we have a duty to contribute towards making the system more efficient.

(b) The E.D.F. ethics is largely implicit. On the one hand, it derives from the customer, who after all is the very *raison d'être* of the business. His and her interests are central to the duties of every employee, and as manager we have a duty to ensure that the customer is in no way disadvantaged by the fact of dealing with a monopoly. On the other hand, the E.D.F. ethics derives from the individual within the company, who - regardless of his or her particular character or beliefs - has a basic right to a career structure and a professional future through the recognition of, and emphasis on his or her qualities and abilities.

(c) As far as the ethics of French society is concerned, I simply outline two elements here which will serve to highlight the first specific instance I shall describe later on.

-   Firstly, we live in a transaction society where under normal circumstances every member is obliged to pay for the goods and services he or she consumes.
-   Secondly, guided by the principles of equality and justice we should strive to ensure that no individual is excluded from society, *i.e.* that each member of the society does enjoy the basic essentials of life, a necessary condition of human dignity. A part of that package of basic essentials is the supply of electricity to the home.

Although this ethical frame of reference can - in principle - deeply conflict with corporate policies, I personally do not face any conflict that would compel me to leave the company, to modify its policies or to adopt the attitude of a mercenary who only hires out his services. Nevertheless, life is not simple, and one senses, rightly or wrongly, practical contradictions between ethics and efficiency. To illustrate these problems, I shall present several examples of situations I experienced in my own company dealing with customers, the environment and personnel.

Example 1: To cut off the electricity supply to bad payers?

Distributors of electricity can find themselves faced with customers who are bad payers. The most certain means of bringing them into line is to cut off their electricity supply. Those who can pay do so immediately. Those who cannot are forced to live without electricity, which is incompatible with their dignity as human beings. Two problems arise:

- How do we define those who genuinely do not possess the means to pay, so as to enable them to benefit from special arrangements?
- Should one go as far as to cut off their electricity?

Despite being urged to do so, we at E.D.F. have refused to assume the responsibility for judging a customer's ability to pay. This would effectively give the E.D.F. employee an unacceptable degree of power over his fellow citizens. Our decision was to refer the problem to the external organisations, both official and charitable, to whom we direct customers who either claim to be or seem to be in difficulties. Along with the relevant administrative bodies and these organisations, a fund was set up, subsidised by E.D.F., to pay for winter consumption of electricity by these social cases, but it is not E.D.F. which decides upon the individual application of these funds.

Our response to the second question took the form of a compromise: We do not withdraw supply in winter, but only in the months from April to October.

Every year we review the system together with our partners. One development will be the establishment in France of a *Minimum Income Level*, which will lead to the assisted subscriber paying a minimal proportion of his electricity bills. This in itself represents a reinforcement of his or her dignity. Furthermore, we foresee an end to summer supply withdrawals.

The solutions of these problems were prepared on the basis of a preliminary internal study, along with the assistance and opinions of other professionals whose interests were not identical to our own. Together we reached a compromise which we know we shall have to continue to develop.

Example 2: Different pricing policies for different industrial customers?

The growth in sales of electricity would doubtless be stronger if E.D.F. were to adopt its conditions of sale to industrial customers according to their individual circumstances. This would be, however, to distort competition and undermine equality of treatment for customers who have no option but to use E.D.F.

The solution is consequently self-evident: a fair, open, and universal pricing policy is necessary. This is something which E.D.F. has maintained rigidly for several decades. For circumstantial reasons - pressure from lobby groups, or priority given to short-term considerations for political reasons - it comes in for regular criticism. We continue to defend it vigorously, because this policy, which is clear, recognisable and independent of the use the customer makes of his or her electricity, is incontestably one of the fundamentals of E.D.F.

The ethics, therefore, does not merely concern individual decisions or short-term tactics, but equally far-reaching and long-term strategies.

Example 3: Safety and environment have no price?

There is unanimous support today for improvements in safety and greater respect of the environment. Some people go so far as to say that safety and the environment have no price. This attitude smacks of irresponsibility, since it is of no assistance in answering the real question: just how far should one go?

Let me give the example of a new high voltage power line which has to be constructed in order to satisfy growing demand. The least expensive routing is not normally the best from the environmental angle: for instance, a straight-line routing placing the pylons on hilltops, which have a lower agricultural value than valley land, will leave them visible for miles all round. A routing making the best topographic use of hill faces may be the most aesthetic, but it is considerably more expensive. And then how do you ensure that private interests - who want the line to pass through the neighbouring village and not their own - do not lead to a universally unsatisfactory routing?

We have been confronting this problem on a significant scale for some years now. Our response, which strives to reconcile our objective as a business with respect for the quality of life, is as follows:

-       to construct the minimum number of new lines, for which an overall long-term strategy is needed;
-       to refer to expert skills and opinions when researching and studying the routings;
-       to aim for consultation, even though this often more closely resembles confrontation, since it provides the opportunity for expressing opinions - which is relatively easy - and for listening to them - which appears to be rather less so;
-       to arbitrate or go to arbitration in the event of litigation, since an indefinite stalemate is ethically untenable. This calls for reference to the spirit and the terms of the relevant laws.

Professionalism, consultation, arbitration, the spirit of the law - these are the factors which contribute to a routing being fixed in such a way as to be a compromise between cost and aesthetics, and between local and general interests.

Example 4: Ethical criteria for information policy

The availability of information to the public raises fundamental questions both on a day-to-day basis or at times of crisis. The public has the right to be informed, but those who oppose our projects will often selectively exploit press and media releases to their own advantage.

Let us take the example of a fire in a power-station housing transformers with a pyralene content, which at high temperatures could - although experts can neither confirm nor refute this - give off toxic by-products, and particularly dioxins, whose mere mention since Seveso is sufficient to alert the public.

We have experienced several situations of this nature. After an incident at Reims, we issued a statement which was carefully worded, somewhat delayed because of the detail contained in it, contradictory because some experts - although peremptorily - had changed their opinions, and essentially scientific. The result was a wave of media comment which was extremely unfavourable to our ethical image.

The subsequent objective analysis gave rise to several straigthforward rules of conduct:

- make information available rapidly, explaining why more cannot be said at this stage;
- admit immediately to any errors, in particular regarding information already given out;
- take the risk of saying too much rather than too little;
- own up to one's responsibilities. Do not call others to account or blame bad luck, and do not fall into the media pitfall of a public search for a culprit or a scapegoat.

A frame of reference of this kind, which, I believe, reflects the ethics of the company, is a considerable help to the representative who finds himself thrown in at the deep end of a crisis.

A fire in Lyon, which was far more serious than the Reims incident, provided the opportunity for these principles to be applied in practice. Paradoxically, E.D.F.'s image was enhanced in the press and in public.

In this way, a constructive ethical analysis enabled ethics and efficiency to be harmonized, where originally there had been a presumption of conflict.

Example 5: How to deal with HIV positive status, full-blown AIDS, drug abuse?

In today's society, phenomena such as drugs or AIDS give rise to new sets of questions whose answers are not to be found in the textbooks. Should there be testing in candidate selection procedures for HIV positive status, for full-blown AIDS, or for drug abuse?

E.D.F.s company doctors carried out a study which sought to reconcile respect for the human person with the defence of the company as a social body, and the need for a more rigorous approach to candidate selection in high security positions.

Here, in a very generalised form, are their conclusions, which today serve as rules of conduct:

- A person who is HIV positive is not a diseased person. He or she can lead a normal professional life and presents no risk of infection in the workplace. HIV testing should therefore not be used at selection procedures.
- A person suffering from full-blown AIDS is a diseased person whose prime need is for care and who cannot guarantee fulfilling regular employment. If the doctor detects symptoms of the disease, which could be confirmed by testing with the candidate's approval, selection is abandoned.
- A drug abuser, inasmuch as he or she has a daily need of considerable sums of money, is also frequently a drugs dealer. There is therefore a genuine risk of the abuse being encouraged and developed by others. If the doctor confirms pathological symptoms of drug abuse, there will be no subsequent selection, unless the candidate is sincerely intending to carry on proper rehabilitation, in which case he or she can be selected, but will be subject to special medical controls. There is, however, no systematic process of detection.
- For high security positions - such as running nuclear power-stations, work with live electricity lines, etc. - a test is not made a condition of employment, but medical checks are extremely strict, since neither drug nor alcohol abuse is acceptable. As for recognised HIV positives, closer medical controls are applied because of the risk of stress-related or behavioural problems.

Conclusion

These examples are based on my own experience in a company whose survival is not in jeopardy. But if that were the case, would we give the same responses? As we all know, for people and social groups alike, morals in time of war are not the same as morals in time of peace.

Ethical problems in business are nothing new, but the complex evolution of society renders them more difficult and more diverse. It would be a mistake to shrink away from them and expect by doing so to avoid internal tensions or losses of efficiency. It is my personal conviction that, in the long term, a company which maintains its own ethical frame of reference is the stronger for it. It enables a workforce to be united by bonds of common values. That provides a framework of consistency - in ideas, of course, but most of all in action. In this way the company is better morally prepared to deal with a genuine crisis.

I have no doubt that senior managers in business would be more at ease in this area if they had received some relevant training for it, either initially or in the course of their careers, and similarly if analyses of management practice integrated the ethical dimension of business more effectively. The exchange and co-operation between academics and businesspeople must be intensified - this is the *raison d'être* of the *European Business Ethics Network*. For the best solution of any problem can only originate from the fusion of knowledge and experience.

USING THE TECHNIQUES OF ETHICAL ANALYSIS IN CORPORATE PRACTICE

Richard T. De George

Why the need for business ethics?

Some issues of business ethics are peculiar to a particular country's historical, social, political, or economic conditions. Yet those in the field of business ethics in different countries and parts of the world can and should learn from one another. Since business ethics in the United States has a somewhat longer history than in Europe, its current status may hold some lessons for those elsewhere.

Unlike business ethics in Europe, business ethics in the United States is presently at a critical juncture. For a variety of reasons business ethics in the United States has had a success that no one starting out in the infant field in the early 1970's could have predicted. Then the term was ridiculed as a contradiction in terms. Now it is a large industry with over thirty textbooks, dozens of case books, more centers and institutes than one can keep track of, and more practitioners than can possibly be qualified. Corporations have rushed to adopt ethical codes; many have instituted ethics programmes for employees; and business ethics is featured in the popular media. Yet, paradoxically, business ethics is threatened by its very success.

From the start business ethics was internally pulled in three directions: *teaching, practical action, and academic research.* The first two concerns have greatly overshadowed the third. When business ethics started as an academic field in the early 1970s in the United States, it had two components that distinguished it from ethics in business or from issues of the social responsibility of business. First, it was a critical discipline. It did not simply take conventional morality and preach it to management or labour. Its aim was not anti-business; but it respected no sacred cows and it aimed at holding up to scrutiny from an ethical point of view the presuppositions and practices of business. Its practitioners admitted they did not have all the answers to moral problems and so insisted on the need for research on some of the complicated ethical issues involved in business to which there was no clear or accepted answer, including the ethical analysis of new business practices as they developed. Especially in the area of practical application on the corporate level business ethics has been replaced by ethics in business and has succumbed to the defect of moral *hubris.* Both those in business and many of those who work with business in this field tend to believe they know what is right and that therefore the problem is *not determining* what is right (e. g., by research) *but doing* what is right and in *motivating others* to do so as well.

Part of the blame for this lies with those business ethics professionals who have failed both to maintain a critical dimension in working with businesses and who have failed to show corporate leaders how the techniques of ethical analysis can help them resolve difficult or disputed moral issues in business. In the United States consultants most often attempt to determine the values of a firm and then implement a programme that enhances those values. The assumption is that the firm's values need no criticism or adjustment, and that ethical issues can and should be resolved by those in the firm without any special training in ethical analysis, without any help from those trained in such analysis, without any research, and without engaging in a broad discussion of the ethics of new practices. They thus reinforce the belief of many corporate leaders that since everyone is expected to act morally, everyone - at least everyone of good will - knows what is right and wrong. As moral people these corporate leaders want their employees to be moral as well, and they are happy to help make them so by setting up programmes to teach them conventional morality, which is too rarely or too inefficiently done in the home, the schools, or the churches. Most workers and most managers, once sensitized to the moral dimension of business, *can* think through the everyday ethical issues they face in business just as they can think through the everyday ethical issues they face in the other areas of their lives. Moreover, people are morally obliged to do what they believe is right, even when they assume corporate roles.

Thus, in considering the question of "People in Corporations: Personal Convictions and Corporate Claims", corporations that wish to operate ethically must respect the right of people to act ethically, and must have channels through which those who are told or forced to act otherwise can make their concerns known and have them addressed with impunity. These generalisations are compatible with running a profitable corporation and we have many models to which we can point. All of this is, I believe, true, not very controversial, and amenable to common sense moral intuitions.

If this is the case, one might well ask, *why does anyone - especially business - need business ethics or those who claim expertise in it?* If we all know right from wrong, what, if anything, does business ethics tell us or teach us, that we do not already know? The answer is that in most cases business ethics does not teach us anything we - meaning the vast majority of moral people - did not already know. Corporations do not need specialists in ethics to tell them that lying, falsifying records, cheating on an expense account, killing a competitor are wrong.

The false conclusion some draw, however, is that there is no need for a critical ethical evaluation of corporate practices or structures or for research on the morality of new issues or practices. As a result in the United States business ethics has had its greatest effect in teaching - both in schools and in corporations. But it has not had much effect on corporate structures or practices. Even the instituting of ethical hot lines and of ombudsmen - important though they are - assumes that individual workers and managers know what is right and wrong and that all that needs to be done is to allow people the opportunity to ask whether an action is ethical or to report when they are being told to engage in an activity they consider unethical. This is surely important; but it leaves untouched corporate structures, industry practices, and national or international policies that may need moral scrutiny and change. There is no ethical hotline for the competitor who has been unethically driven out of business, for the workers who are exploited by the conditions in which they work, for the supplier of raw materials from an underdeveloped country who is forced to accept terms set by firms from the developed parts of the world to their own advantage, or for the firm that must pay bribes to have its trucks unloaded.

I claimed several years ago (De George, 1987) that the easy work in business ethics in the United States has been done. Some of those in business ethics have systematized the application of generally accepted moral norms to business; and in the United States the many textbooks in the field deal with common problems in hiring and firing, advertising, manufacturing and some aspects of workers rights. The major focus in American business ethics has been on big business or corporations. Most are successful, rich and powerful. To some extent, a cynic might say, they can afford to be ethical - whether or not they are. The firms also operate in a social situation in which they are constrained by law, by governmental regulation, by an investigative press, by vocal consumer and environmental advocates, and to some extent by organised labour.

I shall not belabour the point. *The hard work is where the techniques of ethical analysis are most crucial, and it is in helping provide answers and guidelines in these cases that the credibility and usefulness of business ethics will ultimately be tested.* So I shall turn to three present challenges in business ethics that I do not think can be resolved simply by intuitive common sense approaches to ethics and that require hard thinking and the best techniques of moral analysis and argumentation available. It is in dealing with such issues as these that I think business ethics can be especially useful and of some interest to corporations. Response by business leaders or by others is always the response of individuals. But part of my claim is that moral individuals are not enough.

The three topics I shall address are: (1) The resolution of true ethical dilemmas faced by individuals and corporations. (2) The development of ethical guidelines for firms that operate in an ethically corrupt environment. (3) The establishment of criteria to make up for the absence of restraining background institutions on the international level of business.

Resolving true ethical dilemmas by ethical displacement

The literature in business ethics has developed the notion of levels of business and ethical analysis: the level of the individual, the level of the firm or corporation, the level of the industry or of other groups of firms, the national level, and the international level. Each level has its own problems. Adequate analysis of these problems yields the phenomenon of what I shall call ethical displacement, and further analysis of this phenomenon is often essential in resolving true ethical dilemmas.

Many of the ethical problems of people in corporations that arise from a conflict of personal and corporate values are not resolvable simply through ethical intuition. Nor can they be solved if, as most often happens, one takes them at face value and attempts to resolve them at the level at which they appear. Ethical dilemmas, so popular in business ethics texts, are situations in which an individual is caught in a situation in which neither of the two available alternatives seems ethically acceptable. If taken at their face value, there is no ethically acceptable action. And if one stays at that level we should be led to the conclusion that ethical issues are unresolvable, unless we escape the dilemma through some ethical slight of hand reasoning. If we are faced with true ethical dilemmas, they are in fact unresolvable when approached at face value. But our analysis of them should not end there. For a solution is often available by recognising the phenomenon of ethical displacement.

By *ethical displacement* I mean that what appears as an ethical dilemma or even sometimes simply as an ethical problem on one level may only find a true solution on another level. Thus what appears as a dilemma for an individual on a personal level may only find a solution, for example, on the corporate level, in the sense that personal dilemmas may require changes in corporate structures. Corporate dilemmas, in turn, may require changes in industry structures to guarantee fair conditions of competition. Industry dilemmas may require changes in national policies. And national business dilemmas, such as handling pollution, may require changes in structures on an international level.

The true dilemmas of individuals in a firm cannot be resolved by simply acting ethically. For the nature of a dilemma is that there is no ethical option open to the employee. Often there is no ethical option because of the existing structures of the firm. The only way to resolve the dilemma is to rise above the level of individual ethical analysis. Persons faced with such dilemmas will still have the problem of how to act if they cannot effect change on the next level. But the point is that true dilemmas indicate the need for change at the next higher level if they are to be resolved. *The technique of displacement analysis is initially a descriptive technique and then a diagnostic technique.* Any solution that results from it will not be intuitive and will not be easy. For changing corporate structures and policies have a host of implications that have to be considered and worked through. But the idea that ethical issues are easy and easily resolved intuitively by ethical people is precisely what has to be overcome both at the personal and at the corporate level.

These are issues that cannot be solved intuitively because they are *too complex*. Yet too often business executives who would not consider approaching financial problems without an exhaustive study by experts feel that ethical problems should be resolvable quickly and intuitively.

The need to analyse ethical issues in business in the framework of interactive levels is essential in approaching many problems, it is typically not addressed by management, and it requires the careful use of the techniques of ethical analysis that have been and are being developed in the literature on business ethics.

I mentioned earlier the institution of ethical hotlines and ombudsmen as steps in the direction of making companies more ethical and of helping to resolve the ethical difficulties of individuals within the company. If an employee is told by a superior to falsify a record, or if a worker knows that the concrete being used in construction is being diluted below specifications and may present dangers to the users, some means of making those conditions known to top management is important both to the individual and to the firm. It is partially for this reason that firms institute ethical hot lines and ombudsmen.

But rarely do these lead to *structural changes* within a company or to genuine debates about the ethics of a company's practices. Such debates may take place in the board room or in the offices of the top management. But those issues are rarely considered appropriate issues to be raised by lower echelon employees. Ethical hot lines were not instituted to handle complaints that threaten the existing structure of the corporation but to answer or allay day-to-day concerns of employees, usually on fairly straightforward and obvious issues of right and wrong. Where are the gray areas raised and discussed? Who internally challenges corporate procedures or structures from an ethical point of view, or attempts to resolve dilemmas involving ethical displacement, and how might such questioning or attempts at resolution be institutionalised? Are corporations interested in having a devil's (or an angel's) advocate to do just that? To my knowledge this has not been often - if ever - done. Only if it is the explicit task of someone highly placed in a corporation (who thus has other functions) to anticipate worker and consumer complaints and to argue from an ethical point of view for changes in corporate structures and policies will ethics be integrated into a company's operating procedures. *Such a person will need ethical research assistance* and should be rewarded for raising and pressing such issues and penalized for failing to do so, as evidenced by employee whistle-blowing or consumer suits.

Sometimes corporations in a given industry are driven to compete in ways set by the least ethical among them. The dilemma of the individual in the corporation is here repeated as the dilemma of the corporation in the industry. The solution must in such cases be sought industry wide. *Ethical displacement operates at all levels and among all levels.*

The solutions to dilemmas on a particular level that can be resolved only by rising to a higher level are not always intuitive. The solutions that go beyond a corporation's immediate domain of action are often - if properly approached - so costly, time consuming, or unusual that they may not even be raised. To the extent that they involve changing existing structures or ways of doing business they might well be seen as threatening and hostile. To some extent they are. For if they were not, the moral dilemmas involving ethical displacement would not arise. Such moral dilemmas are a symptom of needed structural changes, and must be considered as such, if not by those in business, then by those academics in business ethics. *Here ethical analysis yields both a threat and a possibility for creative corporate action.*

Ethical guidelines for firms operating in an ethically corrupt environment

The notion of displacement leads to the question of what is ethically required of an individual or firm that faces or operates not in a more or less ethically structured atmosphere but in one of corruption. *The problem of operating in a corrupt environment clearly cannot be solved by individuals acting alone or by individual firms acting alone.* When all the players are expected to operate ethically and legally, the rules of the game are usually clear. Do the same rules apply when some of the players do not operate ethically or legally, when extortion and intimidation are the rule, and when government is either ineffective or is itself part of the corruption? In ethical theory there is the *doctrine of a just war* that specifies what nations are permitted to do when unjustly attacked that they are not permitted to do in times of peace. What is lacking in business ethics is any comparable doctrine that applies or might apply to *a company operating in an unjust environment or that is unjustly attacked or threatened.* The option not to operate in such an environment may be an option for multinational corporations that can abstain from entering such areas. But it is no solution for already established and indigenous firms that operate there.

That there is no obvious and easy intuitive solution is an indication that here is a problem that needs careful study and extended discussion. It requires discussion because we cannot expect any individual or corporate leader to produce acceptable ethical guidelines for operating in such conditions out of whole cloth. Any set of principles will have to be developed by discussion, by considering the relevant values at stake, the human needs, the rights of all those affected, the consequences of alternative approaches. To say this is to refer implicitly to *the use of ethical techniques* that provide the vocabulary and the methods of evaluation generated by ethical theory - be it utilitarian, or Kantian, or one based on rights or justice or charity. How does the right of self-defense apply to business, if at all? Is there anything comparable to civil disobedience that might suggest defensible guidelines when government is ineffective against corruption but not itself corrupt? Of course, firms do operate in such environments, and they implicitly claim that it is ethically justifiable for them to do whatever they must to stay in business. From an ethical perspective such a claim is much too broad to be defensible. But *the development of ethically acceptable norms for operating in such an environment is a pressing need and one fraught with potential controversy.*

The ultimate solution, of course, is the elimination of corruption. The interim solution of providing ethical guidelines for operating in such situations and for moving towards the elimination of corruption requires careful analysis and extended discussion. The discussion must involve at least in principle all those affected. This claim may remind some of Habermas's communicative ethics. The difference is that what is needed are techniques for both working and discussing in a corrupt instead of an ideal environment. Corporations interested in acting ethically must take part in these discussions. They cannot expect to resolve the issues or provide generally accepted guidelines without using the techniques of ethical analysis and reasoning. This is *a classical research task*. Yet I know of no company that hires people to do such research, or any ethics center working on such a project. And if any ethics center were initially to propose such guidelines, it is not clear that business would be interested in extensive public discussion of them. The relation between theory and practice here is admittedly delicate.

Suppose that *the paying (not the demanding) of extortion* under certain conditions were morally permissible. Can we imagine any company publicly announcing that it is morally permissible to pay extortion and defend its payments in this way to its shareholders and to the public? Yet, if it is morally permissible, why not? When nations engage in what they consider a just war they do just that: justify the killing, bombing, maiming, and destruction of the lives and property of the enemy. A possible test of the morality of paying extortion in a corrupt environment might well be the condition that it be reported openly for what it is, and that it be justified as necessary because of the circumstances in which one operates. That condition, for instance, precludes paying extortion when it is not necessary; and defining the conditions under which it is necessary is a delicate and difficult job. Publicity as a possibly contributory justifying condition helps open the practice to the forces of public opinion and to governmental and inter-governmental action. This is an example, not a solution. For the point is that any real solution requires careful study and research. Unless those in business ethics do such research, they fail to enter the real world of business in many countries and in many environments. Moreover the rules for small business - so often ignored in business ethics discussions of corporations - may be different from those for corporate giants. The responsibilities of the latter to initiate change may well be greater.

Any serious and effective approach to this topic will almost certainly underline *three aspects of business ethics* that have too often been ignored. The first is that in such situations, *personal moral courage* will be required. When I speak of personal courage I do not exclude corporate courage. The relation of the personal and the corporate is important here. For a corporation cannot act courageously unless those within it, especially its leaders, act courageously. Personal moral courage is necessary when one may suffer serious harm as a result of one's actions: dismissal, destruction of one's property, business failure, or bodily harm to oneself or one's family. Such actions are not to be undertaken lightly, and we can attempt to develop criteria for when such action is mandatory, as opposed to being simply permissible, similar to an analysis we have of the conditions justifying and making mandatory whistle-blowing (see De George, 1990, 200-216).

Second, operating in a corrupt environment requires *moral imagination*. One cannot rely only on fixed rules and established norms. Yet one must not violate the very norms that one wishes to preserve. Gandhi's technique of passive resistance is an example of moral imagination. That technique is not obviously appropriate in a business operating in a corrupt environment. But moral imagination is essential in attempting to resolve the problem of how to act ethically there.

Third, acting ethically will carry with it *some cost for the businesses and corporations with the courage to act ethically*. Ethics may pay in the long run; but it does not always. And acting ethically in a corrupt environment will take some toll on the company, possibly threatening its existence. When must a business or corporation take that risk, if ever? Although we hold human life precious, we think it noble and morally praiseworthy in some circumstances to sacrifice one's life for others, and we think it appropriate in some instances - such as in self-defense - to take the life of another. I have yet to see a *discussion of the conditions* under which a corporation may be *required to acquiesce to threats to its continued existence,* or when it might be morally praiseworthy for it to do so, or when it might use violence to prevent it. A frequent assumption is that a corporation has not only the right but for some reason the obligation to continue to exist (unless it is advantageous for it to declare bankruptcy) for unless it does so it cannot do all the good it might be capable of doing. Is this assumption justifiable? If so, we must have some explanation of why it is sometimes proper to acquiesce in corruption when necessary for business survival.

The need for guidelines for acting in a corrupt environment is predicated on the belief that ethics does not require a company's capitulation to corruption and that competing with unethical competitors or unethical external agents does require other rules than those governing competition with ethical competitors and external agents. Turning the other cheek and martyrdom may be personal ideals. They are not usually corporate ideals. Yet if legitimate self-defense and economic survival are morally justifiable corporate aims, even if the latter is not an overriding norm, *the conditions of justifiability need articulation and defense.*

Ethical criteria for international business activities

Both ethical displacement and corruption are central to the third challenge of operating ethically in the international business arena. The situation is often one of quasi-anarchy and sometimes of unrestrained power. It is because of the lack of legal constraints and other background institutions (organised public opinion, consumer, environmental and workers' groups, an investigative media, and so on) that ethical guidelines are all the more pressing in this area. These cannot be imposed by any nation or corporation unilaterally on others. The absence of adequate regulations and agreements points up the need for an interim set of guidelines in some ways comparable to those needed for operating in a corrupt environment; a second set might serve as the basis for international agreements (such as the guidelines on the sale of infant milk formula); and a third might consist of the actions required by multinationals as well as by nations to help provide structures that will promote ethical actions by multinational corporations.

In 1977 the United States passed the Foreign Corrupt Practices Act. Corporations in the United States have claimed that adhering to that law puts them at a competitive disadvantage in countries in which *bribery* is the only way to get contracts. Some people have criticised Americans for trying to impose their own view of what is ethical on others - in this case the view that bribery is unethical. Yet I know of no country in which bribery with large sums of money of high government officials is not only practiced but practiced openly and justified publicly. I do not deny it is practiced and tolerated. But if it were ethically justified and were an acceptable public practice, then the whole point of paying bribes would be lost. It would be a normal way of doing business, with no special advantages gained from it. Individual corporate giants that have a near monopoly on their desired product - such as IBM once had - are able to operate without paying bribes, even in countries where bribery is endemic. Other companies in more competitive fields find it more difficult to do so.

If, as I believe can be shown, bribery is unethical (De George, 1990, 58-61), then refusal by any individual company to pay the required bribes, although ethical, will not solve the larger issue. This is a clear instance of ethical displacement. The problem could be solved by all the companies of an industry agreeing not to pay bribes and living up to that agreement. Legislation helps secure compliance that an industry-wide agreement may not be able to guarantee. But legislation is only national. *What is necessary is international agreement among multinationals and countries on this policy.*

The development of *the Sullivan principles* for companies - especially American companies - operating in South Africa was another instance of a creative, imaginative approach to an ethical dilemma that was resolved temporarily at least by moving up from the level of individual firms to the level of a code applicable - at least in principle - to all multinational firms operating in South Africa. Leon Sullivan, a Baptist minister, happened to be strategically placed on the Board of Directors of General Motors. His success reinforces my earlier claim of the importance of having someone in the corporate hierarchy whose task is to consider the corporate policy from a specifically ethical point of view.

Those academics in business ethics can play a role by working with business in helping develop international guidelines, by independently carrying out their analyses and producing the literature required for discussion and action, and by taking an active and critical part in the discussions that any such policies will demand before they will be widely accepted or adopted.

The need for a world-wide business ethics network here becomes obvious. If the phenomenon of displacement suggests that individual firms cannot resolve the dilemmas they face in multinational operations, then there must be networks for discussing the dilemmas and seeking solutions beyond the level of the individual firm and frequently beyond the level of the individual industry. Clearly, multinational corporations, governments - both large and small - and specialists in a variety of business areas - including business ethics - must have access to and participate in the network.

The success of business ethics that I referred to earlier has not been completely beside the point. For one positive effect has been that it is now acceptable to raise ethical issues in business and in discussing business practices, the regulation of business, and social policies that impinge on business. Too often, however, these discussions are still conducted at the level of ethical intuition, often with vested self-interest all too blatantly present.

There is an important role for business ethics not only in teaching but also in examining a variety of problems that are intractable if approached only through common sense moral intuition or only by encouraging individuals to act ethically. If approached in this way they lead only to unresolvable ethical dilemmas both for individuals and for corporations.

Clearly, however, analysis is not enough. If solutions and guidelines are developed they must be *implemented*, and they can be implemented only by individuals. *Personal ethical commitments* are not irrelevant to corporate, industry, national, or international guidelines and policies. They are in fact *the necessary starting point* for the discussions that will lead to the broader guidelines and structural changes on a variety of levels. These must cohere with the personal values and ethical beliefs of individuals if they are to be effective and if they are to be followed. Finally in the crisis situations to which I have pointed - dilemmas, displacement, corruption, and international anarchy - personal moral courage and integrity are necessary conditions for ethical economic survival, as well as for implementing the required changes. Ethically courageous companies are a function of ethically courageous individuals. Those academics in business ethics cannot create such individuals, but we can and should celebrate and support them when they appear.

References

De George, R.T.: 1987, "The Status of Business Ethics: Past and Future", *Journal of Business Ethics*, 6, 201-211.
De George, R.T.: 1990, *Business Ethics*, Third edition, New York: Macmillan.

ETHICAL RESPONSIBILITIES VERSUS CORPORATE EFFECTIVENESS

Jonathan L. Gorman

The question "is there such a thing as business ethics?" has been widely discussed among moral philosophers, and all concerned with the subject are aware of one of its central issues, which is whether business and ethics really "mix". The growing success of business ethics both as a subject of academic teaching and as influential in the world outside universities suggests that they do mix. Still, there is a nasty problem lurking in this issues, which has not yet been seriously considered. It has to do with human motivation.

Corporate effectiveness is naturally understood in terms of success in achieving corporate ends, ends which are given at the most senior administrative or managerial or executive level. (Different countries describe those whith the corporate goal-setting functions in different ways). Max Weber, in his sociological theory of of bureaucracy (Weber, 1964), held that the central task of such administrators is the rational adjusting of means to ends in the most economical and efficient way. This is not just an external sociological description of the task, for the administrator himself understands his task in this manner, and regards his function, so understood, as implicitly justified.

We may agree whit Alasdair MacIntyre (1985, ch.7) that the appropriate mode of explicit justification of the administrator's activity lies in the appeal to the administrator's ability to deploy a body of social scientific knowledge. This knowledge permits the claim to expertise in the manipulation of others. Both government and private corporations see themselves as having resources of competence which most citizens do not possess. MacIntyre locates a problem with this claim to expertise in a supposed incoherence in eighteenth century philosophy, but the difficulty is more recent than that.

What "knowledge" is involved in business administration? Plainly there may be large resources of skills and informational data. But these are mere background to the central activity of the rational adjusting of means to ends in the most economical and efficient way. There is a range of social sciences involved here: economics, cost-benefit analysis, and (Bayesian) decision theory. Textbooks of management theory present or assume these, and are used to inform the "best" managerial practice.

The rational economic man assumptions

These social sciences are complex and mathematical in their complete expression, and very few businessmen will be fully informed of all the technicalities. There are, however, certain basic attitudes involved which express a certain view of human motivation. These assumptions are best seen in the foundation laws of neo-classical economic theory, involving what are widely know as the rational economic man assumptions.

A rational economic man is, first of all, rational. *"Rationality"* here is understood in a special way, so that the following are true:

(1) For any individual A and any two options X and Y, one and only one of the following is true: A prefers X to Y; A prefers Y to X; A is indifferent between X and Y.
(2) A's preferences among options are transitive. This means that, if X is preferred to Y, and Y is preferred to Z, then X is preferred to Z; and if A is indifferent between X and Y, and indifferent between Y and Z, then A is indifferent between X and Z.
(3) A seeks to maximise his or her utility, where the utility of an option X is greater than the utility of an option Y for A if and only if A prefers X to Y. The utilities of options are equal just in case the agent is indifferent between them. In other words, more of what you think is good for you is always preferred to less.

One becomes rational economic man rather than just rational man simply by recognising that among the options available to us are the acquisition of commodities, so that following is true:

(4) If option X is acquiring commodity bundle X' and option Y is acquiring commodity bundle Y' and if Y' contains at least as much of each commodity as X' and more of at least one commodity, then everybody prefers Y to X.[1]

Finally, the following assumption is made:

(5) The marginal utility of any commodity diminishes as the quantity increases. Thus, the more you have of something, the more of it you will be willing to give up in order to get something else you want. An additional bag of gold means less to a millionaire than it does to a beggar, for example. (See Dyke, 1981, 35, 51.)

The economist Amartya Sen valuably analyses these claims about self-interested behaviour into the following *three elements* (Sen, 1987, 80 ff.) :

(1) The *self-centred welfare* assumption: a person's welfare depends only on his or her own consumption (with no sympathy or antipathy towards others).
(2) The *self-welfare goals* assumption: a person's goal is to maximise his or her own welfare.
(3) The *self-goal choice* assumption: each choice by a person is guided immediately by the pursuit of his or her own goal.

---

[1] There are a number of ways of expressing the assumptions of rational economic man theory. The present version is an expansion of that appearing in Hausman (1981), 18.

This view of economic theory thus assumes that human beings behave rationally in terms of actual self-interest maximisation.

These assumptions lie behind the standard ways of specifying the purposes of and controlling the activities of business organisations, and we attempt to understand our business and general economic situation in the light of them. Christopher Hodgkinson says "an organisation is a state of inadequacy. It strains to close the gap between what is and what can be. To have a goal is to be dissatisfied, by definition" (Hodgkinson, 1978, 211). So, if I know the relevant considerations motivating the behaviour of others, am well informed as to costs, benefits and consequences, then I can rationally fit together means and ends in the most economical and efficient way. Corporate effectiveness consists in this. As a manipulator of the actions of others, then I can contrive the fulfilment of the relevant initial conditions for them, and produce an outcome through their behaviour.

The firm as a function of individual people and their actions

What is the relationship between individuals and the organisations to which they belong? Business organisations exist to bring about change, to achieve goals. On the individualist assumptions which characterise economic theory in the way that I have explained, firms can be said to cause things to happen if it is recognised that this is just shorthand for speaking of the operations of individual people. Thus firms we understand to exist as functions of individual people and their actions.

A firm comes into "existence" through a number of people coming together with shared beliefs and desires in pursuit of a common stated purpose or set of purposes. The "purposes" of the firm are specified real purposes of individuals. Once specified or adopted, however, members of the firm and outsiders ascribe a personality to the firm (one which legal systems can recognise), and the original specified real purposes of the constituent individuals are also fictionally ascribed to the firm, which remains a hypothetical entity. The firm thus exists as a hypothetical entity in virtue of the actual beliefs and desires of real individuals. The individuals involved have formed the firm by agreement, by contractual articles of association, and the firm thus exists in virtue of what is called in political theory a social contract. The "consent" which may be supposed to warrant the creation of a state or similar large-scale social institution other than a firm is standardly described as "tacit", but in the case of a firm the consent is largely explicit .

The contract or contracts creating or continuing the firm involve a commitment on the part of individuals to act in accordance with the stated beliefs and purposes of the firm, even though the actual beliefs and purposes of individuals may diverge from those of the firm in the course of time. The rules, roles, purposes and offices which the creation of the firm specifies are matters of belief which founding and subsequent members of the firm adopt for themselves in so far as they are members. The firm may then have purposes which differ from those of the constituent individuals in the following way: the "purposes of the firm" are actually purposes which the individuals involved are *deemed* to have. They are deemed to have them in virtue of their commitment to have them, which commitment is a consequence of their obligation under the terms of the contract. This obligation is a prudential and not moral obligation, freely entered into, and as such exists within a framework of positive law. The carrying out of an obligation to the firm is itself a net preference of the individuals involved, althoug the desires and perceived costs which warrant the individual's net preference here are matters outside the firm's stated range of proper considerations.

Differences between the individual's and the firm's perspective

The self-interest maximising or cost-benefit calculation which the individual *actually* has may typically be different from that of the firm, and thus different from the cost-benefit calculation which this individual is *deemed* to have as occupying an appropriate office in the firm. Thus the individual's actual net preference might well depend, for example, on his assessment of the risk of loss of reputation (or even affection) for breach of contract of employment, whereas this could not be included in the cost-benefit calculation of the firm "itself". Firms don't really *exist*; the difference between "firms" and individuals is the difference between "deemed" personality - deemed desires and beliefs - and actual personality - individual desires and beliefs.

Furthermore, the individual may act in part on the basis of moral principles. Such moral considerations may be extended to become part of the goals of the firm itself. The cost-benefit calculations of organisational interest on the part of the firm is a model which the members of the firm are deemed to share, and it is a calculation which is "real", where reality is determined by the truth of an objective economic theory. It is possible for the firm to be characterised by all involved as being an entity of which the rational economic man assumptions are true. In so far as the individuals of the firm carry out its stated purpose they act according to the "real" (firm's) interest-maximising cost-benefit analysis, whether or not they know that they are doing so.

We thus understand *people's actions,* on the approach to human nature now outlined, not necessarily in terms of beliefs and desires they actually have, but *in terms of the beliefs and desires we deem them to have* in the light of *an independent economic theory* and of *a legally constrained objective specification* of the firm of which they are members. We are warranted in doing so by the individuals' commitment to or tacit acceptance of the practices of the institution of which they are members, which institution is a social construction in terms of individuals' beliefs and desires, a construction which is assumed by us, on empirical grounds, to be formulated in terms of the rational economic man assumptions.

It follows, on the rational economic man hypothesis, that *a person (or firm, as now explained) never does what he or she prefers not to do.* There is therefore a sense in which preference is assumed to be demonstrated in behaviour. We may often come to know what a person prefers, in a given situation, simply by observing the choices he actually makes. Thus if a person says he prefers running to cycling, but whenever he is given the choice he opts for cycling, then we will insist that he really prefers cycling to running after all.

Note, however, that opting for cycling does not *prove* a preference for cycling: "A behaved as if he preferred X to Y" means that A chose X instead of Y, but it does not follow that A preferred X to Y. He or she might be indifferent between them, or the rational economic man assumptions may be false. The "demonstration" of preference in behaviour is a mere common assumption, which the economist calls "revealed preference". For real-life economic problems, revealed preference often provides the only evidence for what actual preference is. It is *evidence* for preference, however, not *proof*. To hold revealed preference to *prove* preference would be to hold it to *define* preference, and this would make the rational economic man assumptions collapse into an empty definition of words.

Despite the claim that a person never does what he prefers not to do, it remains the case that, in common sense understanding or ways of speaking, we sometimes allow that *a person may do what he prefers not to do.* Thus he may do his *duty* instead. It may seem as if this fact falsifies the hypothesis that a person never does what he prefers not to do, but it is not quite so simple. The thesis is, rather, that people attempt to satisfy to the maximum their desires as such, whatever those desires or preferences are. A person who acts morally may be taken to demonstrate a preference for moral against immoral action: he prefers morality to immorality, and acts so as to maximise his return, measured in the satisfaction of that preference.

Morality may in this way be held to be just one maximisable pleasure among others. Indeed, it is in exactly this way that moral considerations enter into the theoretical understanding of the operations of firms, and in this way that governments seek to constrain firms to act within moral guidelines by the imposition of nonmarket costs. But whatever may be the case at the macroeconomic level of the behaviour of firms, it is certainly true that *people do not, as individuals, always regard themselves as acting as rational self-interest maximisers,* for, as individuals, moral considerations are not seen as being part of cost-benefit calculations, but rather as constraining the outcome of such calculations.

If we assume in this common sense way that morality is not just another preferable outcome, then the hypothesis that a person never does what he prefers not to do could be held *falsified* by many cases, for while a person may prefer to do his duty, he may often prefer not to (but do it anyway). Many more cases plausibly falsify the hypothesis of rational economic man, where preferences are taken to be for the acquisition of commodity bundles, and no *economic* theorist will think that the detailed individual complexities of real life can be fully represented by this ideal model.

However, it is a familiar claim of positive economists that the "rational economic man" assumptions, while "empirical" in the sense that they can be used to generate falsifiable predictions, *merely "model" behaviour.* People behave, it has been stressed by Milton Friedman, only "as if" they were rational self-interest maximisers with full relevant knowledge of their circumstances (Friedman, 1979). That they also engage in moral reflection would be, on this view, empirically irrelevant: the rational economic man hypothesis is a *hypothesis,* and it is the task of the theorist to discover just when this hypothesis is applicable. In a situation which approximates that of a free market in commodities, it works. In a monastery, it doesn't . It is open to scientific test just how far the hypothesis is applicable between these two extremes. The implication remains that good managerial practice would be ideally rational in this way.

Ethical deliberation plays a motivating role

Do people behave "as if" the rational economic man assumptions are true? If they do, then our economic theories will have empirically correct implications. But our economic theories do not get it right. Even governments fall very far short of being able to predict, let alone completely control, the economy. In so far as we wish to understand the business and economic reality in which we live, we will need a true account of what motivates human behaviour. Even at the macroeconomic level, therefore we must leave ourselves open to the view that better characterisations of human motivation may be available. Part of what is missing from economic theory is the reference to morality as a partial motivation of human action. I think that one must recognise that ethical deliberation does play a motivating role in actual human behaviour, and, moreover, that it does so without making moral duty itself a matter of self-interested preference, as if it were just one discountable interest among others.

Amartya Sen is one of those who wish to alter the rational economic man assumptions, and he wishes this because he thinks that they are empirically false, and that, by contrast, ethical deliberations may make a person violate one or other of the rational self-interest assumptions. Such considerations, he says, include the freedom, rights or real opportunities that a person has, and not just the state of well-being which the person achieves. (Sen, 1987, 18ff., 47, and *passim*).

Of course, Sen allows, to deny that people always act in an exclusively self-interested way is not to assert that they always act selflessly. Self-interest plays a major part in a great many decisiones. Normal economic transactions would break down if self-interest played no substantial part at all in our choices. The real issue is whether there is a *plurality* of motivations, or whether self-interest alone drive human beings; and, Sen adds, the contrast is not necessarily between self-interest and a general concern for all. The mixture and varying balance between selfish and selfless behaviour is an important characteristic of group loyalty.

Sen, however, goes seriously wrong in his next step, for he believes that the ethical theories which philosophers provide are proper attempts to characterise the "ethical" deliberation which actually affects behaviour, and he believes in consequence that economics should move closer to moral philosophy. Note, however, that if we suppose that ethical considerations do affect actual human behaviour, then we are making a *factual* claim. Even if positive economists are persuaded that ethical deliberation does affect human behaviour, why should they try to move economics closer to ethics? For ethics does not describe what our actual ethical deliberation is like.

Motivating reasons and normative reasons

What does ethics do? Relevantly here, we can pick out that understanding of ethics which suggests that structures of *proper ethical thinking* are provided. Proper ethical thinking sets a standard for ethical thinking, and there is no *a priori* reason to suppose that actual ethical thinking, let alone actual motivational thought, is well described factually by ethical theories. To suppose otherwise is to confuse two different senses of reason for action.

Michael Smith importantly distinguishes for us "motivating reasons" from "normative reasons" (Smith, 1987, 37). The claim that a person "has a reason" to do something is ambiguous between a claim about a motivating reason and a claim about a normative reason.

A *motivating reason* is part of a state which is potentially explanatory of an action. It may be motivating without being overriding, but nevertheless motivating reasons are psychologically real, as Smith puts it. The goals that such reasons embody are the goals the person concerned actually has. A motivating reason, although it does explain an agent's behaviour, may reveal little of value in what the agent did, even from his own point of view. An example to illustrate a motivating reason might be this: my "reason" for selling a profitable business at a loss may be to spite my wife.

By contrast, *a normative reason* justifies an action from the perspective of the normative system that generates the requirement. On this view, "to spite my wife" just can't be a "reason" to sell a profitable business at a loss, for the action is *ex hypothesi* an irrational emotional response, and there is no normative system of rationality which will make it a reason. In this way all normative reasons are, to some degree and in an appropriate sense, "good" reasons. There are as many kinds of normative reasons as there are normative systems which generate such reasons: of rationality, prudence, morality, and perhaps others.

A person may thus have a motivating reason to do what *he* has a normative reason to do; *he* may have a motivating reason to do what *he* does not have a normative reason to do; *he* may have a motivating reason to do what *he* has a normative reason not to do; and *he* may have a normative reason to do what *he* does not have a motivating reason to do.

The rational economic man assumptions express norms of rationality, and thus specify normative reasons, which may exist in the absence of motivating reasons. As such, the rational economic man assumptions provide normative reasons which are distinct from the normative reasons which moral codes provide for us. *Both*, however, provide *normative* reasons.

However, whatever the relationship between the rational economic man assumptions and codes of morality, the question which the economist, and the businessman in the real world, face is one about motivating reasons. The theoretical economist asserts that the normative reasons expressed by the rational economic man assumptions simply are the motivating reasons of human beings.

In saying this, the theoretical economist is presupposing a less explicit and, up to now, unquestioned philosophical view of motivating reasons, which is currently know as the *Humean theory of motivation*. This theory is not a theory of normative reasons. According to it, motivating reasons are *constituted* by desires and means-end beliefs.

This is the view which is expressed by Donald Davidson, and he calls a motivating reason a "primary reason" (Davidson, 1980). His analysis is as follows:

> R is a primary reason why an agent performed the action A under the description d only if R consists of a pro attitude of the agent towards actions with a certain property, and a belief of the agent that A, under the description d, has that property.

Michael Smith's analysis is basically very similar (Smith, 1987, 36):

> R at t is a motivating reason of an agent A to F if and only if there is some G such that R at t consists of a desire of A to G and a belief that were he to F he would G.

The essence of these positions is the claim that something x is a *motivating reason* to do something y if and only if x consists of a desire to do something z together with a belief that by doing y one will do z.

On this view we are committed to a Humean theory of the place of morality in motivation. Moral considerations, in so far as they actually motivate us, must be fitted into the sole available category of desire together with means-end belief. Thus we must hold that the clear perception of some moral fact is something that we can have only if we have *certain desires and beliefs of a consequentialist or goal-directed kind*.

But against this I suggest that moral motivation may be, and for some people is, grounded on a belief that something would be good, or on the basis of a desire together with a belief other than a means-end belief. The question is whether a belief that x is good is reducible to a belief that one has a desire or is reducible to a desire. A proper understanding of morality, not as "ideal" moral reasoning (although here, too) but as actually motivating real people, requires that this not be so, and that we recognise alternatives to the Humean position.

Business ethics requires a view of human motivation in terms of which we may be motivated by other than desires and means-end beliefs, namely by *beliefs that something would be good*. Our understanding of the economic reality in which our business operates has to allow for such facts of human motivation, and corporate effectiveness is vitiated if it uses assumption which ignore such facts about motivation.

Logical inconsistency of motivation by beliefs and decision theory

The nasty problem, however, is this: the philosopher David Lewis has proved that the theory that motivation may be by beliefs (for example, the belief that something would be good) is *logically inconsistent* with (Bayesian) decision theory (Lewis, 1988).[1] It follows that one cannot consistently act on the basis of decision theory, or on the basis of other social sciences like economics or cost-benefit analysis which share its assumptions, and at the same time act on the basis of desire-independent ethical values. To put it another way, business ethics necessarily precludes corporate effectiveness, which is what many people have long suspected.

---

[1] For a non-quantitative proof, see Collins (1988).

References

Collins, J.: 1988, "Belief, Desire and Revision", *Mind*, 97, 333-342.

Davidson, D.: 1980, "Actions, Reasons and Causes", reprinted in his *Essays on Actions and Events,* Oxford: Clarendon Press.

Dyke, C.: 1981, *Philosophy of Economics,* Englewood Cliffs, NJ: Prentice-Hall.

Friedman, M.: 1979, "The Methodology of Positive Economics", reprinted in F. Hahn and M. Hollis (eds.), *Philosophy and Economic Theory,* Oxford: Oxford University Press.

Hausman, D. M.: 1981, "Are General Equilibrium Theories Explanatory?", in J. C. Pitt (ed.) , *Philosophy in Economics,* Dordrecht: D. Reidel.

Hodgkinson, C.: 1978, *Towards a Philosophy of Administration,* Oxford: Basil Blackwell.

Lewis, D.: 1988, "Desire as Belief", *Mind*, 97, 323-332.

MacIntyre, A.: 1985, *After Virtue,* London: Duckworth.

Sen, A.: 1987, *On Ethics and Economics,* Oxford: Basil Blackwell.

Smith, M.: 1987, "The Humean Theory of Motivation", *Mind*, 96, 36-61.

Weber, M.: 1964, *The Theory of Social and Economic Organizations,* New York: Free Press.

THE CORPORATION AS AN OPEN ORGANISATION

Juan Cruz Cruz

Recent studies on individual behaviour in business organisations underline the fact that the training and development of each person depend upon the organisation's capacity for accepting, understanding and stimulating his or her freedom. Without this capacity the organisation becomes a rationalistic mechanism far removed from anything human. This result confirms the Aristotelian view of the organisation where free human beings strive to form a rational and open unity as opposed to a substantial or closed unity.

A relational unity is neither substantial nor absolute. Each of the parties involved in this relational whole possesses his or her own activity which is not an operation of the totality itself: thus, a soldier in an army carries out operations which do not pertain to the entire army, or the worker in a firm performs activities which do not involve the entire organisation. Nevertheless the relational unity engages in activities which cannot be reduced to any individual elements involved, but rather it constitutes a whole entity. The relational totality is not a substantial being but a multitude of beings who are associated by a certain objective relation: the concerted nature of their actions is due to a community of ends, to shared values, in virtue of which they find themselves to be dynamically linked as human beings.

The absolute entity, on the contrary, is a simple unity which does not allow to the parts involved any real activities; examples are the mechanical unity of a clock, the organic community of polyps or a beehive. In these cases, the part is for the whole and the action of the part can be considered as an action of the whole. The relational whole, however, is formed by human beings and its unity is a moral one. The state, the family and the business organisation are moral units. In addition, they are dynamic units because they are made up of free human beings who communicate and share their ends. They are determined not only by physical or biological forces but also motivated by their own free will. Therefore, business organisations in general and corporations in particular are relational unities, i.e. *open organisations*. Otherwise they could not even function as economic organisations.

I try to explain this thesis inspired by the monographs of Thomas J. Peters and Robert H. Waterman Jr. *In Search of Excellence* (1982), Peter F. Drucker *The Practice of Management* (1954), Chester I. Barnard *The Functions of the Executive* (1958), and Herbert A. Simon *Administrative Behavior* (1976).

The closed organisation

The closed organisation is dehumanising. There is an erroneous way of ordaining things within human organisations: governing it with inflexible rules of a mathematical nature, as if men were elements of an algorithm which is constructed in a perfectly rational manner. Committees and bureaucracy thus take over the organisation. The designer of a rationalistic organic framework starts from the presupposition that human beings are ill-structured and therefore in need of a system which can guide their activity without surprises or exceptions. He has a mechanical or biological model of organisation. Freedom, involving also conflicts and paradoxes - moments which are not very rationalistic - disturbs the clarity of the system. In other words, if the origin of conflicts and problems is to be found in freedom, a rationalistic system gives little room to individual freedom. The organisation has to be dehumanised in order to function; it is, thus, a closed organisation.

Within the closed (mechanical or organic) organisation what is common, the common good, does not belong to anybody in particular. On the contrary, in an open (moral) organisation, what is common, the common good, belongs to each and every member. The highest element of the "common good" is freedom, whose demise is tantamount to the demise of social vitality.

A closed organisation generates only apparent efficiency. When a firm stimulates bureaucracy and the closed system, it ends up in dehumanising those men who work inside that business firm. Bureaucratisation reaches its zenith when the parties involved, the human beings, become dissolved within the systematic whole. This leads to a loss of efficiency and effectiveness. Bureaucratisation increases the number of management people who say how things should be done but who do very little or nothing themselves. There is a proliferation of "levels" and also of management personnel. Hence each management nucleus, in order to justify its own existence, generates its own bureaucratic work which is a stumbling block in the way of the fluid management of the whole. Although everybody is busy in their own occupations, nobody does anything necessary.

A closed organisation tends to rationalistic and authoritarian rigidity. It leaves little initiative in the different areas of activity. On the contrary, by fostering interpersonal initiative and autonomy at the lower rungs of the echalon, an open organisation creates a weighed system of decentralisation, an apparent lack of co-ordination, a type of chaos which is sought in order to stimulate the spirit of innovation. An efficient order between liberties can seem to be a lack of order. There are some business enterprises whose planning systems, budget or even control systems, are designed in such a way that there can be "leaks" or programmes which are not officially recognised. It is not surprising that in the most booming companies the most active, bustling and prosperous departments should happen to seem to be structured chaos. An authoritarian organisation blocks dynamism. What is most rationalistic and systematic is not always what is most efficient. An organisation has the right to define objectives and ways of attaining them, and expect people to co-operate spontaneously in that attainment. But if a firm is ruled by an authoritarian spirit, it is forgetting that good results are the fruit of "positive co-operation" and not merely the final link of a set of orders that become weaker as they descend down the hierarchical scale. It will expect innumerable forms to be filled in so that the flow of documents on production planning can convert itself into an absorbing task. People will either end up immobilised in tiny unimportant decisions or shying away from the obligations required by efficiency and letting only the upper levels be responsible for the functioning of programmes.

When a business firm is an open organisation it creates an atmosphere in which, on the one hand, each person develops his or her own esteem, and, on the other, each person participates enthusiastically within the whole. In order to attain this, the firm has to be convinced that the set of rules and regulations cannot guarantee enthusiasm for the common project and that political leadership (the *potestas* of the Romans, doomed to limitation and control) cannot replace moral leadership (the *auctoritas* which projects uplifting and attractive meanings). Too many rules and regulations suffocate the freedom and the force of corporate culture. The greatest capital in a firm is the creative freedom of its members. But freedom is actively and responsibly exercised within an open organisation when there exists an uplifting project in which only a few key values and a few key objectives are to be found.

This project, along with its values - whose incorporation is what gives rise to "corporate culture" - permits the reduction of daily instructions because everybody knows what is secondary and what is really important. When there exists a declaration of principles occupying one single page in which a project and those values are inscribed, there is no need for many pages of manuals and rules and regulations. There should be no fear of having ten different procedures for carrying out things in ten different factories belonging to the same firm. In a closed organisation which is strongly rationalistic, we frequently come across the verbs "analyse", "plan", and "specify", whereas in an open organisation we come across the verbs "try out", "learn", and "modify". Any organisation which has survived a great number of years owes its elasticity not to the mode of organising nor to administrative skill, but rather to the power of its convictions and to the attractiveness which these convictions hold for its members. These convictions refer to values, and a successful organisation without doubt has solid convictions upon which everybody bases norms and actions faithfully. In rough times such an organisation can change everything, except its convictions.

A *closed organisation is "mechanical" and "bureaucratic"*, whereas an open organisation is "free" and "enterprising". In any work it always happens that the expert ends up in carrying it out. If this principle based on experience is not recognised, we cannot expect an individual to exercise his or her capabilities in favour of the organisation. This means that an excess of staffing reduces the dynamism of a business concern. We have to let each individual carry out his or her work with time and according to that individual's needs, perspectives and concrete capabilities. The most important persons in a business corporation are not usually those who administer it but rather those who really provide a service or give added value to the product. Within the narrow sphere in which a worker carries out his or her task with a machine, the most authoritative voice to be heard has to be that very worker. Those who best know how business operates are those occupying the front line; it is this we have to ask for he best of their personal innovative initiatives, creative energy and productive service.

The open organisation

An open organisation fosters the feeling of success and enthusiasm. Nobody likes to be considered a failure. An open organisation designs systems which induce and strengthen, among its personnel, the feeling of victory and the achievement of quotas and objectives. In a business corporation in which only 40 per cent of its salesmen reach their fixed quotas in any given year, the other 60 per cent feel they have failed. If in that company a system were designed whereby it is presupposed that there will always be a 60 per cent proportion of lazy or useless salesmen, a disfunctional type of behaviour would be generated which is a copy of disfunction itself: the majority of persons would continue to act as failures. The normal human situation of 5 per cent disfunctionality is generated due to an ill-conceived system.

Furthermore, the open organisation fosters the capacity for enthusiasm by trying, first and foremost, to employ capable and innovative persons and, secondly, trying to have both its objectives and its leaders generate enthusiasm at all levels. Management personnel not only have to be enthusiastic; they must also possess the capacity to generate enthusiasm among their collaborators. It is not a matter of having altruist leaders, but rather leaders able to generate enthusiasm in others, so that the company is shown as an interesting place of work. And since there is no enthusiasm without joy, the company has to try to make work pleasant; when people are not enjoying themselves, it is difficult to provide a quality product and to have a good image. Melancholy and sadness turn off the light of genius. A sustained atmosphere of informality and happiness provokes the spark of innovation and of vigour within work. If a design is not liked nor perceived as being enjoyable, it ends up not being implemented.

An open organisation makes the promotion of leaders possible. The leader strengthens the opinions of others without stifling them. A closed organisation does not generate leaders but rather a kind of slave-master who bosses over others by means of violence. The true leader can only be that person who knows how to lead free men and women, who feel ever freer while following the leader. In the presence of a leader, people feel strengthened and elevated, more powerful and more capable of attaining shared objectives. But the influence of a leader over his or her followers is not blind: the latter will not follow through the sheer magic of the leader's personality but rather because the leader truly encourages them and fosters self-confidence while mobilising social and psychological resources which stimulate and satisfy their motives, needs and objectives. The leader raises the ethical aspirations of the group and encourages the emergence of new leaders. True leadership is an agent of transformation, and is profoundly moral because it elevates the level of human behaviour and ethical aspirations of the follower. This fostering relationship helps the followers to convert themselves into active members who end up as leaders.

Open organisations stimulate those who fail while experimenting. The innovation mutation usually takes place in extra-systematic spheres. Changes occuring within the organisation very often take place at rather low hierarchical levels, and are produced by enthusiasts who sometimes are not a part of the system. Furthermore, very few great innovations have arisen from the original plans. Open organisations protect "bohemian workshops" in which a few persons experiment with greater innovative success than the official research teams. We can even come across the case of firms employing two or more work teams on the same project who can learn from their own failures. Tolerance in the face of failure, if the latter is to have meaning, is substantial for the innovative spirit. Bureaucracy stifles innovation and trial and error. The open organisation backs up the behaviour of those who shun routine to take on risks as roads to success, even knowing that surely there will also be failures along the way. With a prudent sacrifice of the closed order, efficiency is gained as well as more rapid action. Action generated outside the pre-established order fosters experimentation, trial and error, and consequently a new strategic orientation. Big businesses cease to innovate when they rigidly fall back upon themselves and aim at massive production, planning and routine procedures without tolerating, within their strategy, those mistakes which are the result of an inquisitive and experimental activity. If a business ends up being trapped within the mechanics of exhaustive reports drawn up by all the different departments and by a multitude of staff members who have never experimented with nor produced anything, except the corresponding report, it will cease to have vital ideas and responsible personnel.

Open organisations try to combat conformism. Individual initiatives are incarnated in the figure of the "champion" of a product. The bureaucratic administrator is opposed to the "champion", an enthusiast who perhaps is a bit mad but who has faith in the product which he or she has produced with imagination. That a product should fail in the market-place is usually less due to the objective market situation than it is to the absence of a zealous voluntary champion, of a person who is convinced of the success of the task undertaken. If a corporation does not tolerate the presence of a committed creator because, from the organisational point of view, such a person generates friction and because the proposed innovation does not seem too promising, this corporation will not easily convince its clients. Open organisations maintain their innovators, their product champions who, by means of their individual techniques and their lust for constant experimentation, combat the tendency to inertia.

The open organisation seeks to establish personal and stimulating relationships respecting human dignity. Within the closed organisation the differential character of the parts is annulled. In the open organisation the parties involved are configurated as differentiated totalities who freely integrate and tend to be free. Here the main source of increased productivity is not capital nor a set of automatic instruments, but rather human individuals who have to be treated not as parts or elements, but rather as human persons, with respect and dignity. This implies that reasonable expectations be established for the human persons and sufficient autonomy be guaranteed in order to enable them to make the best use of their capabilities. It will be very difficult for a business firm to assume a leadership role, if it does not respect the individual and create a personal sense of self-esteem and success, and if it does not expect people to bring out what they create. In this manner, people produce things that work. Interest in quality replaces concern over costs. Dealings between management and workers become more flexible to the extent that there exists a common shared project. Rules and regulations are replaced by the contributions of all the parties involved. The open organisation holds categorical moral imperatives similar to the following: "Respect the individual!", "Ensure that people be successful!", "Allow people to be excellent!".

In the open organisation, management turnover reduces the establishment of complicated systems. In his *Politics*, Aristotle observes that the optimum government of free people must be by rotation: that the rulers from time to time become governed by others is the only way to guarantee the best organisation among all by means of the persuasive exercise of reason. In some outstanding corporations this organisational principle is observed. They demand, for example, a triennal rotation of their management staff. In this way, the corporation does away with "professional bosses", inventors of complex systems which foster the permanent professionalisation of staff members. This is a principle which goes well with the psychology of human beings: nobody in his right mind sets up a closed and dictatorial bureaucracy whose disastrous consequences will be suffered on a short-term basis.

The open organisation is simple and its hierarchy is structured in a participative manner. The functional system of the organisation is rather simple, with few very high executives. It passes authority down to the lower echelons and confers practical authority upon a large number of persons. In an open organisation, the adhesion to a few key shared values generates a disciplined authority: people feel confident enough to do things, to experiment, to project and innovate. Authoritarianism, however, does away with autonomy and self-discipline, which is much more demanding than discipline imposed from above.

In the open organisation information is shared to the greatest possible extent. Managers and workers communicate face-to-face. By analysing their problems and searching for solutions jointly, they deepen their commitment for the common purpose. To talk back to the boss or to ask a stupid question can be a sign of responsibility. For the management must listen, inform, eliminate barriers, clearly explain objectives, in order to be able to count on the co-operation of all. The open organisation avoids the constant use of written

48

communication, fosters the free flow of questions and answers, the intervention of all parties without fear of interruption, and the stating of matters directly and sincerely. Free initiative increases productivity and is the best control. What is usually not too productive is a team of people who have been haphazardly put together without being able to set their own objectives, who are not able voluntarily to say no to the project. For this reason open organisations know how to exploit the need which each individual feels to forge his or her own destiny. A worker having even a very small amount of control over his or her destiny or task displays an extraordinary amount of energy.

The rationalistic approach to management is "anti-productive" because it does not take into account the degree of identification which a worker can acquire with regard to his or her task if a little bit of decision power is granted: self-generated quality control is more effective than that coming from inspectors. An open organisation is efficient, if its members have access to sufficient and basic information. This access is the basis for self-esteem because it allows each member to compare himself or herself with the others. Thus each member knows at all times if the work is being carried out and who is carrying it out well because each member operates in the light of general objectives and overt values without need for instructions from the boss at all times. Control and management cease to be tasks for the "apparatus". This self-control from below is the most efficient and effective type of control. "Rigid" and "formal" control from above, with huge costs, can become drowned in a sea of documents without having a single product come off the production line.

The open organisation places trust in initiatives being taken outside work hours. It allows, for example, unlimited access to electronic and mechanical equipment on the part of its technicians, who may take them home for their own personal use. Although they may not be using such apparatus for the ends of the company project, such usage opens new possibilities for new applications and strengthens the company's committal to innovation. This is a way of affirming the individual's dignity and worthiness. Some organisations even remove all their time clocks and establish flexible work shifts, thereby offering the opportunity for workers to adjust their work time to their private lives.

References

Barnard, C.I.: 1958, *The Functions of the Executive*, Cambridge, MA: Harvard University Press.
Drucker, P.F.: 1954, *The Practice of Management*, New York: Harper and Row.
Peters, T.J. and R.H. Waterman, Jr.: 1982, *In Search of Excellence*, New York: Harper and Row.
Simon, H.A.: 1976, *Administrative Behaviour*, Third Edition, New York: The Free Press.

THE FUNCTION OF MANAGEMENT CONTROL SYSTEMS IN INNOVATIVE ORGANISATIONS

Raymond A. Konopka

Konopka (1988e) has pointed out that there is an apparent conflict between management control systems and the manifestation of innovative behaviour in organisations. He has attributed this apparent paradox to the dual theoretical problem of a lack of tolerance for intellectual virtue and a lack of moral virtue (which virtue breeds trust); this problem is related to alienation.[1]

Management control and innovative behaviour

At the heart of the paradox of controlling for innovative behaviour in organisations lies a commonly accepted conception of control which is at odds with the nature of innovative behaviour.

Anthony best sums up this conception of control when he defines management control thus:

> "The management control process is intended to make possible the achievement of *planned* objectives as efficiently and effectively as possible, *within the givens*" (1965, 31, emphasis added).

Thus the normal concept of management control assumes known ends of organisational functioning and a given environment. Konopka (1988a) describes three different control paradigms which have governed management control thought throughout the twentieth century. He labels these paradigms as (1) the classic management school, (2) the systems-oriented approach, (3) the behavioural approach. Although there appears at first glance to be some change of attitude in the behavioural management control paradigm regarding the assumptions of organisational goals and operational parameters, in the end the behavioural paradigm falls victim to the same underlying flaws of assuming *a priori* goals, ends, and environments.

---

[1] See definitions in the Appendix

Thus, the management control paradigms which have been dominant throughout this century are based upon two key assumptions that, as we shall soon see, render them totally irrelevant in the context of innovative behaviour. These assumptions are:

1. That organisations know what their goals are, and
2. that organisations know how to achieve these ends.

These two (at least implicit) assumptions are evident in practice by the emphasis that the great majority of control systems place on controlling (or monitoring, or measuring, or rewarding, or what have you) inputs, processes and outputs.

A basic problem with control theory is that it is based on an assumption of "rational man" (Savage, 1954) or "economic man" (see Demski and Feltham, 1976). However, innovative behaviour does not conform to the tenets of rationality (Konopka, 1988d) and the perception of a need for innovation within an organisational context is an implicit admission that the organisation does not know what its goals are, or at least does not know how to achieve them. In short, it is an admission that it does not understand the causal model. If the causal model is not clear, it seems rather silly to control using a management control system which assumes (and indeed requires) a specific causality.

This combination of a reality that is uncertain (at least to the causal model) and a control system which requires certainty (at least to the causal model) in order to be valid can result in the alienation and institutionalisation of individuals within organisations.

Alienation is an exceedingly broad concept, and it can be dealt with at many different levels of abstraction. At one extreme is Christian theological alienation which occurred as a result of man's fall from Grace, and at the other extreme is physical alienation in the sense of the alienation of material property from an individual. In the human and social sciences, alienation is basically concerned with man's alienation from man or from society. In the psychological sense, man may be alienated from himself. Man's alienation from himself, from his fellow men, and hence from his society is what here concerns us.

Marx and Hegel both viewed alienation as "a dependence, a lack of or loss of control" (Tinker, 1985, 148). In the social or humanistic sense, alienation is a lack of control over oneself or over one's relationships with others.

Konopka (1988a) noted that a major advance to accounting or control theory offered by several recent authors has been the observation that accounting is not neutral. However, accounting's "partisanism" runs much deeper than its ability to influence an investment or to arbitrate in the distribution of material rewards or economic goods. As Tinker (1985) has noted:

> "Accounting theory, like any social belief, is not merely a passive representation of reality, it is an agent in changing (or perpetuating) a reality" (p.111).

The ability of accounting to alienate man from himself or from his fellow human beings rests in its function as an aid in the perpetuation of the reality, or better the myth, of the corporation or organisation. This is inherently linked to institutionalisation. There can be no serious argument that accounting and management control, in both theory and practice, aid directly in the perpetuation of the idea that the organisation is something tangible in its own right; that it is an institution. But, as Tinker (1985) has astutely observed:

> "The corporation is an entity only in theory; it is a fiction--a reification--that masks an array of conflicting social interests" (p.181).

Accounting, and management control that is primarily based upon accounting numbers, provide at least some important tools that allow for institutionalisation and the subsequent masking of social as well as personal conflicts within organisations. It does this by dehumanising the organisation through the creation of a common numerical measuring device. Accounting aids in the process of alienation by removing the human element from what is inherently human: an organisational endeavour. Human beings, being human, need to identify with something. If they are alienated from themselves and from their fellow human beings, they are left with only the institution with which to identify. Alienation, in our context, is dehumanisation, and it is an aid in the process of institutionalisation.

> "Whatever its form, ... alienation is an appropriation of the human essence, an obstacle to human growth and development" (Tinker 1985, 172).

Accounting is an alienating phenomenon, and it is inherently so by its nature. The purpose of accounting *is* to reduce human economic activity and economic states to a common and comparable numerical measure (how well it does this is open to debate, but a debate which is beyond the scope of the present discussion). To attempt to place a human face on accounting by, for example, accounting for human resources is self-defeating and indeed is a step backwards. To account in the accounts for human resources is to place a monetary value upon human beings, reducing them to a numerically measurable, quantifiable, and interchangeable phenomenon, and hence enhancing rather than mitigating against the alienating nature of accounting.

Stated differently, we can say that accounting is an alienating phenomenon and it must be accepted as such. Accounting is alienating because it deals with a reduction of vision, and that is its purpose. By reducing economic events to quantifiable data in summarised and easily communicable form, accounting serves to aid the transfer of information. However, by the same process, the coding of reality which is necessary for accounting implies a distance from reality. In effect, by reducing reality to facilitate communication, information transfer, and comparability, a degree of the connection with reality is sacrificed. Through this data reduction process, all parties to the accounting communication process experience a reduction of their vision of reality. It cannot be otherwise; to attempt to do so would be to attempt something which is in conflict with the very nature and purpose of the accounting function.

Management control systems, however, do not necessarily need to be accounting oriented. To be sure, accounting information is an integral component of most management control systems, but the degree to which management control systems are accounting-oriented varies gretly from one organisation to another.

The essence of management control is the ability to influence behaviour. To the extent that accounting systems control the management control system, innovative behaviour is unlikely to occur within an organisation. The essential characteristics of innovative organisational behaviour are deviance and trust, or the fruits of both intellectual virtue and moral virtue (Konopka, 1988e). It would be difficult to develop these characteristics in an organisation that would utilise an alienating phenomenonon as its basic behaviour influencing force. When people are alienated from themselves and each other, there is a tendency towards institutionalisation and away from human values. We would posit that the movement away from human values does not come as a result of institutionalisation *per se*, but that is proceeds from a loss of a clear vision and understanding of the causal model as it exists in reality. This loss of clarity in understanding results directly from the attempt to reduce reality. Whilst it is undeniable that reality must be reduced in order for it to be in any way communicable and intelligible (even within the same organism), it must always be understood that any reduction of reality is alienating because a reduction of reality implies a loss of essence.

In developing control systems, one must be cognisant of the alienating effects inherent and natural in the accounting components of control. The important conception to maintain in mind is the effect of accounting and control systems on the perceived causal model.

Work, like any activity, can become an alienated phenomenon when the focus of the activity is not the human being in his wholeness. Innovative behaviour is unlikely to occur in a situation where the individual is alienated, or divorced, from his work. This statement may not be self-evident. When a person is alienated, it may seem that this state would have little to do with his abilities to imagine, to be creative, or to think, and these are the qualities commonly associated with innovative behaviour. However, in order for creativity, imagination, and thinking to benefit the organisation, these actiivities must be directed towards the benefit of the organisation. An alienated individual may do a lot of creative thinking, and in fact his alienation may in a way be an excuse to do a great deal of creative thinking, but it is not going to be thinking (nor the subsequent necessary action) about ideas to benefit the organisation. Indeed, in an alienated environment, it is only the very few who utilise their feelings of alienation as a catalyst to change the situation for the better (either to their benefit alone or to the collective benefit). Most people do not rise to the challenge of an alienating environment, and instead prefer to use it as a drug to deaden the senses.

In essence, if management desires to create a corporate environment which is conducive to innovative behaviour, it must fulfill its responsibilities to the individual organisation members. These obligations include being cognisant of the learning (or the potentiality for learning) on the part of the organisation members. Employees cannot be alienated from their work and in effect work must become an integral part of the human experience and of human existence. The control system can play an important part in that process.

Alienation, learning and control

Innovative behaviour is based upon positive learning and a willingness to act upon that learning on the part of the individual (Konopka, 1988d). In an organisational context, it is also based upon the acceptance of these actions on the part of the organisation. Systems which contribute to the alienation of the individual and to institutionalisation are not conducive to the manifestation of innovative behaviour within organisations. Alienation of the individual is accompanied by institutionalisation because in an alienated setting the institution is the only thing left with which the individual can identify.

Argyris (1977) has somewhat addressed this area. He has described organisational learning as potentially of two types. The first type he terms single loop learning, and he describes it as consisting of the ability of "the organisation to carry on its present policies or achieve its objectives" (p.116). Argyris labels the second type of learning as double loop learning and describes this phenomenon as the "questioning [of] underlying organisation policies and objectives" (p.116). Thus, to Argyris, double-loop learning is involved with questioning the *status quo*. The concept of double-loop learning also appears similar to the concept of auutonomous strategic behaviour developed by Burgelman and Sayles (1986). Hence, we believe that it is somehow involved with the occurrence of innovative behaviour.

Argyris suggests that double-loop learning is inhibited in organisations because, in most organisations, norms exist which demand of people: "Do not confront company policies, especially those top management is excited about" (p.116). Since to us company goals and objectives seem to be the known, challenging them is to veer toward the unknown, or to act on intellectual virtue (Konopka, 1988e). Thus, according to Argyris, most organisations have norms which inhibit the development of intellectual virtue in the members of the organisation.

Argyris (1977) describes a situation he terms a "double bind", and this is in actuality the turning away from reality by the organisation member. It contributes to that which we have termed the institutionalisation of the individual and therefore to his or her alienation. The organisation member begins playing games based upon the organisation's rules, which then become more important than reality. In fact, they can become so important as to blind the organisation member to reality. Thus, he or she cannot direct his or her actions toward reality (moral actions) and experiencie positive learning simply because he or she is unable to see reality and therefore his actions are bound toward frustration (immoral actions) for either the actor, the organisation, or both. The organisation member is engaged in what we have termed negative learning. The situation described by Argyris indicates a total rejection on the part of management of its responsibilities to the human component of the organisation. Placing organisation members in situations such as this (a moral dilemma) is conducive to neither the organisation member's personal growth nor the organisation's long-term economic growth. It also contributes to the development of institutionalisation of the individual. We shall further deal with the issue of the institutionalisation of the individual later in this discussion.

In this type of environment, moral virtue cannot be developed within the organisation members. Hence, a vicious circle ensues. Since moral virtues cannot be developed given the "games" being played to satisfy the control system, more controls are introduced to counter the game playing, which in turn begets more game playing and a further divergence from reality, which begets even more controls, *ad nauseam*. This would seem to be the cause of the reinforcing dysfunctional behaviour engendered by control systems which was noted by Ashton (1976).

Thompson and Tuden's (1959) classification of managerial decision-making types is insightful for our purposes. They classify decision-making into four categories, based upon the degree of relative certainty of both causation and preference as to possible outcomes. When beliefs regarding both causation and preference of possible outcomes are certain, Thompson and Tuden view decisions as being made by computation. This fits very well with traditional control theory, and with the rational model. Where preferences as to possible outcomes are uncertain, but beliefs as to causation are certain, decision is made by compromise. This fits quite well with control theories which deal with power coalitions (Ouchi, 1980) or administrative theories which deal with power (Crozier, 1963; Crozier and Friedberg, 1977). When beliefs about causation are uncertain, but preference as to possible outcomes is certain, Thompson and Tuden view decisions as being made by judgement. This fits quite well with traditional control systems based upon hierarchical authority.

The interesting decision case in the Thompson and Tuden typology is the situation where both beliefs concerning causation and the preferences as to the possible outcomes are uncertain. In this situation, which seems to be the case of the innovative context, Thompson and Tuden suggest that decisions are made by inspiration. We are unaware of any control theory or system based upon inspirational decision making. Ouchi (1979) has somewhat touched upon this issue. He has posited that in situations where the ability to measure outputs is low and the knowledge of the transformation process is imperfect, the organisation should employ "clan" control. Ouchi's description of this situational context somewhat approaches our idea of an innovative context and his idea of "clan" control contains some elements of what we call moral virtue.

The problem, which cannot be overstated, is that control philosophy is based upon the tenets of rationality (Konopka, 1988c) and innovative behaviour cannot be explained by the tenets of rationality (Konopka, 1988d). Or, as Hopwood (1974) has succinctly stated, "Decision-making by inspiration and net present value hardly appear to be a happy pair" (p.140).

Organic organisations and organisations that allow decision-making by inspiration (which is merely decision-making outside the tenets of rationality, but is by no means irrational) require a high degree of moral virtue on the part of the organisational participants, at least if the ability to decide inspirationally is to be delegated. Organic structure requires moral virtue because it implies that anyone can step on anyone else's "territory", or indeed that no one has "territories", and inspirational decision-making requires trust (the practical product of moral virtue) because when things go wrong, one cannot "hide behind the numbers" as a defence.

Argyris and Schön (1974) developed Model I and Model II theories in action. All the governing variables for action of Model II are conducive to the development of intellectual virtue in the organisation members; all the governing variables for action of model I are inimical to this development. Also, it is interesting to note that all of the consequences of Model II as observed by Argyris and Schön indicate the presence of moral virtue as well as a lack of alienation (minimisation of defensiveness, high freedom of choice, high propensity of risk taking, etc.); the consequences of Model I indicate that the moral virtues are lacking, and that alienation is present. Of particular interest is the observation that in Model I situations there was little public testing of personal theories, whilst in Model II situations public testing of personal theories occurred frequently. A high propensity for public testing of personal theories would seem to indicate the existence of interpersonal trust.

Argyris (1977) indicates that whether an organisation is operating under a Model I theory of action or under a Model II theory of action basically depends upon the attitudes, beliefs, and view of the world held by top management. Gallo (1980) seems to agree with this view. This implies that leadership is an essential component in setting an environment conducive for the occurrence of innovative behaviour.

Leadership

For our purposes, the most interesting theory of leadership is that which has been proposed by Hershey and Blanchard (1977). They entitle their theory *the leadership life cycle theory*. In particular, their theory of leadership confronts a serious problem which is inherent in models of organisational learning, such as that proposed by Argyris and Schön (1974). Particularly, whilst the Model II theory of action proposed by Argyris and Schön seems to function in the presence of intellectual and moral virtue, it is unclear which one precipitates the other.

Hershey and Blanchard's theory of the leadership life cycle sees the appropriate leadership style, or management control style, progressing from Quadrant I to Quadrant IV as the maturity of the subordinate group increases. In effect, we can see the role of management control passing through the following stages, depending upon the maturity of the group of subordinates. The leadership life cycle is depicted in Figure 1.

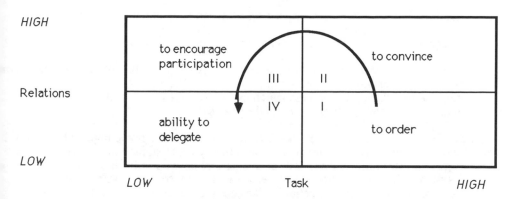

(curve flows in the direction of increasing subordinate maturity level)

Figure 1: Management Control Methode Based on Subordinate Maturity

In essence, the movement of leadership style (or control system requirements) through the four quadrants depicts a method for management to reduce and eventually eliminate alienation from the control system and from the enterprise. It is a method for helping individuals to mature, to grow, and to become more productive for the enterprise, for each other, and for themselves. It is the essence of the internal responsibilities of the corporation noted by Gallo (1980).

Focusing control

In order to develop an innovative organisation, management must be concerned with the whole individual, the entire human being in respect of those groups of employees from which they may desire innovative behaviour. In respect of these employees, the management control system must be one that minimises or eliminates alienation, and that develops and reinforces intellectual and moral virtue. In short, it must be a control system that is concerned with the development, growth, and well-being of the whole individual. The human being must be at the centre of this type of management control system (Konopka, 1988b).

Also, the control system must be controlled by persons with the values, attitudes, and world view that will not be threatened by attacks on the *status quo*. The efficiency of a control system at providing an environment which is conducive to innovative behaviour is very much dependent upon those leading the control system. The leadership style of a person reflects the basic structure of the individual's motivation and needs.

The point that Hershey and Blanchard (1977) miss in their idea of the leadership life cycle is that there needs to be a distinction in leadership (as well as control) as to the object of the leadership (or control) effort. Reduced to its most simple level, leadership is concerned with motivating an action and control is concerned with monitoring the result of the action so motivated. Before one can decide an appropriate level or focus of leadership, it is necessary to define that which is desired as an outcome of that leadership, and therefore that which will be monitored. Monitoring and leadership cannot be separated.

The monitoring or control process can have at least three distinct foci:

1. defining and monitoring the effort of the controllee (what in the literature is currently term the agent in a principal-agent relationship;
2. defining and monitoring the process which the controllee follows; and
3. defining and monitoring the outcome of the process.

The difference amongst the three foci for a control system lies in the implied belief in a causal model. It can be reasonably assumed that in any leadership/control situation there exists a goal, be it implicit or explicit, on the part of he who is leading. That given, a control system which is monitoring the effort of the controllee is assuming a causal relationship between effort of the controllee and desired outcome. A control system which focuses upon monitoring the process which the controllee follows is implicitly assuming a causal relationship between the process defined and the outcome desired.

Only with the third focus of control, that of focusing on the outcome desired, does a system of control approach the necessary requisites to at least not stifle the manifestation of innovative behaviour. Innovation involves the perception and the realisation of new combinations (Konopka, 1988d). It is quite simply absurd to anticipate innovative behaviour to be demonstrated in a system which assumes any given causal model. By definition, innovative behaviour requires that prjudices as to causal models be dismissed. To monitor effort or processis to prejudices the system against the occurrence of innovative behaviour.

Further, we suggest that even the monitoring of outcome may be prejudicial to the manifestation of innovative behaviour in organisations. Innovation generally occurs in society when a provider convinces a consumer of a new satisfaction (Schumpeter, 1955; Konopka, 1988d). In control terms, innovation occurs when a controllee in effect demonstrates to the controller a new preference as to outcome (Konopka, 1988d). In principal-agent terms, an agent is innovative when he or she convinces his or her principal of a new satisfaction preference. Basically, for this to occur requires that management be listening.

In institutional terms, management listens and directs through its control system. The rewards system is its basic directing tool; the accounting and reporting systems are its basic listening devices. If the listening devices focus upon only the output of an assumed causal model, management is simply not going to be attuned to innovation. In effect, the system is maintaining the *status quo* by denying management the ability to sense innovative behaviour as such, and limits management to sensing such behaviour as only threatening deviance.

And so we see our fundamental paradox. We arrive at the question of the compatibility of control with innovative behaviour: energetic bureaucracies or innovative anarchies.

Fiol (1984) has concluded that there is indeed a link between strict financial controls and long-term firm success. This might at first glance seem to contradict our assertions. However, we propose a resolution to this apparent conflict, and link it to ideas previously developed (Konopka 1988a, 1988b, 1988c, 1988d) as well as to Hershey and Blanchard's (1977) theory.

To apply Hershey and Blanchard's (1977) theory to control in the potentially innovative context, it is necessary to speak in terms of a leadership spiral rather than a leadership cycle. The four quadrants proposed by Hershey and Blanchard (1977) to explain the development of group leadership dynamics can operate at various levels depending on the focus of control, as depicted in Figure 2.

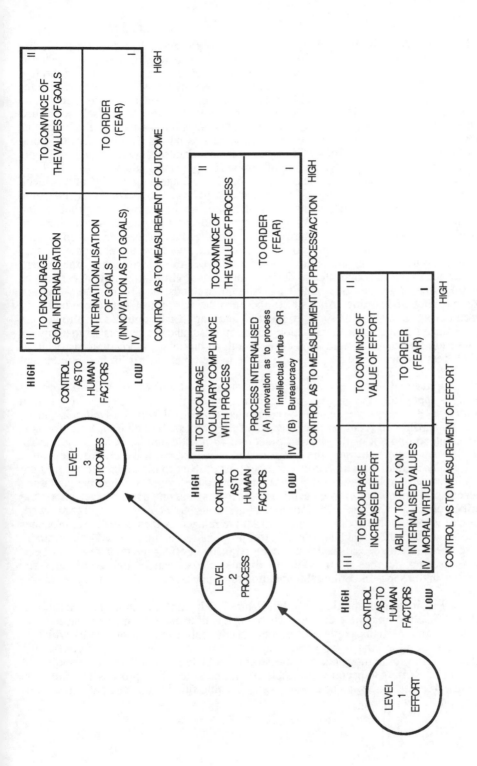

FIGURE 2: CONTROL / MATURITY SPIRAL

If the control is focused on monitoring the effort of the controllee, the leadership life cycle can apply as a guide to the use of leadership abilities to develop the controllee to the point where he is self-controlled *as regards his level of effort*. Basically, moving through the four quadrants of the first level of Figure 2 can be viewed as developing within the controlled individual a feeling of responsibility or conscientiousness in respect of his effort for a particular task. He or she is not self-directed, and therefore not self-controlled as to the task, but his desire to put forward effort becomes internalised. In the terms that we have used in this inquiry, we would speak of this as partial development of moral virtue. In effect, by leading through the stages of the quadrants of the first level of Figure 2, the individual is internalising a feeling of responsibility toward others.

At the next level of the spiral, the quadrants of Figure 2 again apply. But at this level, we are concerned with developing self-control *as regards a process*. This is indeed that to which we refer when we speak of institutionalisation. As the controllee approaches the situation described by Quadrant IV of the second level of Figure 2, he can become self-controlled as to the process because he has internalized the process and given it value *for itself* and therefore fails to question it. If this occurs, we have the phenomenon that we commonly term bureaucratisation. In order to avoid this phenomenon, the system would need to allow the controllee to develop intellectual virtue so that he questions the process.This can only be done once he or she understands the process, so we are in reality speaking of learning. And, of course, in order for him or her to productively question the process, we must speak of positive learning. If the controllee is allowed (or led to) positive learning, bureaucratisation can be avoided, and the stage is set to allow the controllee to advance to the third level of the spiral. At this stage, innovation can occur as to the process for achieving preset goals. There is the potential for limited intellectual virtue.

At the third level of the leadership/control spiral, the focus of the system is on the *outcome* as opposed to the process or the effort. In effect, once the process inherent in the *status quo* has been accepted by the controllee, the organisation or system is free to allow the controllee to focus on the outcome of the process. In Quadrant I, the focus is mainly upon attainment of the desired outcome, with little emphasis upon the human /environmental factors. In fact, the controllee is protected from the environment by a limited ability to interact with the environment, or at least to make decisions and take actions in response to his view of reality. As the controllee moves through the quadrants, and accepts and understands more the desired outcomes, less emphasis is placed upon the prescribed outcome, and more freedom to act in response to the environment is allowed. As control as to outcome and as to ability to act are relaxed as the controllee approaches the situation described in Quadrant IV, the propensity for innovative behaviour is increased because the causal model has been relaxed. In effect the controllee has been given increasing degrees of freedom to dismiss the causal model as he sees fit. Innovation, in the sense of continual renovation of organisational goals, can occur in this situation.

The leadership/control spiral depicted in Figure 2 is in part sequential. For example, it would be difficult to imagine a situation where there is little control emphasis placed upon outcome but much emphasis placed upon effort; the belief in a causal model which is implied in a strong emphasis on effort assumes a desired outcome. But, of course, the three levels of the spiral may operate simultaneously. Stated a bit differently, a subject of control can be learning to become more self-controlled as to effort, process, and outcome at the same time; he or she can be maturing and learning simultaneously at all three levels of the spiral.

Innovative behaviour : A management choice.

Practically by definition, institutionalisation leads to an identification with the *status quo*. The *status quo* is exactly that against which innovation must fight. Institutionalisation is incompatible with intellectual virtue, at least as the latter is concerned with discovering new things, new connections, and new combinations. In short, institutionalisation is incompatible with challenging the *status quo* also leads to more dependence on "the system", as opposed to the individuals within the system. Hence, it is alienating and contraposed to the development of what we have termed moral virtue. It can also lead to men being used as tools. This is fundamentally opposed to true individualism, a necessary component of innovative behaviour.

Obviously, whether or not the upper management of a corporate organisation wishes that innovative behaviour occur within the organisation is a decision which they must make. Whether or not they wish to employ control systems which are conducive to the occasioning of innovative behaviour is also their choice. It is obvious that many organisations can meet the goals of their management and of their owner without exhibiting innovative behaviour. Indeed, for these organisations traditional control systems are probably more easily implemented than would be those required in an organisation needing to realize its innovative potential.

However, it is all too often forgotten in the management control literature that control is a process of value placement, and that therefore values are under the influence of management. For example, Hopwood (1974) states:

> "It is, of course, true that some managers and employees attach a higher priority to the intrinsic interest of the job, or alternatively to financial earnings, but the majority of people seek both intrinsic and material rewards from their work, although with differing priorities in differing situations and contexts." (p.35).

Hopwood's comments are typical of those authors whom Konopka (1988a) classified as advocating the behavioural approaches to management control thought. The basic premise is that control must take into account the differing values, and hence potential motivations and behaviours, of the organisational members. We here depart radically from this premise, and we insist that it is the control system that is in large part responsible for the values of the organisation member, at least as respects their values toward the organisational endeavour (but quite possibly in a broader context).

As Andrews (1971, 38) has noted, one of the major components of corporate strategy is personal values and aspirations. Value placement and development is a component of management strategy that allows this conceptionalisation of situations facing the organisation and their conversion into motives toward action.

Conclusion

Management desiring to develop and exploit the innovative potential within their organisations must recognize that they have internal corporate responsibilities in this regard. This responsibility revolves around the obligation to develop the capacities of the human beings within the organisation for intellectual and moral virtue; to develop a taste for the unknown rather than a feeling of security based in the *status quo,* and a respect for and trust in each other rather than a reliance on the formalisation of the organisation. In short, management has the responsibility to aid their subordinates in maturing as full human beings. The management control system can be instrumental in this attempt; it can be used to promote innovative behaviour within the organisation.

Alienation is the major impediment to the development of the personal character traits and personal growth that are conducive to innovative behaviour. Management control systems can either enhance or mitigate against alienation. Organisations needing to be innovative need to employ systems of management control which push alienation aside, and which develop within the employees the human virtues that breed intellectual curiosity (and hence deviance) as well as trust. Placing these values and attitudes in operative employees through the management control system is an essential component of the strategy of managing for innovative behaviour; to bring the corporation to an innovative tomorrow.

APPENDIX: DEFINITIONS

In this article, several terms are used either for which there is not common agreement on definitions or which are here used in a particular sense. The following are definitions for these terms as they are used in the discussion in this contribution. They are provided in an attempt to avoid confusion.

Institutionalisation - As used here, the term refers to the process of the individual accepting the values of the *status quo* of an organisation for their own sake; accepting the rules, procedures, processes, and prescribed outcomes for their own sakes, without considering why these phenomena should be valued. In using this term, we are always referring to the institutionalisation of the individual, and *not* to the institutionalisation of the organisation. This definition is in accordance with Maslow (1954).

Status quo - That which is presently or that which is presently perceived, including people, power positions, processes, and outcomes. As utilised here, the term does *not* imply anything regarding social position. By definition, in our sense, the status quo *cannot* include any degree of changing. Therefore, whenever the term is utilised, please realise that we are always referring to a degree of *status quo*, since nothing can be absolutely stagnant nor absolutely fluctuating.

Alienation - The state of being divorced in feeling and sentiment (which implies as well being divorced in respect of commitment) from another thing. Specifically, throughout this discourse, alienation refers to a state of being divorced from one's work, from one's fellow, from one's self - indeed it implies being divorced, in greater or lesser degreee, from one's reality.

References

Andrews, K.: 1977, *The Concept of Corporate Strategy*, Homewood, Ill.: Irwin. (Page rreferences are to the Spanish edition, *El Concepto de Estrategia de la Empresa*, Pamplona: Ediciones Universidad de Navarra, S.A.)

Anthony, R.N.: 1965, *Planning and Control Systems: A Framework for Analysis*, Cambridge, Ma.: Harvard University Press.

Argyris, C.: 1977, "Double Loop Learning in Organization", *Harvard Business Review*, September-October, 115-123.

Argyris, C. and D. Schön: 1974, *Theory in Practice*, San Francisco: Jossey-Bass.

Ashton, R.H.: 1976, "Deviation Amplifying Feedback and Unintended Consequences of Management Accounting Systems", *Accounting, Organisations, and Society,* 1, 4.

Burgelman, R.A. and L.R. Sayles: 1986, *Inside Corporate Innovation: Strategy, Structure, and Managerial Skills,* New York: Free Press.

Crozier, M.: 1963, *Le Phénomène Bureaucratique,* Paris: Editions du Seuil.

Crozier, M. and E. Friedburg: 1977, *L'Acteur et le Système,* Paris: Editions du Seuil.

Demski, J. and G. Feltham: 1976, *Cost Determination,* Ames, Io.: Iowa State University   Press.

Fiol, M.: 1984, "Contrôle de Gestion: Par les Résultats et par l'Identité d'Enterprise", Working Paper, Jouy-en-Josas: Centre d'Enseignement Supérieur des Affaires, July.

Gallo, M.A.: 1980, *Responsabilidades Sociales de la Empresa,* Pamplona: Ediciones Universidad de Navarra, S.A.

Hershey P. and K H. Blanchard: 1977, *The Management of Organisational Behaviour,* Englewood Cliffs, N.J.: Prentice Hall.

Hopwood, A.: 1974, *Accounting and Human Behaviour,* London: Haymarket Publishing.

Konopka, R.A.: 1988a, "A Paradox Defined: Corporate Control and Innovative Behaviour", Working Paper, IESE, Barcelona.

Konopka, R.A.: 1988b, "Man and Organisation: An Anthropological Model of Control", Working Paper, IESE, Barcelona.

Konopka, R.A.: 1988c, "Homo Humanus: The Focus of Management Control", Working Paper, IESE, Barcelona.

Konopka, R.A.: 1988d, "Man, Organisations, and Innovation: The Intrapreneurial Phenomenon", Working Paper , IESE, Barcelona.

Konopka, R.A.: 1988e, "Unravelling the Management Control/Innovation Paradox: Deviance, Tolerance, Virtue, Alienation, and Learning", Working Paper, IESE, Barcelona.

Maslow, A.H.: 1954, *Motivation and Personality,* New York: Harper and Row.

Ouchi, W.: 1979, "A Conceptual Framework for the Design of Organisational Control Mechanisms", *Management Science,* 25, 9, September, 833-848.

Ouchi, W.: 1980, "Markets, Bureaucracies, and Clans", *Administrative Science Quarterly,* 25, 1, March, 129-141.

Savage, L.J.: 1954, *The Foundations of Statistics,* New York: Wiley.

Schumpeter, J.A.: 1955, *The Theory of Economic Development,* Cambridge, Ma.: Harvard University Press (original English edition, 1934).

Thompson, J. and A. Tuden: 1959, "Strategies, Structures, and Processes of Organizations", in J. Thompson et al., *Comparative Studies in Administration,* Pittsburgh: University   of Pittsburg Press.

Tinker, A.: 1985, *Paper Prophets: A Social Critique of Accounting ,* New York: Praeger.

ETHICS AND INTERPERSONAL TRUST IN CORPORATE MANAGEMENT

Patrick Maclagan

Those who have written about trust in corporations have usually done so with a particular or partial concern in mind. For example, Fox (1974) seems to be especially concerned about the position of the low-discretion employee, this lack of autonomy apparently denoting management's lack of trust in such workers. Furthermore, Fox applies the same argument to higher status employees such as professional and semi-professional staff whose discretion is eroded as a result of an increase in rules, procedures and controls surrounding their work. This concern for what might be defined as the *rights* of employees differs from that emphasised by most organisation development specialists (e.g. Walton, 1969; Filley, 1975; Culbert and McDonough, 1985). Such writers have advocated the pursuit of high-trust relationships because these lead to more *effective organisational communications*. Admittedly, Fox also points to the counterproductive consequences, for management, of increased controls over employees, in that the lower trust presumed to result from this is undesiderable from the points of view of corporate performance. However, despite the impression that his is a "detached" sociological treatise, one feels that this managerial concern is secondary to his real sympathies.

Fox therefore represents, to use his own term, a "pluralist" position, while by contrast, many writers on organisation development represent an explicit and "unitary" concern for organisational (and managerial) effectiveness. While it is true that the pursuit of improved trust relationships in business firms is a laudable and worthwhile aim, the contributions of organisation development specialists in this respect do not provide guidance for those who, in the *short term* have to manage relationships where there is less than total confidence in, or agreement with others.

Such situations confront both managers and their staff with ethical issues, even if they do not recognise them as such. With that in mind, the purpose of this paper is to suggest a framework for analysis which adopts a different perspective from that found in earlier work on the concept of trust in management situations. The starting point is the proposition that such contributions harbour some oversimplifications. First of all, because of their relative generality, they cannot easily specify the precise grounds on which people distrust others, grounds which are, from a moral point of view, distinctive. Second, they may in some cases fail to take account of the variety of stakeholder interests in an enterprise. In common with so much work in the field of management and organisational behaviour, they tend to deal with their subject matter in either a managerial-technical or a pluralist-sociological fashion, rather than viewing it from an ethical-analytical perspective and giving due consideration to the various competing interests affected by business decisions (e.g. shareholders, suppliers, customers and the local community, as well as employees and managers themselves). Additionally, as noted above, the organisation development approach tends to be concerned with a longer-term programme of relationship-building whereas people quite frequently have to face more immediate situations even before mutual trust has been developed. The dilemma of whether or not to share confidential or sensitive information with others in the enterprise, where this might put at risk an important business contract, is one example.

Dimensions of interpersonal trust in business organisations

We may distinguish first of all between *competence* and *motive* as bases of distrust. Is distrust on grounds of a person's presumed motive different, from an ethical point of view, from distrust on grounds of lack of competence? We should also distinguish between trusting or distrusting someone *in a specific situation*, and distrusting them *in general* (Horsburgh, 1960).

These two dimensions to the analysis of trust give us four possible "ideal-type" situations.

(1) *Distrust in general on grounds of motive.* This indicates a general moral evaluation of a person, implying that he or she is self-interested and deceitful.
(2) *Distrust in a specific context on grounds of motive.* This is not such a serious moral criticism of a person whose motive may, after all, be justified. For example, the person may simply be supporting a different set of interests in that particular situation, and indeed feel strongly that he or she is morally right, but this would still give grounds for others to distrust him or her on grounds of motive rather than competence.
(3) *Distrust in general on grounds of competence.* This is barely a moral evaluation of the person, unless one holds that "being incompetent" is morally reprehensible. This of course may be the position adopted. Downie (1964) talking about the "morality of role-enactment" refers to "the contrast between the careless and the trustworthy or responsible performer..." It is interesting, however, that Downie *contrast* carelessness with trustworthiness in the context of moral behaviour.
(4) *Distrust in specific situation on grounds of competence.* This is not a moral evaluation of the person distrusted, but refers to the suitability of the person for that role or task.

It is also necessary to identify the types of organisational situation where interpersonal trust arises. As will become apparent in the next section, this entails consideration of the various stakeholders' interests, but so far as internal relations within the firm are concerned, Fox (1974) drew a distinction between *vertical* and *lateral* trust relations. This can be used to consider the question *who trusts or distrusts whom?* We can identify three broadly defined possibilities, in each of which the two dimensions just indicated, namely competence and motive, generality and specificity, may be found:

      (a) superior - subordinate,
      (b) subordinate - superior,
      (c) lateral relations between equals or across administrative boundaries.

(a) The first of these (as with the second) refers to leadership considerations, but more particularly to delegation. This includes many forms of job-redesign such as job-enrichment (Buchanan, 1979). It raises the question of how much discretion to grant to subordinates, bearing in mind (i) the level of competence of the latter and (ii) whether there is a risk of deliberate abuse of discretion by the subordinate, this latter possibility implying doubts about persons' motives.

(b) The second type of relationship is also connected to leadership. In any particular situation one can ask, do subordinates trust their leader and if not, why not? They may of course feel that he or she is generally incompetent or untrustworthy, and they may be justified in that view. However a manager cannot always be expected to communicate everything which he or she knows, or consult his or her staff on every decision, for reasons related to commercial pressures or other aspects of the enterprise in which his or her role is embedded. These pressures may suggest prudential reasons, perhaps even related to the interests of the subordinates themselves, for a manager's actions, such as the need for a quick decision. Furthermore, according to the stakeholder model he or she has moral obligations to other interests also, which might on occasion override the interests of subordinates. This would be a question of motive, but arguably a justifiable one, even if subordinates disagreed. Several writers on leaderships (e.g. Tannenbaum and Schmidt, 1958; Wroom and Yetton, 1973) discuss the practical issues raised in such situations, although the ethical dimension is left untouched, with the result that such theory may be accused of bias in favour of managerial control.

(c) Lateral trust relations are affected by administrative systems and structures. As Burns (1966) has pointed out, formal structure and control and incentive systems often generate competition and political behaviour within the enterprise. Organisation development practitioners such as Culbert and McDonough (1985) believe it is possible to create trusting relationships in these situations by facilitating less cynical perceptions by people of others' motives, although this calls for moral sensitivity from all concerned. People may view colleagues as generally untrustworthy, or only suspect them in a particular context. The latter situation offers more hope of a solution to the difficulties, since the possibility of goodwill exists and differences may turn out to be over means rather than ends. The former situation entails a more serious moral criticism of the other party, apparently imputing selfish motives.

Normative implications

It is essential to be clear as to one's ethical concerns. An initial distinction may be drawn between a concern for the person distrusted or trusted, and other concerns, such as overall corporate effectiveness, which brings in the stakeholder model. Such stakeholder or corporate interests would be understood in terms of the *dangers* of misplaced trust in specific others, such as a particular group of employees or an individual colleague or subordinate.

The first of these possibilities suggests a Kantian perspective; the second could be a Utilitarian position, although concern for particular stakeholders might on occasion demonstrate respect for persons in the Kantian tradition. It sould, alternatively, simply reflect self-interest.

The Kantian"categorical imperative" would emphasise respect for the person as an "end". To *trust* someone would be to facilitate their moral and personal development. In general, trusting someone entails a degree of risk, in relation to their competence, their motives, or both. Indeed, to trust where competence or motive is in doubt could be a way of facilitating their learning and self-development. This is what Horsburgh (1960) has called "therapeutic trust" which "aims at increasing the trustworthiness of those in whom it is reposed." (p.348) More specifically, Horsburgh suggested that there are two types of such relationship to be considered, and this distinction is important for the present discussion. In the first type, one can have situations where loyalty or affection on the part of, for example, a supervisor, leads him to exhibit blind faith in the employee in question, perhaps with disastrous results for all concerned. In the second type, a purely moral appeal to the person in whom trust is reposed can often be successful, not just with regard to that particular relationship, but in inducing more general trustworthiness. This second basis for demonstrating trust in someone is also less likely to lead to accusations of favouritism or discrimination.

Trust, as demonstrated in the granting of increased responsibility, could also contribute to a reduction in the degree of alienation from the work-situation (Blauner, 1964), but wheter it would really pave the way towards more meaningful work (Schwartz, 1982) or self-realisation (Nielsen, 1973) would depend on the degree of discretion and responsibility granted.

It could suggested that the provision of trust-relations *within organisations* is a necessary, but not a sufficient, condition for persons' development. Beyond a certain point, development is a very personal matter, perhaps involving the willingness to act autonomously (Cooper, 1970) or at the level of self-accepted moral principles (Kohlberg, 1973). This could even result in the trustee breaking the trust-relationship, as in cases of whistle-blowing, which leads us into the converse issues, of distrust.

To *distrust* a person without good ground would be to inhibit their development, to put them down, to lack respect for them. As Horsburgh observed "The stunting effects of distrust upon moral development can be seen on every side. Indeed it is no exaggeration to say that trust is to morality what adequate living space is to self-expression: without it there is no possibility of reaching maturity" (1960, 351). However it is also most important to realise that *trusting* someone on the false assumption that they are competent, when they are obviously incapable of the task, would be unjustifiable, as it could also set back their development by eroding their self-confidence and damage the interests of other stakeholders. This latter concern can be justified on more utilitarian grounds, to which we now turn.

The Utilitarian position gives rise to several possibilities. *Trusting* someone might facilitate their development (especially in the sense of competence) and so contribute to corporate effectiveness, as in job-enrichment programmes (Buchanan, 1979). It could also contribute to greater all round trust, as in organisation development programmes. Dowie (1971, 118) cites Horsburgh (1960) in an analogous context, noting that "therapeutic trust" helps to build social order, while Fox (1974) makes a similar point from his position as an industrial sociologist. However, as already observed, to place *trust* in someone when this seemed unwise could be to put at risk the performance of the enterprise or bring about unacceptable harm to other stakeholders' interests. Contrary to the Kantian "respect for persons" position and the often optimistic assumption of organisation development writers, there may sometimes be a moral justification for *distrust*, or caution, understood in terms of the more diffuse interests (or "good") of stakeholders (the "greatest number") with an interest in corporate performance. Thus the conflict so often experienced in management situations, between the principle of respect for the individual on the one hand, and more utilitarian concerns, on the other hand, is encountered.

How to solve such dilemmas?

What should one do, faced with such dilemmas? First, one can assess the ethical justifications and imperatives for placing one's trust (or not placing one's trust) in someone or some group. These reasons may be understood in terms outlined above; concern for individual recipients of one's trust, and concern for the outcomes of organised activity in so far as these affect the interests of various different people in the stakeholder group. Where the latter concern entails reserving judgement on the trustworthiness of particular individuals then the basis of this distrusts must be scrutinised. Is it on grounds of motive or competence? Is it general or specific? Does the perceived risk attached to trusting them in a particular situation justify one's action?

A reciprocal consideration is the effect of one's own behaviour on others' perceptions, since in so far as mutual trust is a valued state, one has a responsibility to facilitate this by inspiring others' confidence in oneself. Benveniste (1987, 108-111) lists a number of factors in one's own behaviour that affect others' trust in oneself. These comprise accepting the rules of the game, being predictable and reliable, having integrity, sharing commitments, and being capable. This is a mixture of motive-related and competence-related factors, some of which overlap. Integrity, and in some respects predictability and reliability (e.g. keeping promises) are the more obviously moral qualities here. However some difficulties arise. "Accepting the rules of the game" is problematic, since one might decide to challenge these on ethical grounds. A similar issue arises with shared commitment and promise keeping.

But these possibilities would refer to *specific* situations, rather than to any *general* tendency on one's part to behave in a capricious fashion. Benveniste defines integrity in terms of the fulfilment of promises and agreements and respecting the rules of the game, even if it is not in one's own interests. This fails to make the fine distinction between "selfish" self-interest and justifiable breaking of agreements in exceptional circumstances in order to serve *others'* interests. One might feel under a greater moral obligation to these interests than to previously agreed business policies and arrangements. Such action could be understood in terms of Kohlberg's highest levels of moral development (Kohlberg, 1973) and would not be inconsistent with a definition of integrity involving accountability to personal conscience rather than accountability to externally imposed rules.

In conclusion, therefore, trust relationships have a reciprocal moral dimension. Both roles, namely (a) that of placing trust in, or of choosing to distrust, someone, and (b) that of being the recipient of such trust or distrust, place an obligation on people in business organisations, as elsewhere, to understand the nature of the situation in all its complexity. It is maintained that the difference between a person's motives and their competence, as grounds for distrusting them, may be ethically significant, as may the distinction between distrusting someone on a specific occasion and regarding them as generally untrustworthy. Such analytical bases for discrimination between situations can help to guide action when faced with the conflict between utilitarian justifications for distrusting someone and the "categorical imperative" to respect and trust them. This latter obligation, often confined in management theory to a practical concern for corporate effectiveness, is, from a moral point of view, based on the principle of respect for individuals and the potential good in terms of their personal development which can flow from such demonstrations of confidence in them.

References

Benveniste, G.: 1987, *Professionalising the Organisation*, San Francisco: Jossey-Bass.
Blauner, R.: 1964, *Alienation and Freedom*, Chicago: University of Chicago Press.

Buchanan, R.: 1979, *The Development of Job Design Theories and Techniques*, Farnborough: Saxon House.

Burns, T.: 1966, "On the Plurality of Social Systems", in J. R. Lawrence (ed.), *Operational Research and the Social Sciences*, London: Tavistock.

Cooper, N.: 1970, "Morality and Importance", in G. Wallace and A.D.M. Walker (eds.), *The Definition of Morality*, London: Methuen.

Culbert, S.A. and J. McDonough: 1985, *Radical Management: Power, Politics and the Pursuit of Trust*, New York: Free Press.

Downie, R.S.: 1964, "Social Roles and Moral Responsibility", *Philosophy*, 39,31-33.

Downie, R.S.: 1971, *Roles and Values*, London: Methuen.

Filley, A.C.: 1975, *Interpersonal Conflict Resolution*, Glenview, Ill.: Scott-Foresman.

Fox, A.: 1974, *Beyond Contract: Work, Power and Trust Relations*, London: Faber and Faber.

Horsburgh, H.: 1960, "The Ethics of Trust", *Philosophical Quarterly*, 10, 343-354.

Kohlberg, L.: 1973, "Continuities in Childhood and Adult Moral Development Revisited", in P.B. Baltes and W. Shaie (eds), *Life-Span Developmental Psychology: Personality and Socialization*, New York: Academic Press.

Nielsen, K.: 1973, "Alienation and Self-realisation", *Philosophy*, 48, 21-33.

Schwartz, A.: 1982, "Meaningful Work", *Ethics*, 92, 634-646.

Tannenbaum, R. and W. Schmidt: 1958, "How to Choose a Leadership Pattern", *Harvard Business Review*, 36, 95-101.

Vroom, V. and P.W. Yetton: 1973, *Leadership and Decision-Making*, Pittsburg: Pittsburg University Press.

Walton, R.W.: 1969, *Interpersonal Peacemaking: Confrontation and Third Party Consultation*, Reading, Mass.: Addison-Wesley.

THE PARAMETERS OF ETHICAL DECISION-MAKING IN ORGANISATIONS

John Donaldson and John Sheldrake

Very many external factors serve to limit the capacity of organisations to make ethical decisions, or, if it is preferred, of individual officials in organisations to make ethical decisions. We attempt to identify some ways in which these limits might be moved in acceptable directions. The term "organisations" rather than "business" is used specifically to widen the scope of the discussion beyond the profit-making companies of the private sector alone. Many countries have a substantial public sector, whose role and acceptability varies according to national traditions, cultures, myths and ideologies.

The debate on the role has been most sustained in North America, where the purity of the enterprise system and the idea that the free market is the embodiment of justice are live issues. The "Chrysler loan" in the late seventies and the early eighties provides a typical example. Several papers were devoted to the general topic in the seminal collection of readings to the conference on business ethics in Kansas in the late seventies (De George and Pichler, 1978). The sustained debate in Britain from the forties onwards culminated in the insistent rolling back of the public sector in the eighties. Until very recently Britain possessed a large and growing public sector and many spheres of activity remained in the hands of organisations whose main justification cannot be measured merely in terms of financial profitability (Greenleaf, 1985; Saran and Sheldrake, 1988). Although the recent prominence given to "value for money" considerations has served to change perceptions within such organisations as local government, the civil service, the police, fire brigades and health service, it has yet to reconstruct the underlying organisational cultures of these bodies (Deal and Kennedy, 1988).

We believe that public sector organisations operate under a different set of imperatives from those in the private sector and that of themselves these imperatives establish a different set of ethical constraints (Morrison, 1933; Sheldrake, 1989). Evidence that the present British government shares this view is provided by its determination to divest itself of responsibility for as much of the economy as possible, thereby replacing what it construes to be the complexities of state intervention with the apparently simple arithmetic of the market. The attractions of this rolling back of the public sector are apparent from what has been termed "the world privatisation wave" of the eighties.

We suggest that the range of ethical decisions open to organisations is severely, but not unchangeably, constrained within parameters set, among other things, by law, culture, labour relations, the need to maintain profitability in the private sector and also the generalised need to achieve efficiency of operation. The demands of each of these constraints may, of course, compromise any or all of the others and emphasis will change over time. For example, scientific information may emerge which casts doubt on the environmental acceptability of a particular industrial process. The requirement to improve, or replace, the process may well affect operating efficiency and profitability with adverse effects on labour relations. Although our task is to identify the main parameters within which the ethical decisions of organisations are made we do not claim that these provide an hermetically sealed set of circumstances. On the contrary, we argue that the parameters are permeable and subject to constant invasion and modification. The possibility of making ethical decisions in isolation becomes increasingly difficult as the world we operate in becomes ever more complex and integrated. Nevertheless we believe that personal and organisational autonomy continues to be of paramount importance and carries with it the burden of acting responsibly.

Setting and moving the parameters

The continued presence of many internal pressures and constraints is consistent with shifts in some areas of the constraints and pressures themselves. The search for efficiency criteria and success formulae in the profit sector and in the public sector has in recent years been accompanied by growth of interest in business ethics. We think that the connection is not accidental, nor is it merely a shock reaction to some well-publicised lapses and scandals in both sectors in many countries. The shock reaction effect is undoubtely part of the response, but there has also been a more insistent questioning of the value-neutral approaches offered by the social sciences. That is, the positivist programme carried all before it in the sixties, but its insistent ignoring of the value issues in business and industry generally has permitted an explosive growth of ethical issues (Donaldson, 1989).

As Ryan puts it, in the American context:

> "My larger confidence rests on the belief that the waves of concern are now more frequent and less theoretical, with a lessening of mere exhortation and greater attention to specific suggestions and their implications. I note also the simultaneous convergence of different interests. This is a quantum leap from the earlier cycles of concern, building up a sustained momentum which is bound to develop ethical acuity in business leaders. We have here a maturing of business ethics, which, like the good seed, has the ingredients to improve business behavior a hundredfold" (Ryan, 1988).

The practical areas where improvement has been sought have been mainly:

a) Raising the awareness among managers of ethical issues and concepts.
b) Adoption of codes of practice and institutions for self-regulation.
c) Legislation, and especially the requirements for harmonisation with the European Community.

On the first of these, De George observes:

> "Business ethics can help people to approach moral problems in business more systematically, and with better tools than they might otherwise use. It can help them to see issues they might normally ignore. It can also impel them to make changes they might otherwise not be moved to make. Business ethics will not in and of itself make anyone moral... Business ethics will not change

business practices unless those engaged in the practices that need moral change wish to change them" (De George, 1986, 19).

De George sees a role for government in setting an example in its own practices and in regulation, but, rightly we believe, sees awareness of issues and conceptual resources as prerequisites.

The second mode, the adoption of self-regulation and codes of practice, has become so widespread that some observers have described them as a twilight legislation, serving too often to enable responsibility to be evaded, with legislation effectively passing out of the control of the sovereign.

The third mode raises many unresolved issues of the relationship between international law and state law, generating several *causes célèbres* (Newbiggin, 1984; Adams, 1985).

The primacy of individual action

Organisations, like individuals, seek to maximise their freedom of operation. At the level of theory, market capitalism construes the competitive interaction of self-interested producers as the best means for achieving operational efficiency and, by extension, consumer satisfaction. Similarly, political liberalism claims that the self-interested pursuit of individually selected goals provides the best basis for a "good society". These two notions (viz. market capitalism and liberal individualism) are closely linked in intellectual history having developed in Britain during the 120 years which separated the Glorious Revolution and the Napoleonic Wars (Checkland, 1983). In the writings of Locke, Smith, Paine and Bentham it is possible to discern a common thread which advocates, or defends, the autonomy of the individual and concedes only a minimal, or residual, role for government or the state. Of course, in practice, individual autonomy was closely linked to property ownership and the defense of property against the possible incursions of rulers. Nevertheless the assertion of individual liberty and inalienable natural rights provided a potent ideology which ultimately influenced all sections of society.

The tension between the advocacy of the maximum freedom of the individual and the proper role of government has never, of course, been resolved. The social outcomes of largely unbridled industrial development in early nineteenth century England soon generated the necessity to dilute the principles of individualism through the intervention of government. Even so, such intervention was depicted as a necessary evil rather than a positive good and "progressives" such as J. S. Mill agonised over how far the liberty of the individual might be justifiably compromised in the interests of society as a whole (Sabine and Thorson, 1973). Dissenting voices from what might be called, risking the charge of anachronism, left and right of the political spectrum had from the first been raised against the notions of individualism and dependence on the utility of the market. Rousseau, Burke and subsequently Carlyle and, of course, Marx had all generated potent critiques of what emerged as the prevailing liberal orthodoxy. By the final years of the nineteenth century, partly due to the influence of Hegel and partly as a result of the economic success of Prussia (Germany), there were increasing calls for state action as a means for achieving greater individual freedom throught the amelioration of gross inequality. The rise of socialism in Britain, together with the contemporary phenomenon of New Liberalism, generated a radical re-appraisal of the role of the state and the freedom of the individual within it. It was the impact of these new political ideologies with the unique political circumstances of the First World War which produced, in embryo, what subsequently became known as the welfare state (Vickerstaff and Sheldrake, 1989).

The notion that individuals, entrepreneurs and organisations should operate with the minimum of external constraint remains central to the thinking of the western world and, indeed, continues to gain influence in the wider world including both China and the Soviet Union. Nevertheless, the need for legally enforceable constraints is now widely conceded. During the past ten years in Britain the conservative governments have made much political capital out of engineering a retreat of the state, particularly through such policies as privatisation, contractualisation and de-regulation. This process offered one approach towards a necessary, if sometimes painful for some, corrective for the institutional ossification which had developed during the long period of governmental growth which had continued since the Second World War. Recent evidence, however, suggests that the process of liberalisation is now reaching the threshold where public opinion (particularly relating to health and environmental issues) is undergoing a shift in the direction of greater state activity in order to ensure protection.

Briefly, it is possible to posit a continuum between freedom and security which ranges from the horrors of the Hobbesian state of nature to a stultifying, bureaucratic, totalitarian state. Of course, in modern democracies, goverments are constrained to operate within a consensus which provides them with the opportunity of gaining re-election. This obviously places severe limitations on their freedom of action and reduces the range of issues over which they enjoy control. Indeed, the years of labour government in Britain from 1964 to 1970 and 1974 to 1979, provide potent examples of how goverment action is limited by external constraints and the existence of powerful vested interests. For example, the notion of taking large portions of industry into public ownership in order to protect workers and serve consumers proved untenable in the economic circumstances of the times and was thus tacitly abandoned as a policy option.

The activities of individuals, organisations and governments interact and, in a plural society, generate mutal constraints. The governmental constraints placed on organisations have been thought to be so onerous that operating efficiency and profitability are so badly affected that the enterprise might relocate, limit further investment or even cease trading. Similarly, the unbridled activities of an organisation might severely pollute the environment, compromise national security or grossly endanger employees. As industrial societies mature, the number of external constraints on organisations are likely to increase as aspirations develop and public opinion becomes informed about the environmental costs which often attend industrial and commercial success (Carson, 1988). For this reason alone there is an obvious incentive for major companies to relocate to areas of the world where low wages and the lack of environmental protection provide operating circumstances conducive to profit maximisation without constant concern over externally imposed constraints. This possibility has not been lost on governments who are often forced to compete to attract valuable investment by major companies. Self-evidently when governments desire to attract investment they cannot, if they seek to be consistent, legislate in ways which are likely to drive that investiment away. This situation poses a dilemma and is likely to result in an uneasy trade-off between the desire for industrial and commercial success and the wish to preside over a "green and pleasant land."

Since the seventeenth century the view has prevailed that self-control is to be preferred to externally imposed constraints. Central to this view has been the influence of protestantism with its emphasis on individual responsibility, and, certainly in Britain, an underlying hostility to government and its agents. As we have noted, the intervention of the state was, until the eve of the twentieth century, seen as a necessary evil rather than a positive good and, notwithstanding the influence of the Labour Party and the creation of the welfare state, this view has remained influential. Organisations which operate in Britain have inherited the generalised view that things are best left alone unless a positive abuse is identified. Organisations must constantly consider appropriate courses of action and, like individuals, balance ethical consideration with the promptings of expediency. Like individuals also they are subject to a multitude of constraints which serve to limit the span over which meaningful ethical considerations are possible. In the case of public bodies, for example, their operation is likely to be constrained from the outset by statute.

So far we have examined the evolution of that body of ideas concerning the activities of individuals and organisations which are generally identified as market capitalism and liberal individualism. We have noted that the primacy of the individual and the freedom to enjoy the use of property were gradually eroded by the need for governmental action in the face of generalised threats to society as a whole. We have also noted that maximum autonomy of individual action has remained dominant in the western world. On this view, at the level of theory, individuals and organisations are constantly faced with the task of identifying and justifying their courses of action. In practice the capacity to decide and to make ethical judgments concerning the decision are constrained. Though we claim that the ethical judgments made are *in fact* constrained, few, if any of the constraints are immutable and inevitable "laws of nature". They *tend to be* generated by external considerations rather than by internally generated concerns, but they can be seen - to use Leibniz' phrase - to "incline without necessitating".

Procedures for improvement: Some current uses and limitations

It was remarked earlier that no single definitive criterion for evaluating the performance of organisations has yet emerged. "Profit maximisation" provides a useful starting point for economic theory, but it remains a static concept, unable to provide much of a description of profit-behaviour over time, or to provide decision-rules except in static terms, because the "long-run" remains indeterminate, or at best, arbitrary. It is further weakened by the (empirically obvious) existence of multiple "goals" within and between individuals and their value-sets. *A fortiori* it does not apply in the public sector in those activities where the goods are costly, but not market-driven, such as the police, the armed forces, voluntary organisations, for example. The most that can be said, theoretically, is that "value for money" concepts, though undeveloped, seem to be moving in the right direction. Bits of public organisations can be brought into the market sector, where traditional profit criteria are at least relevant. Shadow prices can be created, but the core activities are there because they are valued. Profit maximising armies, police forces and churches are not part of the official scheme of things, however much their costs need to be monitored. The absence of sufficient criteria in part explains the oscillation between enthusiasm for privatisation and for state control. *In the absence of definitive performance criteria, practical proposals for improvement have, in recent years, concentrated upon (a) raising individual awareness, (b) adoption of codes of practice, and (c) legislation.* There are discussed in turn below.

(a) Raising awareness: Uses and limitations

The idea of raising awareness of ethical issues and the existence of systematic ways of handling them seems to be an essential "gateway" through which improvements in standards can enter. It brings with it a number of problems which replicate those which became evident in the era of "T-groups" and "sensitivity training" in the sixties and early seventies. The first of these is that replacing "sensitised" managers into situations in which others are not sensitised tended to create a mutual puzzlement as the old structures, concepts and behaviour remained in place. Argyris (1974) describes the process in terms of organisations' capacity for "self-renewal", which can clearly be seen to be low in many cases. Educating a few managers and leaving structures intact carries, paradoxically the opposite danger, that of raising expectations that cannot be met, followed by a complete rejection of the process. This latter possibility was visible in the "participation"-movement in the seventies, particularly in Britain. If we are right, the implication is that raising awareness among managers is necessary, but the expected results should not be overstated. Bureaucratic structures, internal politics and career practices all take their toll, and may need to be amended to fit the growing awareness of the issues that they raise. Difficult though change may be, these processes are by no means immutable laws of nature.

(b) Problems with codes

Codes of practice set minimum standards. They are usually set in a form that is offered as highly practical, and are not often, if ever, accompanied by detailed discussion of their underlying rationale. Rather they are protected by their practical form from much discussion. They tend to be mixtures of technical, prudential and moral imperatives. They remove some doubt as to what standards are expected but they vary in the extent to which they can be enforced. A standard objection to professional codes is that they tend to protect, primarily, the professionals from the laity, just as those in use in industry protect suppliers from customers, benefits to customers or clients being subsidiary, though necessary. The problem lies not so much with the codes and their content, but with the procedures by which they are drawn up, applied and amended. A major constraint is provided by the level of willingness or ability of the people affected to participate in the design, operation and revision of codes. For example, when pay restraint codes were regularly imposed by governments, they set "ceilings" on pay-rises. These soon became "floors", or minimum expectations. The limitations on the extent to which codes can contribute to improvement of standards of conduct in business are provided much more by the code-setting processes than by the often claimed cynical ignoring of their provisions by those who are able to do so.

(c) Problems with legislation

Examples of improvement of conduct generated by legislation are legion. Instances in which legislation has the opposite effect to that intended are not difficult to find. It is not our intention to rehearse them here, but two features are worth noting:

Firstly, enforcement of ethical behaviour to a large extent denatures it. It is sound and sensible to reinforce what people ought (morally) to do with prudential motives, such as threats of punishment, but no business system can rely purely on prudential motives. Business is, in fact, redolent of and driven by values, only some of which are enforced by law. Managers (and management text books) spend a great deal of time inculcating values, which are often embedded in what are taken to be matters of purely technical competence. Thus business ethics needs to offer far more than the basis for some new legislation.

Secondly, legislation itself has always been widely regarded as a necessary evil, inconsistent in principle with individual freedom. A corollary of this is the idea that business is so complex that, for example, legislation to reduce the number of *causes célèbres* in financial services must, to be effective, strike a balance between education and training, voluntary codes and compulsion. This is clearly visible in the recent Financial Services legislation in Britain.

Conclusions

Organisations, both private and public, undergo a continuous justification process, which gives them an ethical status. Their capacity to permit ethical decisions to be made by managers is hampered by the absence of definitive performance criteria. The "profit "criterion serves well enough for many purposes in the private, market sector, but it is full of ambiguities and has very limited application in the public and voluntary sectors. The principles of autonomy and the primacy of individual action require that managers and others in organisations should act ethically, as a condition of the autonomy and primacy. They are constrained by some internal forces and many external ones. The latter range from market imperatives to cultural norms, customs and practices, lack of ethical awareness, and inflexible authority structures and attitudes.

Some promising ways forward are supplied by the increase in awareness of ethical issues in business, in the increasing use of codes of practice, and in legislation aimed at curbing some kinds of business behaviour that have been under criticism in recent years. These ways forward have their characteristic limitations, even though evidence of improvement can be found. The limitations are provided less by the cynical and self-seeking nature of people than by real dilemmas and conflicting principles. The need to curb some kinds of behaviour *is* in conflict with the norms of freedom of action and autonomy of individuals. Some legislation *is* counterproductive. Tensions *do* exist between the processes of code-setting and their content.

None of this leads to the conclusion that ethics education is ineffective or that codes and legislation are not helpful. They do need to be proven in practice, and constantly restated in changing circumstances. The structural determinants of behaviour and conduct provided by bureaucratic forms of management are reinforced by cultural myths and norms developed in the absence of systematic ethical reasoning. The external constraints can be moved, but it is unlikely to happen so long as the education, codes and legislation coexist in isolation from each other.

The following additional possibilities are offered in conclusion. (They are treated in more detail in Donaldson, 1989, 189):

1. *Matching values to strategies.* This recognises that some business strategies render difficult, if not impossible, the realisation of some espoused values. Just as there is usually choice of strategies, there is usually choice as to which values to pursue, and which to leave to look after themselves. There is often a relationship between values and strategies which promotes myths to "hard realities". In particular cases the process can be understood and modified acceptably.
2. *Development of commitment from the mutual design of codes.* This is the far from novel insight that has been widely canvassed by the advocates of "industrial participation" from the Hawthorne Studies of the twenties onwards.
3. *Discretionary legislation* to encourage experiment in organisational forms, especially those that help to bring the "official" processes and procedures in industry closer to the "unofficial" or real processes.
4. *More openness in decision-making* to discourage undue restriction of business agendas. This would suggest the modification of bureaucratic and hierarchical forms of business and business-related institutions.
5. *Encouragement and incorporation of research on values.* There are many agencies

which fund research, and industry spends resources on research and development. As has often been pointed out, the explosion of interest in ethical issues in business has not so far been research-based. Some surveys are appearing, and much case material is supplied daily in the mass media.

6. *Recognition* that ethics often requires a balancing of principles that pull in different, often opposite directions.

What these amount to is the view for business ethics as a discipline to raise its influence, it will need to become increasingly integrated into practice as well as theory, at the moral as well as the technical and prudential levels. The constraints are much too powerful for "bolt-on" or "plug-in" ethical modules in business to stand much of a chance. Improvements, however precarious they may be, do occur from a variety of

sources: what happens is not wholly determined by inexorable laws, but not all good ideas for improvement work.

References

Adams, : 1985, *Roche versus Adams*, Glasgow: Fontana/Collins.

Argyris, C.: 1974, *Behind the Front Page*, New York: Jossey-Bass.

Carson. R.: 1988, *Silent Spring*, Harmondsworth: Penguin Books.

Checkland, S.: 1983, *British Public Policy 1776-1939*, Cambridge: Cambridge University Press.

De George, R.: 1986, *Business Ethics*, Second edition, New York: Macmillan.

De George R. and J. Pichler, eds.: 1978, *Ethics, Free Enterprise, and Public Policy*, New York: Oxford University Press.

Deal, T. and A. Kennedy: 1988, *Corporate Cultures*, Harmondsworth: Penguin Books.

Donaldson, J.: 1989, *Key Issues in Business Ethics*, London: Academic Press.

Morrison, H.: 1933, *Socialisation and Transport*, London: Constable.

Sabine, G. and T. Thorson: 1973, *A History of Political Theory*, London: Harrap.

Saran, R. and J. Sheldrake: 1988, *Public Sector Bargaining in the 1980s*, Aldershot: Avebury.

Sheldrake, J.: 1989, *Municipal Socialism*, Aldershot: Avebury.

Vickerstaff, S. and J. Sheldrake: 1989, *The Limits of Corporatism*, Aldershot: Avebury.

Part II

"Empowering" People: End or Means?

THE ETHICAL CHALLENGE TO THE CORPORATIONS: MEANINGFUL PROGRESS AND INDIVIDUAL DEVELOPMENT

Philippe de WOOT

1. Urgent questions

Why is the moral philosophy of business becoming increasingly visible today? It is because the development of the international competitive game as well as the evolution of the strategic power of corporations give rise to a series of problems and issues. The most important of these may be identified es follows:

(1) The globalisation of competition and the need for a "triad" approach (Europe, United States, Asia) often compel corporations to achieve a considerable strategic capacity. The corporation develops its power by creating the key resources needed for its development: international teams, technologies, information systems, networks, contacts, etc. From this perspective, private power becomes more important and increasingly international.

(2) The acceleration of technical progress follows its course: research and development constitute major competitive weapons. In many fields, it is the enterprise which decides the scope and orientation of technical progress. This relates not only to the volume of research, but also to the combination and interchange of disciplines. Such a policy triggers the emergence of new generations of technology which are broader and more complex.

(3) The increased role of the financial establishment in the restructuring of world capitalism provides another example. Without aiming at too rigid a separation between the world of finance and of enterprise, we may wonder if their objectives are sufficiently close, and whether their approaches are always as complementary as some people claim. In some cases, the dismemberment of a corporation for a short term profit may prejudice its long-term development by destroying delicate networks, almost invisible synergia and a common culture carrying a capacity for progress. The stock exchange market does not always adequately reflect the long-term bets of entrepreneurs. If we consider the sums at stake, the intervention of financiers may have a considerable impact: there would be nowadays around thirty billion dollars in LBO funds (Leverage-Buy-out)). If we take a lever of ten, 300 billion dollars seem to be ready for investment, with this procedure, in financial manoeuvers whose industrial purpose is not always visible. If we add scandals and "affairs", we will better understand why some people wonder about the object of this type of game.

(4) There are also "mega-problems" in which enterprises may be involved, either because they are at their origin, or because they may contribute to their solution. We may in particular mention pollution and accidents such as Seveso, Bhopal, Three Miles Island, Alaska, etc. Or think about the development of the Thirld World or Eastern countries: must or can the huge know-how of our enterprises be used to serve these gigantic causes?

(5) Finally, if we define the corporation as a society of individual entities involved in relationships of authority, co-operation and exchange, we understand the magnitude of the ethical questions resulting from the management of an enterprise: Which mode of use of power must one choose? Which policy must we adopt for the development of human resources? Is it possible to reconcile (harmonise) the economic requirements and the aspirations of people working in the enterprise? How does one deal with conflictual interests?

2. Specific function of the corporation

The power of the corporation, the direction of technical progress, financial games, environment, Third World, personal development - there is clearly no "ready made" ethical answer to problems of such a magnitude. General ethics do not enable tus o go deeper into such questions, even if they provide a preliminary orientation. It is therefore necessary to define the scope of reflection and to focus it on the specific function of the enterprise. It is only by starting from the function that the enterprise fulfils exclusively in our society that we will be able to tackle the specific ethical issues engendered by its activities and strategies.

By studying the functioning of corporations, their performances and strategies, research has validated Schumpeter's assumption: innovation alone explains their development and survival. If we observe them over a long period of time, we note that no enterprise has ever been able to survive without constantly renewing its products, processes, markets, methods. It is owing to innovation that they have created and spread economic and technological progress.

It is the active corporation which takes the risk and makes the effort for that progress. It develops within itself the characteristics of Schumpeter's entrepreneurship: foresight of possible achievements, liking for risk sufficient to undertake and implement it, authority and capacity for action enabling the entrepreneur to carry the initiative to its objective, in spite of the risk. Thus, the active corporation systematises creativity and enters into a dynamic process of change. In this respect, to undertake is essentially to change an existing order. If this function takes place in a competitive and open (international) framework, and if we add the various public incentives, we may then understand the essentials of the creative mechanism of economic and technical progress.

In this perspective, we may propose a central concept to describe the specific function of the enterprise: *economic and technical creativity.*

One may maintain the thesis according to which, among major civilisations, Western civilisation has constantly valorised this type of progress and adjusted its endeavours to the level of those activities which it deemed fundamental and worth of attention. If we refer to the great myths at the basis of our culture, we soon notice that they give an important role to economic and technical progress. Is this not precisely the meaning of the myth of Prometheus? Taking the risk of progress, stealing from the gods'fire, father of all arts, endless road..." Prometheus is the embodiment and symbol of the entrepreneur's qualities and dynamism. "One day, in the sacred stem of the narthecium, I have hidden the Spark... I transmitted it... O! Liberating Fire, O! Creative Spring. Master of all arts,

Endless road open to Mankind" (Aeschylus, *Prometheus bound*). Around this central character, other gods and heroes embody the function of economic progress: Vulcan the engineer; Ulysses and Jason, the opening of markets; and even Icarus, the heroe of the ill-calculated risk and aborted progress. Icarus... the Concorde!

And by degrees, the West kept and developed this belief in an achievable and useful progress, sometimes through admiration given to overseas adventures and to discoveries: Marco Polo, Christopher Columbus, Magellan, or by the will to endlessly define itself as an urban society, inclined to international exchanges, open to the sea and all the freedoms it entails. A clue to the growth of our Western civilization is the development of merchant cities involved in business and free enterprise: Athens, Alexandria, Byzantium, Venice, Bruge, Antwerp, Amsterdam, London, New York,...

This gradual growth was that of a movement, a striving towards something new, a relentless questioning of the existing order, the commitment to a fast evolution which we accepted with sometimes the impression that we were leading the process.

"For those who spread well their sails to the breath of the Earth, a new wind rises and compels to always take the high seas" (Teilhard de Chardin, 1956). True, one of the characteristics of the Western world is that it has often accepted a need to take to he high seas, whether it be for international exchanges, arts, institutions, knowledge and thinking.

Pondering over the extraordinary capacity of renewal of Western artistic creation, André Malraux defined it as the "art of the great navigators". Do not we find the symbol of that collective attitude in the moto of the Hanseatic league: "Navigare necesse est"?

For more than two centuries, the corporation has been the most dynamic agent of that movement in the economic field. Its creative function was for a long time part of the general strive of the whole society towards a different future. We may consider that the corporation was more than a mere social phenomenon. In the Western world, it was an element of civilisation.

"Listen to the worries of mortals and to what I did for these weak-willed children whom I led to Wisdom and the strength of Reasoning... Before, men had eyes in order not to see. They were deaf to the voice of things, and like characters in dreams they moved around in the disorder of the universe... They did not build houses in the sun. They did not know about the brick or how to manufacture beams or boards. Like ants, they were hiding underground, shutting themselves in the darkness of caves... They did not foresee the return of seasons, since they were unable to decipher the signs announcing winter, or spring with its flowers, or the ripening summer sun. They did everything, knowing nothing. Until the day came when I invented for them the complex science of the rising and setting of the heavenly stars. Then, I introduced them to the science of numbers, queen of all knowledge, and to the assembling of letters, memory of all human thoughts, vector of human labour... Then, to alleviate their pain when labouring the soil, I taught them how to harness wild animals. The horse submitted to its rider, drove the cart, became the pride of kings. The ox bent its neck and drew the plough. And to cross the seas, I gave them the ship with its cloth wings. These were my inventions. The man who freed mankind did not find the way to his salvation" (Aeschylus, *Prometheus bound*).

3. Goals and values: two examples

Economic and technical progress does not constitute an end in itself. To give a meaning (or value) to economic progress, we must go further and try and find an answer to the following questions: (1) What for ? (2) For whom ? (3) How ?

3.1 Meaning of economic and technical progress

Today, we perceive more clearly the limitations, costs and dangers of uncontrolled technical progress. We also see that it can only be a means, and not an end in itself.

Technical progress transforms into an Apocalypse the threats of nuclear war, it does not prevent thousands of human beings from dying of hunger; it does not in itself suppress social inequalities. In its pride, although rather short-sighted, Prometheus, the "Saviour of Mankind" claimed "I have abolished the anxieties of death". We all know that this is not the case. We also realise that Prometheus must be subject to a political order which supersedes and leads him at the same time.

Such an orientation can only be given by well oriented progress. We must go beyond a too exclusively economic and financial approach to come out with social and political values and a definition of common good or general interest.

"It stands to reason that science and technology have provoked irreversible degradations to the environment, an economic unbalance and moral laxity... Nobody has seriously doubted that this process was necessary. This attitude, often nonsensical, involves a blind mercantile instinct and an unbounded thirst for comfort and consumption. But there is also a much more powerful mechanism: the conviction, deep-rooted in the heart of Westerners, at least since the days of Athens, that the intellectual quest must proceed, that such an impetus is in conformity with nature and deserving in itself, that man is dedicated to the search for thruth. The "Tally ho" of Socrates bringing his prey to stand re-echoes all over our history. We open the row of doors of the Castle of Bluebeard because they are there and that each of them leads to the next one, according to a process of intensification in which our Mind defines its own nature. Leaving one of these doors closed woud be not only an act of cowardice, but also a gross treachery, a mutilation of the inquisitive, searching and unquenchable instinct of our species. We hound reality, wherever it is leading us to. Risks, disasters are obvious...".

"What I have in mind goes far beyond the current concerns of the scientific community regarding issues such as environment, armaments, the unconsidered use of chemical substances in the organism. The real problem is to know whether we must persist in certain research activities, whether human society and mind are, in their present stage of evolution, able to endure truths to come. It is possible - and here we come to dilemnas unprecedented in history - it is possible that the next door will open on realities which are, by their very nature, contrary to our mental balance and our weak mental reserves. Jacques Monod has publicly formulated a question that others have asked in private: must we persevere if genetics were to disclose, regarding the differenciation of races, secrets which may have moral, political and psychological consequences exceeding our understanding? Are we free to explore those neurochemical and psychopathological paths which lead to the partly archaic regions of the cortex, if that study reveals that racial hatred, the liking for war or pulsion of death mentioned by Freud are based on heredity? Many other examples may be quoted" (Steiner, 1986, 151-152).

3.2 Development of the individual in the corporation and the use of power

Research in the social sciences indicates clearly the will of those who work in a business enterprise to give meaning to their activity and to be able to develop themselves. The concept of *responsibility* is at the centre of the debate. Whether it be the need for self-fulfilment brought to light by American researchers, or the will to create and control, underlined in particular by Touraine, the exercise of responsibility in one's job seems to be the cornerstone of genuine social progress.

The conditions of a responsible work have been underlined in numerous books (see in particular Argyris, 1958). They mainly aim at developing :

- competence
- a feeling of being useful
- a feeling of being valued
- experience of success
- sufficient freedom in the following fields: expression, research for information, control over standards and the result of one's work.

The results of such research activities correspond almost word for word to the great moral appeal of John XXIII in *Mater and Magistra* (1962), to such an extent that we can only ponder over this convergence.

Pondering over the conditions which need to be fulfilled for a social and economic system to be considered as "just" from the Christian point of view, John XXIII puts at the heart of his answer the concept of responsibility.

"If the structures and functioning of an economic system are of such a nature that they endanger the human dignity of those who belong to it, blunt their sense of responsibility, deprive them of any personal initiative, we consider that system as wrong, even if the wealth produced reaches a high level and is distributed according to the laws of justice and equity" (p.91).

This obviously implies an exercise of power oriented towards individuals. There are two concepts of power, in Europe. One is cynical, cold-blooded, shrewd, amoral. The other is humanistic, cordial, democratic, permeated with ethical values. It is no longer a dominating power, but the power to serve: the purpose is to moderate a collective game and to lead it, instead of dominating. Moral qualities play therefore an important role and leaders of this type rely more on their authority than on their exclusive statutory power.

4. Personal ethics

The problems described here will certainly be illuminated by a vision of the specific function of the corporation, as well as by some general goals. However, this will not suffice: many decisions will be guided exclusively by the leader's personal ethics. In this respect, the recent books of Jean Moussé (1989a,b) propose a concrete approach which may be adopted by a "committed" leader.

In a divided society, where the concept of good is more and more relative, is there a basic principle, of sufficiently universal character to serve as an ethical basis? Many works have been written on this topic:

"Kant is close to us when he proposes his imperative 'Do what you must, because you must'. Unconditionally, since you are free and responsible, able to determine personally what is good or wrong. There is no other ethic than that of freedom... That assurance characterised by Saint Paul when he wrote that everything is permitted, even if everything is not convenient".

"Everyone judges for himself". It also inspired Saint Thomas Aquinas when he wrote that the law of conscience dominates all human laws, including the law of the Church... But, in all the cases, the strength of the statement presupposes a lengthy personal march fed by many reflections. It is precisely this itinerary which gives strength to certain men who are utterly right, incorruptible and, at the same time, perfectly respectful of others.

The two principles proposed by Kant are unambiguous: "Act in such a way that the rules of your action can be transformed into universal rules". Here we come to the very principle of universality. And the second principle: "Act in such a way that never mankind, be it yourself or others, be used as a simple means, to reach your purpose" (Moussé, 1989a, 28-29).

"Human Rights", following other approaches, *e.g.* the Gospel, endeavoured to clarify and materialise that respect towards human beings. They define some preliminary and indefeasible rights, such as freedom, justice, equality, truth... rights which ought to be respected by any reasonable man.

Jean Moussé believes that we should go further and base our professional ethics on the unconditional recognition of others as free persons. This must be done *unconditionally* and we "must not satisfy ourselves with providing a personal answer to the movement of recognition coming from the others. It is the only means to break the cycle of violence in relations between groups, as well as between individuals" (1989a, 44).

At the individual level, there may be religious, moral and civil beliefs and values. But in a pluralistic and divided society, the concepts of good and wrong become less absolute: emergence of an ethic implying choices ("menu"), rejection of ideologies (it is forbidden to forbid).

In our present society, the "convictions" of the participants are often different. Their conception of "good" varies considerably. Nevertheless, participants cannot force their ideology or ideal, or system of values, upon their partners. This is clearly explained by Jean Moussé: "Personal convictions may bring people together in specific associations, benevolent, spiritual or cultural. Their members act like ferments in our society. They participate in transfomation. They must not for all that impose their ideal on all their fellow-beings. The rules of good are not those of justice. What is good is not what is right. In a given society, justice relates only to the establishment of rules enabling people to come to a fair agreement to live and work together. In an enterprise, it means that tasks and responsibilities must be defined while taking into account its objectives, so that everyone will understand what is expected from him as well as what to expect from others... But this excludes the interplay of ideological opinions, of good or ill feelings, preferences or antipathies, under the pretext of the pursuit of good... The good that the legislator pretends to impose becomes wrong if he no longer respects the concept of freedom, since there can be no good without freedom. This respect is therefore a prerequisite and imposes its law and organizational rules." (1989a, 116).

In such a society, the ethics based on conviction leads more and more to an ethics centered on responsibility (Moussé, 1989a, 87). It does not suffice to act according to one's convictions, we must answer for the consequences of our deeds. In fact, ethics are embodied in actions. "This is why a responsible man starts from convictions, freely elaborated and strengthened by his experience, and discovers the inexhaustible complexity of the world in which he does his job. His convictions bring him back to the constantly updated analysis of facts, without which he cannot deal with them and this analysis, in its turn, sends him back to convictions which give a meaning to his deeds. Man is never totally independent, since his experience continues, as do his relations with the world and with others, while his encounters, readings, lessons derived from failures and success constantly open new perspectives and generate new questions". "The true decision-maker", explains I. Adizes, "scans the mist and decides amidst uncertainty. It is precisely his decision which partly dissipates the clouds of uncertainty, both as regards himself and his surroundings... He does not wait until he knows everything before taking the risk to act. It is for him a supplementary reason to appreciate the scope of his deeds" (Moussé, 1989a, 87).

Finally, it is necessary to organise *"links"* at the level of professions and business. Each profession - medicine, teaching, business, judges - has its own specific problems:

- A first link is constituted by associations of leaders and managers who will attempt together to identify ethical problems and open a debate on principles and approaches susceptible to throw light on the choice of solutions.
- A second link is made up of industries or sectors: advertising, pharmaceutical products, defence industry, etc. For each trade, we may be more specific and deepen the analysis and orientations.
- A third link is that of the corporation itself, with its own specific problems, culture, history, etc.
- Finally, the fourth link is that of individual conscience. Due to the complexity of problems and issues, we cannot avoid making individual ethical choices, on a case by case basis.

"From any initial situation, each of us can work towards the establishment of a meaning... Interrogation relative to ethics finally sends each of us back to the network of concrete relations in which freedom may find an answer, always incomplete, never final. Thus, to express an ethical attitude is to act freely, according to convictions which are always in process of elaboration; during an evolution determined by history, both personal and collective. The reflection which is at the basis of the ethical attitude is fed by numerous contributions from others. Nevertheless, it is personal, the fruit of an autonomous and responsible freedom" (Moussé, 1989a, 31). François Guiraud speaks of distributed responsibilities, distributed ethics.

Improvement of the ethical level of a society or profession will not take place by decree. It will result from a living and well-structured process of reflection and commitment, by an increasing number of participants.

References

Argyris, C.: 1958, *Personality and organization*, New York: Harper.

John XXIII: 1962, *Mater et magistra*, Paris: Spes.

Moussé, J.: 1989a, *Fondements d'une éthique profesionelle*, Paris: Les Editions d'Organisation.

Moussé, J.: 1989b, *Pratique d'une éthique profesionelle*, Paris: Les Editions d'Organisation.

Steiner, G.: 1986, *Dans le château de Barbe-Bleu. Note pour una redéfinition de la culture*, Paris: Folio.

Teilhard de Chardin, P.: 1956, *Le phénomène humain*, Paris: Seuil.

THE INDIVIDUAL DIMENSION IN CORPORATIONS

Francisco López-Frías

1. Background

1.1 The experience

My teaching and research activity is centered in ethics as that part of philosophy which is concerned with the morality of human behaviour. It is a highly speculative field, but this does not free the ethicist from the necessity of formulating practical questions. Between 1981 and 1985 I taught ethics and professional deontology at the training school of a savings bank in Barcelona (*Escuela de Formación Profesional de la Caja de Pensiones para la Vejez y de Ahorro (la Caixa), founded in 1906). It was my first opportunity to use theoretical knowledge in dealing with the concrete activity of banking employees. The course outline consisted in the study of specific cases chosen from hundreds of real situations - carefully disguised to avoid identification - which had occurred in the various offices of the company, in the light of certain principles of ethics.

The students were employees who also attended courses in other subjects. They came to class at the end of their working day and, in many cases, had to travel far. They didn't want to waste time, and so their main preoccupation in the ethics course was the material to be dealt with. They were very happy to hear that it was not going to be a moralistic sermon, but rather an analysis of the morality of behaviour, and that we would try to carry out this task using Aristotelian methods (obviously I saved this vocabulary for later in the course) with the help of which we would try to *arrive* at primary principles rather than starting with them (see Aristotle, 1900, 1926).

Excellent material was available, as I have said, for stimulating interest in discussions and setting into the main themes. The actual cases were very striking because some of them might easily have happened to anyone attending the class. But we had to avoid the sessions becoming casuistic analysis which would have led us to situational ethics or relativism.

The experience lasted four academic years and the programme included two complete courses. In the first course the students acquired some theoretical knowledge of values, work, the common good, justice, utility, rights, duties, property and contracts. The second course was the application of those principles and concepts to the concrete relations between the employee and his or her institution. We studied mutual knowledge, integration, confidence, loyalty, fidelity, image, professionalism, professional duties, rules and institutions, the principle of authority and its abuse, negligence, security, professional secrets, intimacy, relationships with clients, obeying the law, and so on. The fruit of these classes was the publication of two books (López-Frías *et al.*, 1984a, 1984b).

1.2 The problem

By the second course, the student-employeees usually had enough confidence in the teacher to deal with the topics without reserve. All of them were conscious of belonging to a prestigious, responsible firm with an excellent public image and a well-defined organisational structure. The doubt - as they put it - was whether it was a firm where they could develop as individuals or, on the contrary, where their personalities were going to be annihilated. They wanted to know, definitely, if what the firm offered them was *work* -in the socio-ethical sense of participation in a common task - or simply a job (cf. López-Frías, 1983)

The big question at all of the sessions was how was it possible to reconcile the interests of the individual with those of the firm. At first sight the confrontation seems very unequal in that the firm can clearly impose its own conditions. Does the firm have any other interest than making profits? The corporation we were concerned with does not pay dividends to shareholders and all profits are used for social causes; but were the employees being sacrificed to these objectives just as they might have been in any other firm? Some student-employees argued that what we talked about in class did not fit in with the real world and gave examples to support their view that the corporation can only justify its existence if it makes profits. This being the case, they argued, ethics has little to do except perhaps ease the problems or camouflage them in more presentable clothes.

1.3 The arguments

There were many ways to attack this attitude of resistance with logical arguments and I think I tried almost all rationally defensible ones. I frequently played the devil's advocate, defending positions I didn't believe in, so as to bring into perspective attitudes critical of the firm. In some groups - not all of them gave the same results - this atmosphere was developed in a few sessions.

In our class nothing impeded deep moral reflection aimed at getting a clear idea of what we could do as individuals joined in a common task. On the other hand, personal participation and respect for individuality were, at this level, a premise accepted by the majority of firms which think about the future and *invest* in the moral and responsible enrichment of their employees as one of the most profitable assets in the balance sheet.

1.4 The thesis

In this article I try to show that true *individuality* is a matter of social integration and that all individuality that excludes the social dimension is pathological and is the main source of conflict in corporations. I arrived at this certainty - which is the central nucleus of this paper - as a result of the discussions in the seminars. I made a point of supporting the arguments of those who said that it was important not to be engulfed by the firm or annihilated by the force of rigid structures, authoritarianism, or pressures of any type. But I had to be careful not to support disguised individualistic behaviour which frequently pursues actions not as ends in themselves but simply as means to achieve egotistic designs. These various forms of individualism frequently hide psychological or moral defects.

The reasoning, the nuances and even part of the vocabulary which I used in the development of this thesis was to a great extent conceptually coined to convince the students that, in spite of the difficulties, we have to opt for being individuals with all the consequences this involves, whilst unmasking egotistical individualism as a psychic disease, a social pathology or, in the majority of cases, a moral limitation.

2. Theory of individual and social life. Between society and the corporation

2.1 The individual and the collectivity: History

The individual is the essential ingredient in the functioning of the social reality and rarely does a corporation or firm ignore this important truth. But the individual becomes a disruptive influence when this individuality takes the form of egotistical individualism. Since the words used to designate such opposite concepts are so similar some clarification is in order, as well as an examination of this typically modern phenomenon which arose as a response to the general spread of an extreme collectivism, committed to the dissolution of the individual, especially after the 19th century.

Our object is to show that social life is a kind of individual life. All the richness and complexity of the social contribution "contracts" and is lodged in the individual who thus becomes not only the beneficiary of these riches but also the supplier to society of these same gifts, now enriched with his contribution. It is a reciprocal relationship through which the individual can pay back with interest what he has received. Individuals do not all respond to the same extent in this relationship, but the important point is to show that individual and society are ingredients in the same body. An isolated individual is an abstraction because it does not exist in reality; if we want to speak of individuals we most include in this concept the unavoidable social dimension.

Because of this social dimension, humans do not need to occupy themselves with routine questions which are necessary to live but which, when confronted as problems - petty as they may be - cause a great loss of time needed for other more important and creative labours to develop society. This is the great difference - of quality and not only of degree - between human and animal life, although being confined to such things, is not a serious problem for animals, since they possess sufficient and adequate instincts. The paradox, and the reality, is that a human can be an individual *because* he or she has the time and opportunity to do so, that is, *because* he or she is social.

2.2 Egotistical individualism and individuality

By way of contrast, the best way to appreciate the true social dimension of the individual is to study its pathological form which is egotistical individualism - the cult of the individual. It is a defect, as we shall see, and there are some confusions about it which are best cleared up immediately. The most general of these can be defined as an incapacity to accept the general will and thus a difficulty in adapting to collective enterprises. Many hide this incapacity behind the alibi of not wanting to be gregarious, rather as if their "excess" of personality kept them from accepting the discipline of a group. We must be wary of such individualistic attitudes because they frequently hide a grave deficiency.

Rather than being a re-affirmation of personality, they are often the last recourse of those who lack it.

What is involved here is an attempt to keep others from recognising this deficiency which becomes obvious with any participation in a collective enterprise. Individualism in this sense is a radical negation of social life *because it is fundamentally* a negation of individual life. The egotistical individualist resists associating in order to hide his or her lack of being an authentic individual. This form of individualism is, in conclusion, the resort of those who have nothing to give to others. Sometimes, finding others in the same or similar state of personal vacuum, such people may form a group ready to follow some charismatic individual.

Two concepts are involved here:

- *Egotistical individualism* is the inability to take part in a collective enterprise. It is a phenomenon which acts as a defence mechanism to mask this deficiency. In reality it is real negation of individual life, and thus of social life.
- Authentic *individuality* is personal development, a passion for the distinctive, recognition of difference (not necessarily superiority), cultivation of genuine features, and a capacity for understanding others.

Every attempt at individualisation is an affirmation, then, of the self; but either this attempt is justified, that is to say, springs from a true desire to individualise through an effort to take some specific course of action, or it is simply a capricious attitude which tries to affirm individuality *without doing anything* specific at all to gain it, beyond making the gesture. In the first case, individuals realise themselves, they become masters of themselves and, when through their social dimension they come in contact with others, they form a social group perfectly defined by individualities and united (by consent, not by force) through common interests - something which helps to overcome egotism and bring acceptance of differences. In the second case, individuals go no further than affirming an individuality which is never consummated and with which they manage to organise the kind of group, lacking authentic individuals, in which we find, rather than consent, the abdication of personality that clings pathetically to any charismatic individual. This is not a particularly rare phenomenon and is indeed especially common in times of crisis.

2.3 Individuality as a guarantee of integration

A group of individuals is more difficult to manage but its stability is superior. The leader directs the others and succeeds in doing so with individuals of developed personality as well as with those of gregarious temperament. He or she can manage the latter, but a group thus constituted does not have lasting coherence. Alternatively, however, the dynamic relationship among the personalities can create a collaboration (through conflict or debate with positive results) which enriches all of them including the leader, who finds himself or herself continually challenged and obliged to maintain constant vigilance in order not to lose his or her position. In this case, leadership must be maintained with something more than mere force. A group or company so constituted excels precisely because individual initiative is not limited or cut off but integrated.

One might think we are speaking of an ideal society, but nothing is further from the truth. Human relations are always *somewhat* imperfect and so is society, but it is not so much the ideal society we are seeking as a better society; the first is an abstraction but the second is a feasible possibility. We should not be discouraged before the impossibility of perfection, which in human matters must remain only a reference. We must continually urge more individuality and accustom everyone to demand it from himself or herself so that this obligation is not considered a social imposition. Being an individual has a price (not strictly economic) and is one of those things in which all men and women are now on an equal footing.

2.4 Collectivity without individuality is unstable

Collectivism constitutes the greatest risk of the impoverishment of social life. In reality we do not find pure collectivism because - notwithstanding some of the examples of authors such as Spencer - no human group is comparable to the collective mechanism of a beehive or an ant-hill. There are, however, many human situations which are greatly impoverished as far as their social level is concerned. It is often thought that these situations belong to other epochs and are incompatible with modern society, but the fact is they continue to occur although, perhaps, in new forms even more dangerous because they are more subtle.

Typical forms of collectivism have been mobs ("cabilismo") and gangs ("banderías"). These are strictly collective phenomena with no elements of individuality, a mass of people united not by convictions but by loyalty to a leader, and thus of little stability. In effect the organisation of the mob is based on a leader to whose individuality the members adhere, since they lack their own. This type of *collectivity without individuals* is extremely fragile since the union is produced by superficial interests. The appearance of this structure is monolithic, with no cracks, but it can fall apart as if by magic at any moment because it lacks the flexible joints which are the result of the free, spontaneous contributions of *each one* of its members. Without them it is continually exposed to sudden dissolution. In this social arrangement, nobody worries about affirming his or her individuality in relation to others, so no social fabric is created in the form of institutions. The only way to keep this kind of group together is by the moral or physical force of its leader.

2.5 Organisation as a necessity: The person who makes demands on himself and the gregarious person

Individuals who live in an unorganised society without institutions find themselves obliged to improve it themselves because humans need society in order to enjoy their own individuality. In the corporation, the company life is, in the same way, impossible without a minimum of organising effort, but not all the individuals feel this necessity with the same force. It is thus necessary to distinguish between the person who makes demands on himself or herself and the gregarious person.

The first contributes his or her effort and the second is a freeloader. Both have the same objective of living well in the society which shelters them, and this is a motive for conflict because it is not easy to reconcile opinions as to what each one should contribute and receive in the community. It is the old problem of just distribution, more burning than ever today in so far as social doctrines are highly egalitarian when they are based on the collectivism that we have been dealing with.

The liberal ingredient is crucial to an understanding of this issue: according to this, no one should be forced to do what he doesn't want to do, but if someone does do this he should be recompensed. The just state or corporation as it is conceived of today, must take into account the needs of the most helpless, though not to the point of becoming a charitable body, in order to support equal opportunity and create conditions which permit each one freely to be what he or she wants to be and can be. It is not a question of belonging to a particular social class since the qualitative and moral criteria are directly related to each person's own conscience.

3. Final considerations

Corporations function in accordance with the theoretic scheme we have outlined. The important thing is to understand, with all its implications, that any collectivity is made up of individuals. This seems obvious, but is necessary to pay special attention to it because the relationship between the individual and society is dynamic. This means that the situations are not always the same; they have a certain elasticity wich can significantly influence the functioning of a group, for good or for ill.

A corporation is small enough - in comparison with society in general - to allow internal relations oriented to optimum functioning to be effectively regulated. But this facility can at the same time be a problem. As has been affirmed throughout this paper, the dynamic ingredient of any group, which is in reality a harmonious combination of perfectly differentiated parts which of necessity find themselves together, must not be forgotten. Its inevitable instability is at the same time the source of either its innovative power or its stagnation, since it creates a need for action, not just any action, but fitting measures which respect both the individual and the corporation.

An excess of confidence in the whims of each individual person can only result in disorganisation and failure. If, on the other hand, corporate planning is excessively regimented, the individual feels excluded and unstimulated. The first situation denies the corporation - and thus the individuals which make it up - the minimum stability needed if workers are to be offered the support, based on experience, which would make it unnecessary continuously to come up with solutions already familiar through accumulated practice and inherited knowledge. Individuality is more efficient if it forms part of a disciplined situation which facilitates the creativity of individuals. In the second situation, the evils are not as immediately evident because the external organisation acts like a corset which controls the group in such a way as to postpone the discovery of problems until they are, in some cases, irreversible. In this case the annihilation of individuality can cause a reaction and provoke egotistical individualism, a serious problem since, as we have seen, this is a form of pseudo-individuality very dangerous to any corporation.

A healthy corporation is characterised by a rising level of individuality and independence in each member along with the responsibility and careful attention which this entails. The manager of such an enterprise will not be the only creative and responsible individual in it, although he or she will assume the burden for all.

References

Aristotle: 1900, *The Ethics of Aristotle*, J. Burnet (ed.), London: Methuen.
Aristotle: 1926, *The Nicomachean Ethics*, H. Rackham (ed.), London and New York: The Loeb Classical Library.
López-Frías, F.: 1983, "Una distinción. Trabajo y colocaciones", *La Vanguardia*, Barcelona, February 11.
López-Frías et al.: 1984a, *Principios de Deontología Profesional*, Barcelona: Ediciones de la Universidad de Barcelona.
López-Frías et al.: 1984b, *Etica aplicada*, Barcelona: Ediciones de la Universidad de Barcelona.

HUMAN DEVELOPMENT AND THE IMAGES
OF THE ORGANISATION

Domènec Melé

Ethics, like moral theology, sees personal development, or the complete development of the person, as a *self-standing value* to be attained through all life's activities and not just by specific training processes. Ethical consideration of personal development in an organisation is thus centred on the person rather than on the results of the production process.

However, the starting points of organisational and personnel management theories are often particular views of man and organisations. These views have a decisive bearing on our conception of human development. We will attempt to show that these images are unidimensional and closed, while human beings are multidimensional, spiritual and open to transcendency.

Human activity in organisations

It is not difficult to realise the relationship between personal development and effectiveness at work. In fact, both in the processes of personnel recruitment and promotion and in day-to-day business activities there are universally appreciated qualities, such as responsibility, punctuality, industriousness, desire to excel, honesty, loyalty, etc. The problems caused by laziness, disinterest in one's own improvement, alcohol abuse or the willingness to accept bribes are equally well-known. These aspects reveal the state of development - or underdevelopment, or even of deterioration - of people's moral qualities or virtues. However, people are also influenced by the results of the work itself.

Very often, people in organisations are treated as just one more resource, one of the inputs involved in the technological process. However, human activity is what really makes the production process work, generating three different types of effects: (1) *material effects,* (2) *social effects,* and (3) *personal effects*. The material effects or results are brought about by the transformation of materials, financial funds, technology and information into products or services (sometimes also into by-products and pollutants), into profits or losses, and into additional technology and information. Part of these results are made available to society, while the rest is fed back into the organisation. Human action in organisations also gives rise to social and personal effects on the people performing the actions, and through them, on society.

The various observable changes brought about by personal effects include somatic changes (health, physical condition), and changes in feelings and attitudes, in skills (psychomotor and intellectual), in knowledge, and in moral habits.

Aristotle was the first philosopher to describe the internal changes caused by action, when he said that "like activities produce like dispositions" (*Nichomachean Ethics,* II, 1: 1103b 20). Aristotle called *hexis* (habit) the increase in the power and scope of the operative principles. Habits are "dispositions", one of the deepest parts of a person's being. Later on, positive psychology has described habit formation as "learning", and cybernetics has generalised the phenomenon, calling it "positive feedback".

Personal development

In a wide sense, all the changes caused by human action may lead to human development (or degradation). However, from a more limited viewpoint, human development is only concerned with what is more specifically human, what is concerned with human's rationality or spirituality and its operative principles.

In other words, human development is the germination and growth of a human being in what is essential to his or her being; it is becoming "himself" or "herself", that is, fulfilling the potential inherent in man's rational nature. Human development involves a process of shaping a human being through the use of what is his or her by right, trying to attain his or her specific good. In other words, human development affirms the values that are inherent in human nature.

All activities performed by human beings have some effect on them, but these activities have not by themselves a capacity to improve the person, regardless of the intrinsic goodness of the action and of the agent's intentionality. Thus, to be skilful in the use of a tool or in typing involves the development of human capabilities, but this is not necessarily human development. These skills may be used to do good or to do evil. Skill in using a tool to open safes, or in typing to forge documents are not improving acts for a human being. Nobody would say that stealing leads to human development, and yet there is no doubt that the act of stealing develops specific skills.

A similar statement could be made about knowledge. Without doubt, intellectual knowledge and skills enrich a person, but being knowledgeable is not necessarily identified with human quality. Human development or human quality in its strict sense should be sought in good moral habits or moral virtues, which are habits inherent in the character behind the actions by which man develops as a man. Consequently, virtues are something closely bound to a person, like a second nature, and so to a certain extent they make the human being more human.

Thus, human development is basically moral development, or the perfecting of each person's moral quality, and not just the acquisition of knowledge, manual or intellectual skills - although, as we have said, these are closely connected with moral virtues.

Virtues are not automatically acquired when a person performs ethically correct acts; certain dispositions in the person are required for them to take root. According to Aristotle (*Nicomachean Ethics,* II, 4), in order to acquire virtues, the agent

- must act in full consciousness of what he or she is doing,
- must "will" his action and will it for its own sake, and
- the act must proceed from a fixed and unchangeable disposition.

Human development occurs because the person wishes it and acts only after considering the action in all its depth. Thus, we can only speak of human development insofar as human beings *know* what they are doing, and act *freely* (identifying themselves with their action) and in accordance with the intrinsic ends of their rational nature, that is to say, *responsibly*. In other words, human development is a *conscious, freely-willed* and *responsible process*.

Human virtues are such to the extent that they are moved by a freely chosen love for doing real (not apparent) good.[1] If this is so, human development will be caused by acts freely performed out of service and generous love for others. When the action is aimed at the receiver's good, it not only favours the receiver but, above all, perfects – humanly develops – the person who performs the action, in the same way that acts of injustice, hatred or simple indifference to others degrade the person. This is equivalent to Socrates' statement: "If it were necessary either to do wrong or to suffer it, I should choose to suffer rather than to do it" (Plato, *Gorgias,* 469 c). Thus, the agent becomes a "better person", achieves his or her humanity to the exent that they transcend themselves in their actions in service to others and looking for other people's good. The same conclusion can be reached from Christian theology.[2]

When awareness of service to others through work becomes negative, the human degradation this gives rise to must become apparent within a relatively short period. This occurs when people act without caring to give a true service to the customer, or when they make or sell harmful goods, or use dishonest means, or work at the expense of basic family duties, etc. In the same way, working with a true awareness of the service given to others, or combining it with love for family, or with some other noble reason, gives a deeper meaning to work and develops the humanity of the person carrying out such work.

Images of human beings and organisations

The study of the organisation theories currently prevalent suggests that they are informed by certain images of man and organisations which, as we will try to show further on, are a reductionist view of man's true nature and barely consider the characteristics of human development previously stated.

Morgan (1987) proposes a number of images which seem to be apparent in the operation of organisations. There are basically four images of man and organisations which, either alone or in combination, have heavily influenced organisation theories and the management practice: (a) the engineering image, (b) the psychological image, (c) the sociological image, and (d) the political image. These images will be the subject of our subsequent discussion, in relation to several well-known organisation theories and personnel management schools of thought.

---

[1] On this point see C. Cardona (1987). This Spanish philosopher concludes: "That which most radically and definitely comprises the human act as such, and therefore man as such, is love as an act of freedom" (p.116).

[2] The teaching of the Roman Catholic Church is that, in order to attain true development, man must not lose sight of "mankind's reality and vocation according to his own internal measure (...) which is in man's specific nature, created by God in his own image and likeness" (John Paul II, 1987, n. 29). This includes transcending oneself, since "man cannot achieve plenitude save by sincerely giving of himself to others" (Second Vatican Council, *Gaudium et spes,* n. 24). Within the same line of thought, Thomas Aquinas says that charity –love – is the root and form of all virtues (*Summa Theologiae,* II-II, q.23, a.8).

a) The industrial engineering school and the decision-making theory: the engineering image

The *industrial engineering* school maintains that efficiency and productivity are the result of economic remuneration and of a strict and systematic management, whose purpose is to match technologies and human abilities using technical criteria to monitor performance. Man is considered as an input-output system motivated by money and other rewards.

This gives rise to an engineering image in which the worker's activity is governed by management standards aimed at making his or her work more productive. A typical expression of this image is the *mechanistic approach* of the school of *scientific work management,* first expounded by Frederick W. Taylor (1911) at the turn of the century. The philosophy of the scientific management school consists of a number of rules for work organisation, and a recommendation to develop skills and employee-management co-operation. Taylor considers co-operation to be the essence of scientific work organisation. This co-operation no doubt strengthens the organisation's unity but, on the other hand, requires that the worker forego all initiative and creativity - it is rare for a worker's action not to be preceded and followed by a management action. Although the worker is trained according to his or her ability to improve his or her productivity, this training is no more than the development of highly specialised technical knowledge which often brings about fatigue, monotony and distortion of body rhythms.

Fayol's *management principles* (1916) also use an engineering image. Fayol's theory, presented as a series of management principles drawn from experience, conceives an extremely rigid hierarchical structure without any workers' participation. The human element is almost forgotten, with the exception of the need to act with equity (justice applied with good will) as stated in one of his principles. Nothing is said about the attention that should be given to individual motivation or human development, or about the role of leadership, or to the formation of informal groups.

A more refined engineering image is that presented in the work of Herbert Simon and his followers. This image takes into account the human ability to ascertain and decide on satisfactory solutions. According to Simon (1956, 1979), man's way of thinking is governed by programmes that organise an enormous amount of simple information processes. The task is then to find out the limitations of such processes and to try to change them, either by acting on the person (skill-forming, re-focusing values, etc.), or by making the organisation more amenable to rational ways of doing them (Simon and March, 1958; Cyert and March, 1963; Simon, 1976). This approach, known as the *decision-making* approach, attempts to organise and co-ordinate human decisions (and not merely physical actions, as Taylor suggested), and assumes that the employees' performance will be improved if they act more "rationally".

The chief contribution of the decisional approach is to provide an insight into human cognitive processes, but it reduces man's inner life to a kind of "computer thought", little more than a kind of artificial intelligence.

The application of the engineering image to organisations could be summarised as using the worker in such a way that he and she acts to achieve the goals set by the management, which offers higher wages or other rewards for obeying orders, for achieving goals, or for taking a decision in line with the programme established beforehand. This generates reponses in workers which lead to a certain degree of development of several skills: psychomotor skills in the mechanistic approach, and mental skills in the decisional approach. However, as Carlos Llano explains (1979, 72-82), these approaches are basically a transposition of Cartesian rationalism to the analysis of practical action, ignoring its basic ethical and cultural dimensions.

b) The individual behaviour school: the psychological image

Within the human relations school, the individual behaviour theories are based on human action as a result of psychological tendencies aimed at satisfying individual needs within an organisation. This school pays particular attention to psychology, leadership, power, authority, responsibility and the person's subconscious. In the classical theories, as in the school of industrial engineering, the goal is to achieve efficient work by means of appropriate management guidelines, but without any consideration of the worker's personal goals (except remuneration) or of the satisfaction of his or her needs. In the psychological image, however, the satisfaction arising from the achievement of personal goals associated with empirically verifiable basic needs and tendencies is a key element. It is chiefly concerned with the individual's feelings and impulses and with the way in which they affect his or her work.

The psychological image was conceived at the end of the thirties, mainly by H.A. Murray (1938) and A.H. Maslow (1943, 1954), and was subsequently developed by F. Herberg (1959, 1968), L.W. Porter and E.E. Lawler (1966), D. McClelland (1961), and others.

In the individual behaviour theories, the human being is only seen through his behaviour, as reflected in psychological tendencies which interact with the organisation. The theories focus not on human overall development, but only on the way to satisfy psychological tendencies and needs, conceptualized and evaluated in relation to productivity, through organisation and motivation - although some authors include among the needs a general concept of growth.

The human development that can be achieved by implementing the psychological image is dependent on the quality of satisfaction whose achievement is desired, that is, on its matching or otherwise with personal improvement. Thus, to satisfy the desire for success, or the ambition for power or money does not help to make a better person, although they are not incompatible with human development. For this reason, it is very possible that the motivation of "achievement" present in individual behaviour theories will not always lead to a true human development.

c) Group behaviour and organisational development schools: the sociological image

The *group behaviour* school is concerned with social interaction and interpersonal relationships. The theory states that group behaviour is of decisive importance for co-operation and success. Its chief exponents are, among others, Douglas McGregor (1960), Rensis Likert (1961, 1967), and William Ouchi (1981). The Tavistock Group (Emery and Trist, 1969) has also made significant contributions based on a sociotechnical approach, pointing out the importance of initiative and autonomy at work for improving productivity.

The *organisational development* school (Huse and Cumming, 1985) applies knowledge of human behaviour in the organisation in order to plan and strengthen corporate strategies, structures and processes and to improve their effectiveness. This school bears in mind the need for people to exchange opinions on common difficulties, and argues that workers can often manage themselves better than their managers.

The sociological image of the organisation is centered on the organisational structure and its influence on economic performance. Some of the authors mentioned above have contributed to humanising work conditions by considering the relational aspect of the human beings and by emphasising participation. However, they are only seen in terms of their relationships with the organisation, which are basically work relationships.

d) The labour relations school: the political image

For the *labour relations* school, the key to any situation is to be found in politics and labour legislation. The human being is seen as an individual with hierarchical relationships, a certain power within the organisation, and some duties and rights to be respected, but also with the ability to establish influences and claims which must be answered. It is a sort of political image.

The forerunner of the socio-political image is Max Weber (1922), who introduced several organisation typologies to account for differences in structure and behaviour. For Weber, bureaucratic management basically means the exercise of control legitimised by the possession of knowledge. "In Weber", writes MacIntyre, "the contrast between power and authority, although it is maintained in one's speech or thoughts, does in fact vanish as a special case of disappearance of the contrast between manipulative and non-manipulative social relationships" (1984, 44). The bureaucratic authority conceived by Weber is really no more than the triumph of power.

Subsequently, Alain Touraine (1956, 1962) challenged the conception of the company as a bureaucracy by emphasizing the de-bureaucratizing role of technology and the increasing autonomy of the professional technician. Touraine argued that the company should be viewed as a political institution.

In the political image of organisations, the worker is generally portrayed as someone with interests and a certain amount of power, either in his or her own right or through his or her group relationships or links, subordinated in turn to the interests and power of others in the organisation. The exercise of power is not justified by its service to people, but as a requirement of laws and policy and, above all, by its effectiveness *per se.*

In spite of these limitations, the image of organisations as political systems provides insight into human interdependences and into the influence of outside conditions on human activity within companies. This could have been used to study in greater depth the social conditions that favour human development. Unfortunately, the followers of this line of thought rarely conceive the company as a community of people working together, bound by strong moral links, and able to assist or impede personal human development. Rather, they prefer to concentrate on the analysis of interests, power relationships, social conflicts and equilibriums, labour laws, collective bargaining, economic principles governing cost and salaries, and other similar subjects but have paid little attention to approaches able to promote human development.

The oneness, wholeness, transcendency and spiritualness of the human being

No doubt, all these images portray significant aspects of the situation as it exists and have made major contributions to the progress of management. However, in all of them the worker appears as a mere "human resource" which, as opposed to the inert resources, must be suitably controlled through some of his empirically determined characteristics. But there is no consideration of the human being as *one* and *indivisible.*

This suggests that the above-mentioned authors have not really made a serious attempt to answer the questions proposed by Chester I. Barnard in 1938, at the start of his famous book *The Functions of Executive*:

"I have found it impossible to go far in the study of organizations or of the behavior of people in relation to them without being confronted with a few questions which can be simply stated. For example: 'What is an individual?', 'To what extent do people have a power of choice or free will?' The temptation is to avoid such difficult questions, leaving them to the philosophers and scientists who still debate them after centuries. It quickly appears that definetely we cannot evade them" (p.8).

To ask and to answer these anthropological questions is not only a basic requirement for designing and managing organisations, but also a demand for ethics. The behavioural rules for achieving human development on all levels require going beyond the images that have been conceived for human behaviour and attempting to know the human being as he really is, to the extent that this is possible. Otherwise, the result will be the development of a particular facet, while neglecting the others.

a) Oneness and wholeness

All the engineering, psychological, sociological and political images respond to *unidimensional* and *closed* views of man.[1] The human being is "focused" under the light of engineering, psychology, sociology or politics and projected onto a single plane. Using this single-plane projection, a theory is formulated, and conclusions are drawn which, at best, are synthesized with the conclusions drawn from other planes. Thus, the multidimensional richness of the human being becomes compressed into one or two planes and reduced to a kind of intelligent machine, a being with tendencies or needs, or a mere component of a social or political system.

Obviously, the psychological reactions and tendencies and the sociological facts that we may observe in human behaviour in organisations are real and must be taken into account, but they do not provide a total explanation for human activity, nor do they necessarily help in human development. The major error of working with images is to ignore the fact that the human being is not divisible into factors because he and she is a single *entity*.

A unified view of the human being could be obtained by means of a logical formalisation of human action, involving its various dimensions as shown through their technical, economic, social and personal consequences. Such a formalisation would be a huge step forwards, but it would also be incomplete, as the human being is more than a system interacting with his or her environment. In addition to being one (*in-dividuum*), the human being is also complete (*insummabile*) in itself. He or she is composed of physical, psychic and spiritual elementsa and is neither any of these elements nor their sum, but something that is complete in itself.

b) A spiritual being open to transcendency

In the unidimensional and closed views previously mentioned, no reference was made to the human being as a spiritual being open to transcendency, with an unlimited desire to

---

[1] The idea is taken, *mutatis mutandis*, from Viktor Frankl (1984, 15-18), who, when discussing the psychotherapy schools, compares man with an open vessel projected onto several planes (dynamic psychology, behaviourism, etc.), which necessarily lead to projectional and closed views of man.

know and love. Instead, an image is fabricated of it from a few empirical data, and then he organisation is conceived on the basis of these data. However, no matter how many empirical data are collected, it is not possible to deepen into one's understanding of the human being without considering his or her transcendent and spiritual nature.

The main features of the human being are his transcendency and spirituality (Fabro, 1955; Wojtyla, 1980). Transcendency means going outwards beyond the subject of the action. The human being is not subject to the limitations of the material universe. He or she has rational knowledge and free will, he or she is able to say *I know who I am* and *I know what I want*.

The human transcendency and spirituality are phenomena that can be easily reached through common experience. When one performs an action, one knows what it is that one is doing, at least to a certain extent; one also knows that it is the person who is performing the act. At the same time, one discovers the transcendence of the act on one's environment and knows that one acts because one wants to, fully accepting the responsibility that this involves.

By transcending himself or herself, the human being realises the ethical values inherent in action: justice, solidarity, service to fellow men and women, friendship, co-operation, love for one's family, love for God, etc. People continually reflects on and seek meaning for their actions in other people and act on the basis of what they see. As V. Frankl said (1984, 28), "The world towards which human beings transcend themselves is a world full of meanings (which are the reasons and motivations for acting) and of other human beings (which are the reasons for loving)".

Organisational theories and practice should be considering that, as Mons. Escrivá de Balaguer wrote (1985, n. 48), "Man's great privilege is to be able to love and to transcend what is fleeting and ephemeral. He can love each other creatures, pronounce an 'I' and a 'you' which are full of meaning".

Responsibility expresses the sense of freedom, the *wherefore* of his or her action. The human being is fully committed in his or her freedom of action by virtue of his or her self-determination to act. Her transcendence not only leads her to a specific intentionality, but also to the self-control and self-possession of her acts. This is a specifically human way of being, which confers on human beings a unique dignity by showing that the person is an end in herself and not a means for anyone. As Spaemann explains (1989), human dignity comes from the nature of the human being understood as self-transcendency: open to the Absolute. Consequently, the conception of the human being as a person precludes any perception as a mere utilitarian value, whether by viewing him and her as a production resource or instrument, or by considering them solely as beings with needs, instead of beings open to transcendency, with an absolute value and an intrinsic dignity.

Nor is it possible to accept the postulates of the philosophy of action that identify the human being with his or her action. This is contrary to the internal experience of human beings during action: human action is human performance. Knowledge of the action leads to knowledge of the person, but the person comes before the action. On this point, therefore, we are in agreement with the Classics, where they state that acting comes after being (*operari sequitur esse*).

Toward a comprehensive anthropological conception of the organisation

The subjectivity present in human action and in what happens in its inner being is expressed by the notion of *person*. If we consider the human being as a person, we obtain a globalising notion that is ontologically consistent in its unity and totality, beyond empirical divisions and aggregations.[1]

In short, the problem is not one of choosing between one image or another, but of taking a globalising view of the human being as the starting point. A correct anthropological approach should be sought neither in the sum of a large volume of projectional data, nor even in achieving a logical and coherent formalisation, but on the human being as a person, with easily observable fundamental goals and operations that are inherent in his or her rational nature (intellectual knowledge, free will). Given this starting point, the next task is to study the *changes* that human beings experience through action - and these changes may be measured and quantified, at least to a certain extent, by the methods of the various sciences of human behaviour (psychology, sociology, etc.).

In fact, current thinking in business management is a reflection of the western philosophy that came into being after Cartesianism. The being - and particularly the being-person - has been forgotten and replaced by a multitude of images that cannot easily be assembled into a whole. At most, the judgemental logic of reason accomplishes a mere copulative composition of being (joining images) without managing to capture the unity and totality of human beings.

Fortunately, it often happens in business practice that the notion of person is restored – with his and her dignity and fundamental rights – thanks to business managers' *common sense* that, when necessary, puts aside current theories and concepts. The employers' sense of realism and their constant interaction with other people lead them to discover many aspects of human nature much more effectively than many business management philosophers and theorists. Reinhard Mohn, president of Bertelsmann (a German multinational with 42,000 employees and an annual sales turnover of 6 billion dollars) has stated that "any social system that claims to be effective and have continuity (...) must reflect the ends and the intrinsic nature of the human being" (1987, 34).

The engineering, psychological, sociological and political images are still very powerful today, but human being is gradually coming to be considered as a whole, leading to a progressive humanisation of business organisations and to better opportunities for personal development. To paraphrase Bernanos,[2] one would say that an inhuman organisation must be based on a false or incomplete definition of the human being.

Since the forties a number of authors have advocated co-operative approaches and the integration of individual and corporate goals, albeit from the psycho-sociological standpoint. In the fifties and sixties the corporate social responsibility movement was developed (Gallo, 1980) and many of its concepts have been integrated into the conception of business and its strategy. In addition, since the Second World War, the human rights movement has led to a greater recognition of the human beings in their workplace (Byre, 1988; John Paul II, 1981, chap. IV). The consideration of the dignity of the person and of the rational human nature is a solid foundation for human rights (Finnis, 1980).

---

[1] According to Boetius, person means individual substance of rational nature (*rationalis naturæ individua substantia*). Other meanings of person are included in this definition (Mondin, 1983, 257-274).

[2] "An inhuman civilization is obviously a civilization based on a false or incomplete definition of man" (Bernanos, 1989, 75).

From the seventies onwards, human values and corporate responsibility have been progressively incorporated into business strategy. Subsequently, there has been a growing awareness of the importance of a corporate culture that includes shared beliefs and values (Schein, 1985) as a result of interpersonal activity within the organisation. Nowadays, corporate ethics is enriching corporate culture. As Alejandro Llano states, "a business' culture, its cognitive and ethical style is judged above all by how it treats its employees and by how it ensures their development" (1988, 164), so that the conception of organisations as communities of people in which the latter may achieve their development as human beings is gaining increasing acceptance.

An overall view of human beings is not only an *ethical requirement* derived from human dignity but also a reality that must be accepted to avoid the *inefficiency* and *ineffectiveness* that result from an incomplete conception of the person. Juan A. Pérez López (1981, 1988) has highlighted the incompleteness of the mechanistic and organic paradigms of organisations (Burns and Stalker, 1961), which include the theories criticised above. In their place, he proposes an anthropological paradigm[1] based on a global view of the person. It is thus clear that the other paradigms are special cases that may provide an explanation for organisations in particular situations, but they can by no means be applied universally.

Conclusion

A realistic view of human beings and organisations that takes into account ethics and economic efficiency requires that the human being be examined under an all-embracing light, that is, as an individual being with specific aims and operations, including freely taken decisions, openness towards transcendency, and also the changes produced during working activities. This means rejecting images that reduce the human beings to just one of their dimensions, but instead considering them in their wholeness. From this point of departure and with the valuable contributions of engineering, psychology, sociology, economics and other sciences, we can go on to examine the activity of the human beings in organisations.

----

[1] In fact, in this paradigm man is conceptualized as a free agent or freely adaptive system, which is consistent with the basic human characteristic of being free.

References

Aristotle: 1961, *Nichomachean Ethics,* Translation J. A. K. Thomson, Baltimore, Maryland: The Penguin Classics.

Barnard, Ch. I.: 1938, *The Functions of the Executive,* Cambridge, Ma.: Harvard University Press.

Bernanos, G.: 1989, *La libertad, ¿para qué?*, Madrid: Encuentro (*La liberté, pour quoi faire?*, Paris: Gallimard, 1953).

Burns, T., and G. Stalker: 1966, *The Management of Innovation,* London: Tavistok Publishing Co.

Byre, A.: 1988, *Human Rights at the Workplace*, London: Policy Studies Institute.

Cyert, R. M., and J.C. March: 1963, *A Behavioral Theory of the Firm*, Englewood Cliffs, NJ: Prentice Hall.

Cardona, C.: 1987, *Metafísica del bien y del mal*, Pamplona: Eunsa.

Emery, F. E. and E. L. Trist: 1969, "Sociotechnical Systems", in F.E. Emery, ed., *Systems Thinking*, New York: Penguin.

Escrivá de Balaguer, J., 1985: *Christ is Passing by*, Second Edition, Dublin: Four Courts Press.

Fabro, C.: 1955, *L'anima. Introduzione al problema dell'uomo*, Roma: Editrice Studium.

Fayol, H., 1916: *Administration industrielle et générale*, Paris: Bulletin de la Société de l'Industrie Minérale; English translation, International Management Institute: Genève, 1929.

Frankl, V. E.: 1984, *La idea psicológica del hombre*, Fourth Edition, Madrid: Rialp (*Das Menschenbild der Seelenheilkunde*, Stuttgart: Hippocrates Verlag, 1954).

Finnis, J.: 1980, *Natural Law and Natural Rights*, Oxford: Clarendon Press.

Gallo, M. A.: 1980, *Responsabilidades sociales de la empresa*, Pamplona: Eunsa.

Herberg, F., B. Mausner and B. Snyderman: 1959, *The Motivation to Work*, New York: Wiley.

Herberg, F.: 1968, "One More Time: How Do You Motivate Employees?" *Harvard Business Review*, Jan.-Feb., 53-62.

Huse, E. F. and T.G. Cumming: 1985, *Organization Development and Change*, Third Edition, St. Paul, Minn.: West.

John Paul II: 1981, *Laborem exercens*, London: Catholic Truth Society.

John Paul II: 1987, *Sollicitudo rei socialis*, London: Catholic Truth Society.

Lawrence, P. R. and J.W. Lorsch: 1967, *Organization and Environment: Managing Differentiation and Integration*, Homewood, Ill.: Irwin.

Llano, A.: 1988, *La nueva sensibilidad*, Madrid: Espasa-Calpe.

Llano, C.: 1979, *Análisis de la acción directiva*, Mexico D. F.: Limusa.

Likert, R.: 1961, *New Patterns of Management*, New York: McGraw Hill.

Likert, R.: 1967, *The Human Organization*, New York: McGraw Hill.

MacIntyre, A.: 1984, *After Virtue*, Second Edition, Notre Dame, Indiana: University of Notre Dame Press.

Maslow, A. H.: 1943, "A Theory of Human Motivation", *Psychological Review*, 50, 370-396.

Maslow, A. H.: 1954, *Motivation and Personality*, New York: Harper and Row.

Mayo, E.: 1933, *The Human Problems of an Industrial Civilization*, London: MacMillan.

McClelland, D.: 1961, *The Achieving Society*, Princeton, N.J.: Van Nostrand.

McGregor, D.: 1960: *The Human Side of the Enterprise*, New York: McGraw Hill.

Mohn, R.: 1987, *Al éxito por la cooperación. Un enfoque humano de la estrategia empresarial*, Barcelona: Plaza y Janés (*Erfolg durch Partnerschaft*, Berlin: Wolf Jobst Siedler Verlag).

Mondin, B.: 1983, *Antropologia Filosofica*, Roma: Urbaniana.

Morgan, G: 1986, *Images of Organization*, London: Sage.

Murray, H. A.: 1938, *Explorations in Personality*, Oxford: Oxford University Press.

Ouchi, W. G.: 1981, *Theory Z. How American Business Can Meet the Japanese Challenge*, Reading, Ma.: Addison-Wesley.

Pérez López, J. A.: 1981, *Management and Leadership*, Barcelona: IESE, Research Paper No. 56.

Pérez López, J. A.: 1988, *Approach to the Management of Human Resources*, Barcelona: IESE.

Porter, L. W. and E. E. Lawler: 1966, *Managerial Attitudes and Performance*, Homewood, Ill.: Dorsey Press.

Schein, E. H.: 1985, *Organizational Culture and Leadership*, London: Jossey-Bass.

Simon, H.: 1956, *Models of Man*, New York: Wiley.

Simon, H.: 1976, *Administrative Behavior: A Study of Decision-Making Process in Administrative Organizations*, Third Edition, New York: Free Press.

Simon, H.: 1979, *Models of Thought*, New Haven: Yale University Press.

Simon, H. and R. G. March: 1958, *Organizations*, New York: Wiley.

104

Spaemann, R.: 1988, *Lo natural y lo racional. Ensayos de antropología*, Madrid: Rialp (*Das Natürliche und Vernünftige*, München: Piper).

Taylor, F. W.: 1911, *Principles of Scientific Management*, New York: Harper.

Tomas Aquinas: 1957, *Summa Theologiæ*, Westminster, Maryland: Christian Classics.

Touraine, A.: 1956, *Essai sur la qualification du travail*, Paris: Marcel Rivière.

Touraine, A.: 1962, "L'organisation professionelle de l'entreprise" and "Pouvoir and décision dans l'entreprise", in Friedmann and Naville, eds., *Traité de Sociologie du Travail*, Paris: Colin.

Weber, M.: 1922, *Wirtschaft und Gesellschaft. Grundriss der Verstehenden Soziologie*, Engl. transl.: *Economy and Society: An Outline of Interpretative Sociology*, New York: Wedminster, 1968.

Wojtyla, K.: 1980, *The Acting Person*, Dordrecht: D. Reidel.

EMPOWERING PEOPLE AS AN END FOR BUSINESS[1]

Norman E. Bowie

Alternative theories of the function of the corporation

In the past decade business ethicists in the United States have called into question the classical formulation of the purpose of business, *i.e.* , the purpose of a corporation is to maximise profits for stockholders. In place of the profit maximisation view a number of alternative theories of the function of the firm have arisen such as:

1. The corporation should seek profits so long as it does not cause avoidable harm or unduly infringe upon human rights (for example, Simon *et al.,* 1972) ;
2. The corporation should seek to do social good (correct social problems) as well as seek profit (for example, Davis, 1975);
3. The corporation should seek to produce life sustaining and enhancing goods and services (Camenisch, 1981);
4. The corporation should seek to maximise the interests of the various corporate stakeholders rather than simply the interests of the stockholders (Freeman, 1984).

Each of these alternative definitions has much to be said for it. All recognise that there is more to business than making a profit. Yet I am convinced that each of the alternative views to a greater or lesser degree omits or gives insufficient emphasis to something essential - namely the main purpose of the corporations is to provide meaningful work.

For example the "seek profit while avoiding harm" view simply argues that corporations should follow a moral minimum required of all individuals and institutions. It puts constraints on the competitive profit-seeking game. There is a concept of unnecessary roughness in football. Similarly there are concepts of unnecessary roughness in profit-seeking. To recognise this fact is important, but under this view the essential function of business remains profit. Management is simply reminded of the rule against avoidable harm.

The second alternative that urges corporations to do good by correcting social problems is vulnerable to all of Friedman's (1962) well know criticisms, and to charge that the obligation to do social good is too open ended.

---

[1] The thesis of this paper was originally proposed in Bowie (1988).

First, who is going to define what the social needs are and which get priority? If business begins to decide what social needs are good ones, that would mean that some executives who are in their position because their major forte is managing are now being asked to decide what are and what are not "worthy needs". Thus, utility-minded managers will be asked to make decisions that might not be best made by employing utility considerations.

Second, business with its good intentions unduly influences social priorities that are best left to the government or the people's representatives. Government agents in principle are accountable to the citisen who elected them for the way they allocate resources. The business manager is accountable to no one. Thus, allocation of funds - the taking of profits away from the business or the stockholders to fill social needs - can be constructed as taxation without representation. What recourse do minority stockholders have if they do not approve of the "cause" or "charity" to which their company is giving support?

Third, although we all have duties as citizens, these duties are not open-ended. The injunction to take social responsibilities into account and to assist in solving societal problems may make impossible demands on a corporation. At the practical level, it ignores the impact that such activities have on profit. At the theoretical level, it turns every action into a moral action and hence makes the moral life too demanding. The relation between ethics and business should be realistic; "pie in the sky" ideals or demands confuse obligations with actions that are above and beyond the call duty. Such idealistic demands yield little or nor results. For these reasons, it seems unwise to suggest that business has a moral responsibility to do good.

One of the criticisms of the third alternative is that it focuses on human beings as consumers rather than as producers. One of the common complaints against ethicists who criticise distributive justice under capitalism is that these ethicists ignore production at the expense of distribution. Goods can't be distributed unless they are produced. There is much merit in this criticism but ironically the business community has forgotten its own insight. In selling to consumers, far greater attention is directed to increasing sales than to increasing the productivity of the employees. Perhaps the quality and quantity of goods and services would improve, if more attention were placed on employees and the environment in which they worked.

Moreover, as the social commentator David Bell (1976) has pointed out, current attempts to increase consumption creates paradoxes that threaten capitalism itself. Specifically, the set of values business encourages in consumers is inconsistent with the values business wants to instill in its workers. The attitudes that make Americans good consumers are not the attitudes that make Americans good workers. Business wants workers who are loyal to the company, who will delay gratification, and who will exhibit the attributes associated with the work ethic. But business urges consumers to buy and enjoy now and to pay later on credit. Thus we have in Bell's memorable phrase, "The cultural contradictions of capitalism."

Perhaps the interests of all stakeholders should be treated equally? This seems to be the view of Freeman and others who take the stakeholder approach. Since I wish to argue that the interests of employees often take priority over the interests of other stakeholders, I reject the view that treats all stakeholder interests as equal in all cases. Indeed, in some cases the interests of the stockholders or suppliers might be given priority. Which stakeholder interests deserve priority in any case depends on both economic and ethical considerations. Employee interests take priority far more often than is commonly thought.

Hence, I argue that the primary purpose of business is to provide meaningful work for employees and that if managers focus on this goal, business will produce quality goods and services for consumers and profits as beneficial by products.

Meaningful work as the goal of corporations

Philosophers would argue that an emphasis on the individual employee is just what ethics requires. For example Kant, in the tradition of Aristotle, recognises that only human beings are capable of being motivated by the moral rules. It is human beings that place values on other things; these other things have conditional value because they only acquire this value as the result of human action. Human beings, on the other hand, have unconditional value, that is, value apart from any special circumstances that confer value. Since all human beings and only human beings have this unconditional value, it is always inappropriate to use another human being merely as a means to some end - as if they had instrumental value only. Hence, Kant argues, one should always treat a human being or a person with unconditional value as an end and never treat a human being merely as a means toward your own ends. Each person looks upon himself or herself as possessing unconditioned value. If one is to avoid inconsistency, one must view all other human beings as possessor of unconditioned value as well.

Kant's principle of respect for persons can be applied directly to business practice. A Kantian would take strong exception to the view that employees are to be treated like mere equipment in the production process. Human labour should never be treated like machinery, industrial plants, and capital, solely in accordance with economic laws for profit maximization. Any economic system that fails to recognise this distinction between human beings and other nonhuman factors of production is morally deficient.

It is one thing to argue that persons ought to be respected, it is quite another to specify how that is to be done in the employment context. A full discussion of this issue would take us into psychology - an area where I am at best an amateur - as well as into ethics. However, the following psychological generalisations are common in the popular literature and are consistent with the "respect for persons" principle. I will take it as given that people do not feel fulfilled unless they are gainfully employed in jobs that they find meaningful and important. If robots could do all our work, utopia would not have arrived. People would be unhappy and frustrated. People need to work. As A. Gini and T. Sullivan (1987, 652) point out, work helps people define themselves because work organises and structures our lives and in part determines our identity.

However, not just any work will do. The work must be seen as useful - as making a contribution to society. Secondly, it must challenge the worker. One of the problems with the assemply line is that it is hard to see how putting six bolts in a car door is useful work. It is also boring and fails to challenge the worker. Many European businesses discovered these truths before the Americans did. Volvo never really had an assembly line technique and the Japanese innovations are now widely discussed and often imitated in the United States.

Moreover, the employee must be able to exercise judgment and creativity. A job where the employee simply follows orders and where all the employee's action result from orders has no autonomy. This denial of autonomy shows lack of respect.[1] In the corporate context autonomy can be honoured through teamwork when each employee has some say in goal formation and implementation.

In summary, I take it as a psychological truth that all human beings need to be engaged in rewarding work where rewarding work is defined as work that is useful, challenging, and respectful of individual autonomy. Moreover, providing meaningful work is more

---

[1] A similar point has been made by Schwartz (1982).

important than the producing of goods and services. It seems obvious that a person can be deprived of nearly any product or even most of the products industry produces without suffering severe psychological harm. But if a person is denied meaningful work, the psychological harm is very great. That is why I argue that it is morally more important for business to focus on the employee rather than on the consumer or on most of the other stakeholders.

It should be pointed out, however, that this approach does not ignore either profit or the production of quality goods and services for consumers. As I pointed out, one of the characteristics of meaningful work is that the work must be seen as useful - as making a contribution to society. One of the best ways to convince an employee that he or she is making a contribution to society is for management to emphasise quality control. An excellent way to ensure quality control is for management to assist employees in perceiving themselves as professionals.

Traditionally the motive for professional conduct is the service motive; the professional skills are service skills that benefit mankind. Doctors, lawyers, teachers and the clergy - the standard paradigms of professionals - exercise a special skill for the benefit of human beings. To the extent that doctors and lawyers do well, financial reward is ideally supposed to be a by-product of professional service. If the professional service model were extended to business, professional work would be exhibited by the production and distribution of quality products and services that customers need. Business persons that take a professional attitude would not be in business simply for the money. Rather their work, like the professional would be intrinsically rewarding.

Should profits be a goal?

But what about profits? Won't a company that fails to focus on profits become unprofitable and ultimately fail? I think not.

One of the more interesting philosophical paradoxes is the so-called hedonic paradox. Hedonists believe that happiness is the only good and that everything should be done with the aim of achieving personal happiness. The hedonic paradox contends that the more you seek happiness the less likely you are to find it. Consider the following situation. You awake at 7: 00 a.m. and as a good hedonist you resolve to undertake each of the day's activities in order to achieve happiness. The achievement of happiness is your conscious goal in everything you do. I submit that if you adopt that strategy your day will be most miserable - probably long before noon. If you want to be happy you must pursue and successfully meet other goals. Happiness accompanies the successful achievement of those goals. To be truly happy, you must focus on consciously achieving your goals. In that way the hedonic paradox can be avoided.

I maintain that a similar paradox operates in business. Many business persons believe that profit is the only goal of business and that everythig should be done with the aim of obtaining profit. I contend that the more a business consciously seeks to obtain profits, the less likely they are to achieve them, despite the argument that business persons believe you should always keep your eye on the bottom line.

But if profits are the result of a focus on the employees, aren't the employees just being treated as a means rather that as an end? Aren't the employees just being manipulated? The companies behave morally because there is a payoff for doing so.

There are essentially three ways to seek happiness. One can set out consciously to do so. Hovever, to seek happiness in that way leads directly to the hedonic paradox. Such behaviour is self-defeating. One can seek to achieve successful intermediate goals realising "in the back on one's mind" that in so doing one will be happy. Finally, one can seek to succeed in achieving personal goals and in the process one will discover that one is happy. This latter means to happiness clearly avoids the hedonic paradox.

What about having happiness in the back of one's mind? Is that sufficient for avoiding the hedonic paradox? Psychologically, I think we have a borderline case. Whether or not the paradox is avoided depends upon how far in the back of one's mind the ultimate goal of happiness is.

Similar comments can be made about management's attention to employees. If the management is creating conditions for happy, healthy employees in order to make a profit, they are simply using employees as a means to their own end. Thay are not motivated by the respect and dignity of personhood. Hence, the motive of such managers is not moral even if the results are good.

Moreover, devices like quality circles or management worker teams that were introduced in order to increase shareholder profit would probably fail. Why? Suppose that the management-worker teams objectively improved the condition of the workers. Isn't that sufficient? No. We know that individuals refuse a bargain they perceive to be unfair even if the bargain would make them better off (Guth *et al.*, 1982). If the workers believe that stockholders already keep too much of the profits, then a programme that increases stockholder wealth even more may be resisted even if the workers are better off as a result. The workers see the increased wealth to shareholders as unfair.

On the other hand if the firm consciously focuses on the individual self-realisation of the employees, the employees are likely to recognise this and to respond appropriately. Will such moral motivation on the part of management yield good results? Within the firm, the answer, I believe, is certainly in the affirmative. Given a stable external environment, the firm will do best by focusing on the employee. Of course, changes in the external environment affect profit too. There is no guarantee that moral motives will yield good results.

Perhaps the best strategy is for management to focus on employee self-realisation while keeping profits in the back of its mind. In that way management can respond to trends in the environment. But such an approach has dangers of its own. If profits aren't sufficiently in the back of management's mind, the employees will develop the same kind of cynicism found when profit is the conscious goal of "moral" behaviour.

Before leaping to the conclusion that this last strategy is the only practical one, keep in mind the folowing distinction:

1. Management A says to its workers: you will never be fired without cause, but if the economy turns sour, some of you will have to be let go. (Moral behaviour with profits in the back of the mind.)
2. Management B says to its workers: you will never be fired without cause nor will you be fired in the event of an economic downturn. If the company should go under because of circumstances beyond our control, we will all go under together. (Moral behaviour with profits as a happy result.)

Wouldn't the employees in company B be less cynical, more productive and hence wouldn't the profit seeking paradox be less likely to occur in company B? I for one would invest my money in the stock of company B.

Considerations like these indicate why Friedman's view on corporate responsibility cannot be adopted as management's position. It is likely to be self-defeating. A product or service is the result of the efforts of a number of stakeholders - shareholders, managers, suppliers, customers, employees, and the local community. Friedman's view commits the manager who is the fiduciary agent of the stockholders to manage all the other stakeholders so that profits are maximised for the stockholders. Such a position seems patently unfair. The task of the manager is to motivate all the stakeholders to increase productivity (profits) and then the total increase is to be distributed solely to one group of stakeholders, *i.e.*, the stockholders. On what ethical grounds can such a distribution be justified?

Traditionally the stockholders argue that they *own* the corporation and hence are entitled to the profits. The ownership argument will not convince the other productive stakeholders. If we assume that the higher profits were at least in part a result of increased productivity on the part of employees, the employees believe they are entitled to a part of them. Total distribution to stockholders could be perceived as unfair.

A standard stockholder response is to argue that higher salaries, increased benefits, and more pleasant working conditions justify the distribution of all profits to stockholders - a company health centre, or day care centre represent the rewards for the employees; better quality products represent the reward for customers; and the local community and suppliers gain the reward of increased security that a profitable firm brings. The stockholders happen to get their rewards in dividens. Maximising stockholder dividends really maximises the interests of all corporate stakeholders. A rising tide lifts all boats.

Even if this argument were true, and I doubt that it is, two further points must be noted. First, at best we have a situation of reciprocal altruism. All the other stakeholders strive to increase stockholder dividends only because they themselves will be better off. Moreover, these other stakeholders know they get the increased salary, benefits, security,etc., because management has to provide them on prudential grounds. Otherwise output would not be maximised because the other stakeholders would shirk. The manager is only concerned with their interests because it enables the manager to do the job of maximising stockholder dividends. If the manager could ignore their interests or give them less and increase stockholder dividends, he or she would do it (is obliged to do it). No wonder some members of the United Auto Workers are suspicious of management-employee teams in the auto industry.

For these reason I don't think managers should try to provide meaningful work in order to increase profits. They should do it because it is the right thing to do.

Some implications of the correct understanding of the function of corporations

If the notion that the chief function of the corporation is to provide meaningful work is to be implemented, what are the implications for traditional business values and business practice? First, we have to de-emphasize competition. The football and war metaphors have to be replaced. Elsewhere I have suggested the family metaphor as an appropriate device for seeing how a corporation ought to functions (Bowie, 1985). Co-operation must be emphasized over competition because co-operation is necessary to provide the cohesiveness necessary for the practice of morality. It is harder to be a free rider if you see your associates as colleagues or teammates rather than as competitors.

On change in corporate pratice might be the introduction of a notion of group merit to replace or supplement individual merit. When an economic downturn occurs, everyone could be put on a reduced work week rather than placing the entire burden on the few who are laid off. A profit sharing system should supplement or even replace the traditional wage structure.

Second, we must give up our excessive commitment to individualism. In a market economy it is very difficult to overcome free rider problems. A rational individual, in situations that require co-operation, knows that he or she does best when every one else co-operates and he or she does not; he or she then free rides on the co-operative activity of others. But if every one reasons this way, then the co-operative activity will not occur or will occur at a level below optimum. Since morality is essentially a co-operative activity, it easily falls victim to free rider problems.

The importance of institutions as an aid in helping avoid free rider problems is seen in the work of the anthropologist Mary Douglas (1986). Her interest is in group solidarity or how it is that people manage to sacrifice their own interests for the public good. Douglas contends that market behaviour cannot be based on completely self-regarding motives.

Her argument, oversimplified here, is that the individual doesn't calculate as general equilibrium theory requires. An individual identifies with other individuals in an institutional setting. We take on the thoughts of others and they take on our thoughts. An institutional culture develops. An individual in a business situation does not maximise his or her individual self-interest but rather makes the decision from both individual and institutional interests. The institution's norms and interests become the individual's norms to the extent that an individual will follow institutional norms even when it is not in his or her interest to do so.

Third, we should abandon the hierarchical view of management. Sharp criticism of the view that the manager is a boss and that employees should follow orders is now a common place. There are strong moral and psychological reasons for abandoning a management tradition where a boss gives orders. If employees are to be convinced to develop institutional loyalty and to put the interest of the group ahead of their own self-interest, they must feel part of a team. Inability to participate in the setting of goals certainly doesn't contribute to a team concept. In this case psychology is buttressed by morality. In the absence of an opportunity to help set group goals, there is no moral reason for a person to sacrifice his or her self-interest for the interest of the group. Many autocrats talk the language of team loyalty, but the employees know that in such cases team loyalty is nothing more than loyalty to an autocratic boss. My arguments for team loyalty and firm loyalty must not be misunderstood. I am *not* calling for blind loyalty. I am calling for loyalty to a total co-operative enterprise. If the culture of the firm is autocratic rather than co-operative, loyalty to the firm can neither be expected nor morally demanded. But if employees are treated as professionals and given opportunities for meaningful work, they will be loyal and loyal employees make the business more profitable. However, if this strategy is to work, the emphasis must be on the employee rather than on the profit.

Conclusion

I have argued that business should see its central function as providing meaningful work. By so doing business will be doing good consistent with the demands of morality. However, if business shifts its focus they are more likely to be profitable. In doing good they are also likely to do well.

References

Bell, D.: 1976, *The Cultural Contradiction of Capitalism*, New York: Basic Books.

Bowie, N.E.: 1985, "Should Collective Bargaining and Labor Relations Be Less Adversarial?", *Journal of Bussiness Ethics*, 4, 283-291.

Bowie, N.E: 1988, "The Paradox of Profit", in N. Dale Wright (ed), *Papers on the Ethics of Administration*, Provo, Utah: University of Brigham Young Press, 97-118.

Camenisch, P.: 1981, "Business Ethics or Getting to the Heart of the Matter," *Business and Professional Ethics Journal*, 1 (Fall), 59-69.

Davis, K.: 1975, "Five Propositions for Social Responsibility," *Business Horizons*, XVIII, 3 (June), 19-24.

Douglas, M. : 1986, *How Institutions Think*, New York: Syracuse University Press.

Freeman, R. E.: 1984, *Strategic Management: A Stakeholder Approach*, Boston: Pitman.

Friedman, M.: 1962, *Capitalism and Freedom*, Chicago: University of Chicago Press.

Gini, A.R. and T.J. Sullivan: 1987, "Work: The Process and the Person", *Journal of Business Ethics*, 6, 649-655.

Guth, W., R. Schmittberger and B. Schwarze: 1987, "An Experimental Analysis of Ultimatum Bargaining," *Journal of Economic Behaviour and Organization*, 3, 367-88.

Schwartz, A. : 1982, "Meaningful Work", *Ethics*, 92, (July) 634-646.

Simon, J.G., C.W. Powers and J. P.Gunnemann: 1972, *The Ethical Investor: Universities and Corporate Responsibility*, New Haven, CT: Yale University Press.

ON THE DEMAND FOR MEANINGFUL WORK

Joanne B. Ciulla

> "Suppose that every tool we had could perform its function, either at our bidding, or itself perceiving the need," and "suppose that shuttles in a loom could fly to and fro and a plucker play on a lyre all self-moved, then manufacturers would have no need of workers nor masters of slaves". (Aristotle, 1979, 31).

It is over 2300 years since Aristotle mused about a life without work. Today the tools and machines that Aristotle dreamed of are the furniture of everyday life in industrialised countries. The demands of a competitive market catapult us towards a world in which machines replace or simplify most jobs. Aristotle might have rejoiced at this. But Americans don't. Instead of greeting this era with joy, we cling ever more tightly to our work. Ours is a work-oriented society, one where "all play and no work makes Jack a big jerk". We live in a paradoxical culture that both celebrates work and continually strives to eliminate it. While we treasure economic efficiency, we seek humanly interesting jobs that will offer fulfilment and meaning to our lives. Perhaps the demand for meaningful work grows because we see the supply shrinking.

In his paper "Empowering People as an End for Business" Norman Bowie (1989) asserts that business ethics should redefine the function of the firm so that "The main purpose of the corporation is to provide meaningful work" (p. 1). In this paper I argue that work may already promise to contribute more to a person's life than most jobs can possibly deliver. I don't think that a corporation is capable of providing meaningful work for all of its employees. However, I do believe that companies have a moral obligation to offer employees a work arrangement that allows them to find meaning either in their work or their free time.

The "loaded" meaning of work

As things now stand, we have gone beyond the work ethic, which endowed work with moral value, and now expect our jobs to be the source of our identity, the basis of our individual worth, and the mainspring of happiness. Furthermore, we want our work to substitute for the fulfilment that used to be derived from friends, family and community. Over the past sixty years, modern management has capitalised on this " loaded" meaning of work. The social engineer has replaced the time-study man - corporations have become "cultures" that seek to transform employees into a happy family. The problem of alienation has been licked by "entertaining" that encroaches on employees' leisure time in the guise of business dinners, corporate beer busts, and networking parties. Managers, charged with the task of "making meaning" create new ways to persuade employees to invest more of themselves in their work than the job may require (Howard, 1985). It is ironic that in an era of hostile takeovers, corporations seem to want more commitment and loyalty from their employees. So, banal work is sometimes dressed up to look meaningful, or as sociologist P. D. Anthony (1977) observed, "A great deal of the ideology of work is directed at getting men to take work seriously when they know it is a joke" (p.5)

Under the old school of scientific management, the alienated worker did what he or she was told, got paid and went home. The work might have been boring, the wages unfair, but at least everyone knew where they stood. Today the transaction is not so honest. While we still trade our labour, we are also required to give away a slice of our private lives. Workers of the past were often overworked; today many of us are over-managed. The exhaustion that pains the faces of office workers at the end of the day may not be physical but emotional, because management demands more of the self than the actual timely and efficient performance of the task at hand. In part this is due to the emotional labour that is required from professionals, white collar workers and service workers.[1]

Work determines our status and shapes our social interactions. One of the first things that Americans ask when they meet someone new is, "What do you do? " (This used to be considered a rude question in Europe, but in recent years it's asked more and more - even in polite circles, where it's asked politely). To be retired or unemployed in a work-oriented society is to be relegated to the status of a non-entity (Mowsesian, 1986, 15). Young people fanatically pursue careers as if a good job were the sole key to happiness - whether that happines is derived from the status of the job itself or the wages that they believe will eventually buy it. They are willing to take drug tests, wear the right clothes and belong to the right clubs, all in the name of obtaining a position that will eventually give them freedom to choose. Many argue that they will work a seventy hour week, make their fortune and retire at forty - few ever do. This attitude has taken a social toll in terms of loneliness, divorce, child abuse and sometimes even white-collar crime.[2]

A consequence of this loaded meaning of work is that people willingly put their happiness in the hands of the market and of their employers. Unlike social institutions such as the church and community, corporations frequently do not possess a clear moral vision of what is good for people. As Erich Fromm (1971) observed, "Since modern man experiences himself both as the seller and as the commodity to be sold on the market, his self-esteem depends on conditions beyond his control. If he is successful, he is valuable; if he is not, he is worthless" (p.38). But large salaries and success on the job no longer equate with happiness - people want something more. Modern managers in this environment are challenged to find ways of motivating people who want jobs that satisfy a variety of abstract desires and needs, such as self-development and self-fulfilment. While there doesn't seem to be much consensus on what "self-development" means or what people self-develop for, many feel that this is what they should want. So managers, consultants and psychologists guess at employees' needs and develop programmes and policies, which carry the implicit promise of fulfilling them. This results in a vicious circle - employees desire more, management promises more, and the expectation for

---

[1] For a discussion of emotional labour see Hochchild (1984).

[2] The impact of careerism on children is well documented in Fuchs (1988).

finding meaning in work rises. Both sides grope in the dark for ways to build a workplace El Dorado.

The evolution of the meaning of work

The practical question is, How did we end up in this situation? To answer this we need to look at the way that the character of work has evolved over the past century in the United States. The 1880s saw the rise of heavy industry and an influx of immigrants. America was a country where it was possible to work hard and get ahead. The next change occurred around the time of World War I when the United States underwent an internal migration from the countryside to the city, and suburbs and ghettos grew. The workers of this era were male and blue collar. In the third phase, programmes like the New Deal accelerated government controls over the labour force. Trade unionism and collective bargainig helped redistribute authority from employers to the government and the labour unions. This trend was carried on by social programmes of the nineteen-sixties and seventies.

The fourth phase of the nineteen-sixties marked a change in the attitudes and expectations of workers. This new orientation was dominated by two themes, personal self-fulfilment and political rights (Kerr, 1979, IX-X). The first theme was psychological in nature - it expressed concern for work as a source of self-respect - while the second was concern for individual rights and power (Kanter, 1978). Political power in the workplace and the right of co-determination has not been pushed as hard in America as it has in European countries with socialist traditions. While many writers wrote about workplace democracy in the nineteen-seventies, it was not an issue that excited workers. At this time American workers had a hard time connecting individual power with group effort. Often the desire to keep unions out led managers to seek new ways to satisfy employees. By the eighties, worker participation and quality of worklife programmes were viewed more as management tools, than the result of employee demands.

In 1971, the Department of Health, Education and Welfare did a massive study on work in America. The study concluded that many Americans were dissatisfied with their jobs because the workplace had not kept pace with the changing education levels and affluence of Americans. In this last stage, the emphasis of change was on redesigning jobs. The report stated that many Americans "were now in a position where having an interesting job is now as important as having a job that pays well."[1]

The central theme of the sixties and seventies did not concern the ethics or politics of work, but focused on the aesthetics of work (Kerr, 1979, XI). People wanted better jobs, meaning jobs that were psychologically satisfying, interesting, clean, safe, well-paid, prestigious and that offered good benefits. Improvements in the workplace led workers to expect an even higher quality of work life and this has led to another problem. According to a study by Daniel Yankelovich and John Immerwahr (1981) on work in America, workers of the new breed believe that they are entitled to jobs, but don't feel the need to earn them by giving them all their energy.[2]

---

[1] Special Task Force to the Secretary of H.E.W. (1973, XVI).
[2] For a good description of the needs of the new technoservice worker see Maccoby (1988).

Immerwahr and Yankelovich concluded that workers still believe in the work ethic, but need to be provided with the right incentives. However, these same employees are increasingly suspicious of managements that manipulate them under the guise of caring, or try to excite them with the latest management fad. Unlike the organised workers of old, the new worker doesn't exert power by picketing with his or her colleagues, but instead stages his or her own silent strike of passive resistance.

What we have seen in the nineteen-eighties is the moral crisis of work, which I would also characterise as a crisis of meaning. Over the past twenty years, the workplace has become more appealing to people's tastes and lifestyles. But we are discovering that some of the values that have emerged from business life are not very attractive or satisfying. Corporate scandals and employee crimes have forced us to rethink the values that have been bred in the work place and the market place. Hence, there has emerged an intense interest in business ethics in the United States and Europe, together with discussions about meaningful work. Bowie's suggestion that corporations provide meaningful work addresses both of these issues.

Corporations as providers of meaningful work

One of the major questions in business ethics is: Can the corporation act like a Kantian moral agent? Can it really have a good will? Is it possible for it to treat employees as ends? The authenticity of a corporation's moral commitment is questionable if the drive for meaningful work is merely another motivating tool or a mask for authority. Yet it appears that some companies have already jumped on to the motivation-through-meaningful-work bandwagon. In *In Search of Excellence* and the management genre that followed it, managers were charged with the task on "making meaning". Peters and Waterman (1982) wrote, "We desperately need meaning in our lives and will sacrifice a great deal for it to the institution that provides it for us" (p.56).

Bob Howard interviewed employees of the Silicon Valley high technology companies that promise equality, efficiency, and meaningful work. Not everyone found their work meaningful or better than the old style work place. In his book, *Brave New Workplace* (1985), he concluded that "this corporate utopia for work denied the essential fact that work in America is a relationship of unequal power, that conflicts of interest are endemic to working life, and that this new model of the corporation, much like the old, is founded on a systematic of influence and control to the large majority of working Americans" (p. 9). The major difference today is that the control Howard refers to is control over needs and values. Managers in this environment are supposed to be more like holy men than muscle men. If corporations control the meanings of work, then they also control the voice of workers. On the other side of this picture are the employees who want the corporation to provide meaning because they are too passive to seek it on their own terms.

What is meaningful work?

Even if we put aside the potential of a company to use meaningful work as a method of control, we still need to ask, what *is* meaningful work? Is it something that an institution can define or is it something that people discover? Is it an objective or subjective phenomenon? William Morris (1985) offers some interesting insight into the nature of, what he calls "worthwhile work." Morris stated that work can be either a "lightening to life" or a "burden to life." The difference lies in the fact that in the first there is hope while in the second there is none. According to Morris, it is the nature of hope that makes work worth doing (p. 20). He says, "Worthy work carries with it the hope of pleasure in rest, the hope of pleasure in our daily creative skill" (p. 21).

The concept of hope is a useful one for understanding the nature of meaningful work. Academics who write about work often make the mistake of assuming that everyone wants work like theirs. Interview a variety of workers and you soon discover that this simply isn't true. There is a wide variance in the kinds of work that people like to do and the ways in which they find meaning. Morris's characterisation of worthy work has both a subjective and objective element to it. It is subjective, in the sense that hope is a potential, which people may or may not actualise. It is objective, in the sense that leisure, usefulness, and the exercise of skill require that these elements be present in the nature of the work. He asserts that "If work cannot be made less repulsive by either shortening it, making it intermittent, or having a special usefulness to the man who freely performs it, then the product of such work is not worth the price" (p.38).

Morris used the craftsman as his paradigm of worthy work, while Bowie uses the professional as his model of meaningful work. Both the craftsman and the professional have a moral and technical commitment to their craft that is independent of their employer. Bowie equates meaningful work with rewarding work, which he defines as being challenging, useful, and respectful of individual autonomy (Bowie, 1989, 6). A person's job could have all of these qualities and not be meaningful, or have none of these qualities and be meaningful. What Bowie has articulated are conditions that allow a person to seek meaningful work. Institutions provide general frameworks for meaning, but it is up to individuals to interpret these meanings for themselves. For example, our liberal society guarantees life and liberty, but it only offers us the *pursuit* of happiness. If a corporation provide meaningful work, it would take away the freedom of employees to find it.

Corporations do have a moral responsibility to do all that they can to redesign jobs and carefully think through the impact of technology on employees. Where jobs can't be made more satisfying, firms need to think of ways to accommodate employees so that their jobs do not stand in the way of their leading a satisfying life outside of work. Morality requires that corporations first recognise that employees have a right to a meaningful life. One task of business ethics is to help corporations rethink policies and practices that interfere with this right.

I believe that the major issue behind the current malaise of workers is the desire for more power and an independet voice.[1] Discussions of meaningful work really mask the fact that in the past ten years the balance of power and control in the workplace has tipped drastically in the direction of employers. If the corporation wants to create an environment where employees can find meaning, they have to be honest about the work relationship and give employees the freedom and discretion to pursue this quest. Henri De Man realized this as long ago as 1927, when he wrote, "The old struggle for the rights of man was taking on a new form as the struggle for joy in work." (p.221)

---

[1] This argument and most of the discussion of meaningful work in this paper are adopted from Ciulla (1990).

References

Anthony, P.D.: 1977, *The Ideology of Work*, London: Tavistock.

Aristotle: 1979, *The Politics*, translated by T.A. Sinclair, New York: Penguin Books.

Bowie, N.: 1989, "Empowering People as an End for Business", chapter 13 in this volume.

Ciulla, J.B.:1990, *Honest Work*, (in progress), New York: Random House.

De Man, H.: 1927, *Joy in Work*, New York: Henry Holt and Company.

Fromm, E.: 1971, *The Revolution of Hope*, New York: Bantam Books.

Fuchs, R.: 1988,*Women's Quest for Economic Equality*, Cambridge, MA: Harvard University Press.

Hochchild, A.: 1984, *The Managed Heart*, Berkely, CA: University of California Press.

Howard, R.: 1985, *The Brave New Workplace*, New York: Viking Press.

Kanter, R.B.M.: 1978, "Work in a New America", *Daedalus*, Winter.

Kerr, C.: 1979, *Work in America: The Decade Ahead*, New York: Van Nostrand.

Maccoby, M.: 1988, *Why Work?*, New York: Simon and Schuster.

Morris, W.: 1985, *Useful Work and Useless Toil*, London: Socialist League Office, Socialist Platform Number 2 (first published 1885).

Mowsesian, R.: 1986, *Golden Goals and Rusted Realities*, Far Hills, N.J.: New Horizon Press.

Peters, T. and R. Waterman: 1982, *In Search of Excellence* , New York: Warner Books.

Special Task Force to the Secretary of H.E.W.: 1973, *Work in America*, Cambridge, MA: MIT Press.

Yankelovich D., and J. Immerwahr: 1981, *Study on Work in America*, The American Enterprise Institute.

ETHICS AND LABOUR CONTRACTS: AN ECONOMIST'S POINT OF VIEW

Antonio Argandoña

Labour contracts have always attracted the attention of economics and business moralists. Wages, job conditions, unemployment, discipline, labour atmosphere, strikes, the rights of workers, unionism, and many other issues occupy a central place in the agenda of ethics scholars.

These questions also attract the attention of economists. Nevertheless, a disparity is evident between both sciences in that, although they focus on the same problems they do not give attention to each other's contributions.

Economics rests on some basic assumptions about human behaviour in relation to human action. Ethics also rests on the same kind of assumptions. Then, both disciplines are supposed to show a high degree of coherence in their conclusions, so that ethics would be the *equilibrium condition* of the economic systems, be they the man, the family, the firm, the country, or the world economy.[1] This means that in case of conflict, ethical criteria should prevail, as they are the only ones coherent with the non-degenerative maintenance of economic systems.[2]

But the purpose of this article is to show not how ethics should guide economics when studying labour relations, but how labour economics may throw light on ethics, because the study of what *should be* is in danger of being restricted to some general, useless rules if not accompanied by an adequate knowledge of what *is*.

The content of labour economics is too broad; this is why we will restrict our analysis to some themes related to labour contracts, and will leave out many other questions of ethical interest. Moreover, economics is not a unified science. This is why we will restrict our analysis to the neoclassical paradigm, the more widespread and, at the moment, the more complete one.[3] Then, we assume that employers and employees are rational

---

[1] I have developed this point of view on ethics in Argandoña (1985),(1987), (1989b).

[2] Nevertheless, there are different theories of ethics, based on different ideas of the human being, and not all of them are compatible with the criterion given in the text.

[3] An excellent survey of labour theory in this paradigm is Ashenfelter and Layard (1986). Other recent surveys that are of interest for the purposes of this article, are Azariadis (1981) and Rosen (1985), both on implicit contracts; Killingsworth (1983), on labour supply; Becker (1975), a classic on human capital theory; Rosen (1977), also on human capital, and Cain (1976), on internal markets. From now on we omit the bibliographic references to the specific subjects.

individuals who are able to have optimising behaviour, at least as a tendency, with some restrictions, including limited information and transactions costs.

In the following sections we will show the ethical implications of the modern labour contracts theory, non-specific and specific human capital formation, and implicit contracts as an employment insurance. The conclusions summarise the content of the paper.

Labour contracts

For many years labour economics followed the model of auction markets, as if potential employers and employees were to meet each day in a hypothetical labour market under the direction of an auctioneer to bargain on the exchange of hours of work for wages. The result of this daily bargain would be a unique wage, at which supply and demand would equalize. Every worker eager to accept a job at the current wage would find one, and every employer would find exactly the number of hours demanded at the current wage.

The level of the real wage per hour would depend on the marginal productivity of work, *i.e.*, would be equal to the increase in income that results from having one additional hour. And all these would happen spontaneously, through the free play of market forces, provided that enough competition could be ensured. The ethical contents of these relationships would depend on the justice of the exchange, *i.e.*, on the level of wages. Or, for some economists, there are no relevant ethical issues in the play of a competitive market.

This approach had the advantage of simplicity, at the same time as identifying the relevant variables for the resulting equilibrium: from the demand side, the desired level of production, the current technology or state of the arts, the quantities (or prices) of other productive inputs, the output price, etc.; and from the supply side, the number of potential workers, the prices of consumer goods, the preferences and tastes, etc.

But labour bargaining is a collective, union-mediated task. And workers' decisions are long term ones, and take into account a vast array of factors, from schooling and on-the-job training to the age of retirement and pensions. Firms' criteria are also long term: in fact, contracts are not renegotiated every day, but have a long - often indefinite - duration. Finally, work is not a homogeneous item, like wheat or Treasury bills, but every worker - and every job - is different.

The consideration of those factors is the basis of the modern theory of *implicit contracts*. Both employers and employees desire to establish long term relationships, so that every party promises to carry out some actions that seem desirable to him or her in the long term, although sometimes in the future one party or the other might deem it more profitable in the short term to act otherwise.

When theorising about labour contracts, economists do not study them as they exist in the legal framework of the different countries,[1] for even the explicit contracts take into account only a limited number of relevant circumstances, so that the great majority of clauses are still implicit (otherwise contracting would be too expensive).

The ethical content of the problem is then manifest: as many clauses are not explicit,

---

[1] This does not mean that legislation is irrelevant, but that economists take it as an external restriction to contracts.

there are many degrees of freedom that the parts may use in several ways.[1] Likewise, the enforcement of the implicit contracts is limited. This poses two kinds of problem: one that affects the *efficiency* of contracts - this is the subject of economics -, and another that refers to their *morality* - as studied by ethics.

Non-specific human capital

Economists look at human capital formation as a productive process in which potential or actual workers use some internal or external inputs (hours of study or work, time and knowledge of other persons, the content of books, etc.), according to their capacity, to obtain an output - education, training, learning, professional qualification - capable of giving to them and/or to the society an economic return and a general increase in satisfaction.

Investment in human capital is usually carried out outside the labour place, i.e. in family or school. But jobs are also excellent places for educating people, as they acquire skills, capabilities and knowledge, learn team work, and develop the virtues of work and sociability . And this is an inevitable process: men and women learn when doing, and every activity they do is an occasion for personal learning and improvement - or worsening.

Then, in addition to wages, the implicit contracts offer the opportunity of human capital formation, for the benefit of both the employer and the employee. *On-the-job* training is often a certain kind of public good (it is within everybody's reach, nobody may be excluded from it, and the consumption of it by one worker may not reduce the quantity available for others). But sometimes it is a real private good: *e.g.* the apprentice's learning or the technician's knowledge about the production process of the firm. In any case, on-the-job training is not free, but it produces some firm's and worker's expenses in time and materials. The ethical and economic problem is then how to share out the costs and benefits of this education, so that the requirements of justice be fulfilled, efficiency be enhanced, and motivation be optimised.

Human capital may be specific or not. The non-specific capital acquired in one job may be used in other jobs or firms with full profit (*e.g.*, the professional knowledge of a machinist). The firm, when investing in non-specific human capital, incurs some costs that it will not recover if the worker leaves the firm. Then, it is obvious that the employee has to bear these costs, and that he or she is free to use those skills and knowledge in another job. This is the explanation for the low wages of apprentices and trainees - specifically that their wages are lower than their marginal productivity value. The firm's behaviour is ethical and efficient, and the employee is free to leave his or her job, not being tied by the learning commitment to the firm.[2]

---

[1] In interpersonal relationships there are no ethically neutral acts; so, every aspect of the labour relationship should be studied in the light of ethics (although in this paper we are only interested in the potential contributions of economics to ethical issues).

[2] This has more implications; for example: (1) the productive process or the organisation of a firm may make it specially suitable for a formative task; then, it will have a high proportion of young employees, low wages and a high turnover, without this deserving a pejorative moral judgement. (2) With increasing age and knowledge, workers prefer higher wages and less formative jobs. (3) The indefinite period contract is not the natural form of labour relationship, and there is a place for a broad range of terms and conditions, so that both the interests of the firm and of the worker may be met.

Which is the right amount the firm may charge to the apprentice for the education costs in the form of a lower wage? This question brings us to the discussion of a more general, interesting problem.

Economists assume that firms make expenditures on their apprentices' non-specific capital formation until the return of the last unit of money invested in it is equal to the return of the last unit spent in any other use, and equal too to the labour productivity increase that results from that investment (taking wages into account). Competition guarantees the long term equilibrium between wages paid to marginal workers of different categories, their respective productivities, the costs of on-the-job formation and its return.[1] The firm charges to its trainees the formation costs including a (normal) profit, and the apprentice makes an investment in human capital now whose normal, competitive return he or she will receive during his or her working life, in the form of higher wages.

This is the economic framework of the relationships between employer (trainer) and employee (trainee), as studied by economists. Its moral qualification is the same as the market economy, of which it is a special case.[2]

But new ethical problems emerge when we observe that the efficiency conditions are based in certain assumptions on competition, information, absence of external effects, etc. For example, wages may be unjust if there is not enough competition in the labour market. Or the time necessary to bring up the economy to the full equilibrium may be so long that some ethical problems may arise during the transition. And the lack of information may also cause ethical concern.

Going further into this, the economist's description and explanation of the problem suggest a content of the implicit contract: the respective commitments of employer and employee, the quantities of money and services to be exchanged, the compensations every party expects to receive from the other, etc.; *i.e.*, their mutual rights and duties.

This jump from the general theory of labour contracts to the specific relationships in a contract defines the new kind of ethical problems which real individuals face up to, in addition to those previously defined. For example, in the outlined theory, firms and workers "sign" implicit contracts of work and formation attending to the *normal* or *average* circumstances: the employer expects to have average workers, who will devote a reasonable effort, and to whom he will provide a normal amount of on-the-job formation, etc. But, should the parties in real life take into account the special circumstances? For example, should the employer pay more to a high-productivity apprentice or worker? Should the worker devote more effort if the firm pays him a better-than-average wage?

The answer of an economist will be inspired by efficiency criteria: it is convenient to treat every case separately if the benefits of doing so are higher than its costs. For example, firms often agree on a general rule for some categories of workers, but treat all other categories, e.g. managers, as individual cases.

Obviously, the personnel policy of a firm should be dictated by both ethical and economic criteria. This means that a personalised policy that may seem to be the best from a general ethical point of view, may be neither efficient nor ethically desirable in some circumstances. In any case, the policy should be just, the treatment decent, and the pacts have to be observed. Then, the employer should make clear to his potential employees the personnel policy he or she will apply (or at least the points in which this policy will

---

[1] The process should take into account a long term view; then, in place of every cost and income, the current discounted value of expected costs and incomes should be considered.

[2] I have expounded this subject in Argandoña (1989c).

depart from the current practices or the legal prescriptions), even in an implicit way (*e.g.*, when paying relatively low wages to new entrants, the firm is showing that it will not consider the case of high productivity workers separately). And this will define the content of the implicit contracts.

Let us come back to the economic treatment of non-specific on-the-job human capital formation. There are many ways other than lower wages to charge the employee with the costs of training. For example, the employer may compel him or her to work a number of years compulsorily, so that the firm may recover the costs of training; or impose a bond to prevent the employee from leaving prematurely, etc. Nevertheless, these are inefficient solutions.[1]

Specific human capital formation

The specific human capital, *i.e.*, the knowledge the worker may exploit in the firm in which he or she learned it, but not in another, needs a different treatment. The knowledge of the customers' personal features, or of the specific production processes of the firm is useful for the employee, because of his or her higher productivity; and it is also useful for the firm, as the departure of the employee will oblige it to make new investment in human capital.

The efficiency argument shows that both the employer and the employee should share the costs and returns of this investment. The firm that bears the whole cost takes the risk of losing its investment if the employee leaves the job. And if the wage the firm pays is just a little over the one the worker would obtain in another job, the employee loses the return on his investment. As in every bilateral monopoly, the gains should be shared.

The *efficiency* question requires that the wage be put between a maximum level - which the firm would benefit from if the worker is dismissed and a new one is hired, even when the costs of his or her training are taken into account -, and a minimum one - the opportunity wage of the worker in another firm, even if his or her non-specific human capital becomes unproductive.

When studying the *ethical* question we assume that the wage should be related to the worker's productivity. But the amount of this productivity is not well known in advance. In any case, the minimum level mentioned before does not seem just (although the worker will be ready to accept it), because the firm should not harm the good faith of the employee, who made an investment in on-the-job formation with the expectation of having a return from it. And the same may be said of the maximum level.[2]

The *costs of searching, contracting, hiring and firing* of both the firm and the worker are also a kind of investment. The employer has to bear the costs of advertisements,

---

[1] A less efficient solution may sometimes be fairer because ethics should take into account the specific, individual circumstances. For example, if capital markets are imperfect so that it is not possible to consume future incomes in advance, a commitment may be preferable to working several years for the firm. These less efficient solutions may be desirable if there are external restrictions. For example, the minimum wage legislation may block the access of young workers to on-the-job formation, because the firm cannot charge the costs of formation in the form of lower wages. Then, a second best solution will be necessary, *e.g.* a bond or a long term contract.

[2] There are also other possible solutions. For example, if one of the parties breaches the contract he or she may be compelled to compensate the other (although the efficiency costs may be high).

interviews and tests, administrative or legal procedures, etc., and the employee also incurs costs in terms of money and time. The expenses of the employer are probably greater, so that a low wage for beginners is justified from the ethical and economic point of view.

The *long duration* of the contract is desirable for both the firm and the worker, in order that they receive the whole return on their investment in specific human capital. This is one of the reasons why mobility is low when people have been a long time in a job.[1]

A consequence of the preceding argument is that the wage paid to a worker in his or her first job - or in the first months in a new job - should not be related to his or her productivity, because the efficacy of the employee is known only after some time, and also because the costs of hiring and contracting should be recovered, and the investment in on-the-job training remains part of the wage. As the time passes, the relationship between productivity and wages will be normal, and the latter will grow even more than the first, to recover the initial negative difference. This means that the labour relationships should be contemplated in the long term.

Labour contracts as job insurance

Empirical evidence shows that labour relationships are in many cases relatively stable, although employers would like to reduce the personnel in recessions (if specific human capital is not important). In the same way wages are relatively stable, although workers would like to increase them in booms. This is why economists assume that there is an implicit contract in which employees renounce high wages in booms for a greater stability of jobs in slumps, and employers maintain jobs in recessions in exchange for stable wages in times of bonanza.[2] Then, wages include an *insurance premium* to be paid by workers in booms and to be received in times of slump, because workers dislike taking risks more than firms do, and they are also less able to manage risk.[3] And these facts have important economic and ethical consequences.

In the first place, firms differ greatly in their ability to manage risk, according to the circumstances of sector, competition, impact of macroeconomic policies and disturbances, etc. Then, they may follow one of the following opposing strategies (or any other in between): (1) firms may pay high wages in booms, let the workers bear the risk and fire them in slumps; or (2) they may pay low wages in every stage of the cycle, and hold up the jobs even in depressions.[4]

The theory assumes that unemployment is recurrent and inevitable for individual firms and workers. Then, on an aggregate level, if both parties know the characteristics of the contract, it seems morally correct that the firm should offer either high wages and the risk of frequent dismissals, or low wages and job stability, provided the contract is

---

[1] If excess mobility in the jobs is costly, the firm may pay low initial wages to discourage potential mobility-prone workers, and high wages later on. This is efficient and not ethically bad.

[2] The theory assumes that the stability of consumption in the life cycle is optimum.

[3] The employer has less assorted sources of income (frequently a sole wage), less financial wealth to diversify risks, more urgent needs (that make him risk-averse) and less knowledge about how to protect himself from risks.

[4] There are other reasons for wages not falling in depressions. The *efficient wages theory* shows that the level of wages and its changes may have important effects on the motivation, morals, and efficiency of employees. Cf., *e.g.*: Yellen (1984).

actuarially fair, *i.e.* the discounted present value of the higher-than-average wages when employed is equal to the discounted present value of the lost wages when unemployed, and the same happens with the other alternative.

Nevertheless, the ethical problems do not vanish here. Firstly, the firm pays high wages to every employee, but dismisses only a number of them (we suppose this to be really necessary for the survival of the firm). On average, the relationship between wages and employment is just, but the sacked employee will be relatively harmed, and the unsacked employee will benefit.[1]

Secondly, the insurance is usually not fair, in the actuarial sense: risks are not perfectly forecastable, the limited size of the firm prevents it from being a full insurer, there are non-insurable risks, etc. Then, there are considerable costs and benefits that fall on one party or the other.[2]

The third ethical problem is the incentive to breach the contract (opportunist behaviour). When demand is high the employees may fight for higher wages, and when demand is low the employers may dismiss workers. Moreover, the objective assessment of the content of the contract may be difficult to make as it is implicit, *e.g.*, to judge if the request for higher wages is justified or not. And this kind of difficulty is likely to be very frequent, especially when law or collective bargaining imposes the same conditions on firms or employees that would like to follow different strategies.

This argument may explain the uneasiness of firms and workers when unintended changes occur that depart from the normal state of affairs, so that every party may think that the other party is breaching the contract. This happens in the case of high inflation of the kind that reduced the stability and predictability of labour incomes from the late sixties to the eighties; it happens when there is pressure to increase wages to protect workers from inflation; with the dismissals and the reduction of working days by firms in order to stand up to the oil crisis; with the high level and duration of unemployment (in European countries); with the increasing rigidity in labour markets, etc.

Other difficulties derive from the problems of moral hazard and adverse selection. There is moral hazard when the behaviour of the insured may increase the insurer's costs without his or her being able to recognise that behaviour and avoid it (*e.g.* the person who drives imprudently because of having a full-risk policy). So, an employee may carry out reprehensible actions with greater impunity if the firm follows a strategy of job maintenance.

There is adverse selection when a high-risk potential customer has more incentives to contract, without the insurer being able to identify him (*e.g.* the seriously ill person who conceals his or her situation when applying for a life insurance). So, workers with a high propensity for mobility may search for a job in one of those firms that maintain employment in recessions, and leave it in the following boom, earning the compensation but not paying for the premium.

---

[1] Utilitarians maintain that the total of the damages of the unemployed should be not less than the total of the benefits of those who are not fired. But this cannot be a valid criterium in individual cases.

[2] The firm may maintain employment in a moderate recession, but not in a deep one, or if permanent disturbances occur in demand, technology or costs. This is probably what happened in Europe in the seventies: the firms were expected to maintain the jobs, according to the implicit contracts, but the disturbance was critical and the dismissals reasonable - and yet in spite of that, the workers felt frustrated.

There are also moral and efficiency problems due to asymmetric information. So, the employee may not know if a dismissal is due to an unexpected and serious drawback in business, in accordance with the implicit contract, or if it is a breach of it.

The previous comments show us that ethical behaviour is always beneficial to individuals and society, at least in the long term. For example, the repeated fulfilment of contracts gives reputation, so that the distrust and the demands of the other party may be reduced, and the costs of contracting and enforcing lowered.

The existence of implicit contracts isolates the workers from transitory disturbances in employment, so that they are less sensitive to external circumstances, creating a wedge between their wages and the prevalent tendencies in the market. Then, there is a possible case for behaviour which displays a lack of solidarity with colleagues elsewhere.[1]

Finally, our previous comments call the desirability of profit sharing into question. There are strong moral arguments on this issue: integrating the worker in the firm, making him or her more responsible and co-operative, giving him or her a voice in decision-making, etc. Nevertheless, economic reasoning is against this policy, as it concentrates the whole income of the worker in a single source, and loads a higher portion of risk on him. In practice, workers usually prefer a higher wage to a contingent profit participation. Then, both economists and ethicists have to face up to the challenge of finding a satisfactory solution to this contradiction, perhaps in the way of workers-stockholding, pension funds, etc.

Conclusions

In this article we have studied some aspects of the neoclassical theory of labour markets, showing how it may throw light on ethical problems. The modern theory assumes that labour relationships are designed for the long term, and are inspired in confidence - implicit contracts.They are employment (and remuneration) stabilizers in the economic cycle, and also as incentives to the accumulation of specific human capital.[2]

We also studied the fairness of charging the worker with the cost of on-the-job non-specific human capital accumulation. As for specific human capital, we concluded that there is a band of possible wages, between a maximum and a minimum, although both limits of the band are excluded for ethical reasons.

Economists offer interesting solutions to the efficiency problems in labour relationships. And as a general rule, these solutions are ethical, *i.e.* there are not strong

---

[1] An *internal market* may arise, and a wedge between the internal and external wages appear, when the costs of specific human capital, or of hiring and firing, are high; but the cause may also be the defensive attitude of workers, that makes it difficult to hire new colleagues. In these conditions, the promotion policy, a certain *esprit de corps*, low dismissals and turnover, and the use of violence (e.g. a strike to stop new hirings) may protect the internal market. One of the explanations of the so-called *hysteresis* of unemployment - its resistance to diminishing once its causes have disappeared - is related to the existence of internal markets: the *insiders* retain their jobs in slumps, and get higher wages in booms, blocking the creation of new jobs. Cf.: Blanchard and Summers (1987).

[2] There are other important elements in implicit contracts, as for example the quantity of effort the worker is expected to apply for the duration of the contract, and the conditions of the job. Cf. on this subject Argandoña (1989a).

arguments against their morality. But the ethical problems should be solved not in general but in specific cases.

This means that we apply to institutions like the labour market, and the implicit contracts that are "signed" in them, the potential morality of the market economy . Then, they are compatible with ethics in the average case, or in the aggregate. But the specific relationships between a firm and its workers should take other details into account, if they diverge from the average. So, we identified several moral issues regarding the stability of employment, when treating labour contracts as insurance contracts: the dismissal (or not) of a specific employee in a recession; the lack of actuarial fairness; the existence of non-insured risks, moral hazard, adverse selection, etc.; the information asymmetry, and the incentives to breach the contract, among others.

The issue of justice in the level of wages is not simple. We cannot say that it is "fair" to increase wages by 4.5 per cent and not by 4 per cent, or that a wage of 100 is just and another of 95 is not. If we do not understand the complex relationships between employers and employees, and how they are related to the operation of labour markets, our judgment on ethical questions will always be arguable. It is in this sense that economics lights up moral subjects.

Labour relationships are customarily long term. This does not exclude temporary relationships, but they have an important component of information and training. So, we cannot judge a concrete labour relationship if we do not know what the contracting parties have implictly agreed: for example, the sharing of the costs of training, on-the-job learning, employment insurance, and also other issues not dealt with here, such as incentives to effort and compensation for the conditions of the job. Every person should seriously face up to his or her specific moral problems, and economics does not give a unique solution to them.

Likewise, there is not a strict correspondence between a worker's productivity and his or her remuneration in the short term. This is why we should study labour relationships as long term ones, including even the years of schooling and those of retirement. It is also legitimate that two employees working in different conditions receive different remunerations in one specific period of time; this makes it difficult to implement the principle of the same payment for the same work.

Finally, the observance of moral rules has, in any case, beneficial effects on the private and social costs of labour contracts. Even ignoring its contribution to the individual's self-realisation and society's good, virtues pay. This is why we assumed that ethics is the equilibrium condition of individuals and societies.

References

Ashenfelter, O.C. and R. Layard, eds.: 1986, *Handbook of labor economics*, 2 vol., Amsterdam: North Holland.

Argandoña, A.: 1985, "¿Qué es la Economía?", *Enciclopedia Práctica de Economía*, Barcelona: Orbis, chap. 120.

Argandoña, A.: 1987, "Trabajo, economía y ética", in F. Fernández, ed., *Estudios sobre la Encíclica Laborem Exercens*, Madrid: La Editorial Católica.

Argandoña, A.: 1989a, "Los problemas éticos de los contratos de trabajo: El punto de vista de la economía", Research Paper No. 165, Barcelona: IESE, april.

Argandoña, A.: 1989b, "Relaciones entre economía y ética", Research Paper No. 166, Barcelona: IESE, april.

Argandoña, A.: 1989c, "Presente y futuro de la economía de mercado", forthcoming in *Cuadernos del pensamiento liberal*.

Azariadis, C.: 1981, "Implicit contracts and related topics: A survey", in Z. Horstein, J.Grice, and A. Webb, eds., *Economics of the labour market*, London: H.M.S.O.

Becker, G.S.: 1975, *Human capital*, Second Edition, New York: National Bureau of Economic Research.

Blanchard, O.J. and L.H. Summers: 1987, "Hysteresis in unemployment", *European Economic Review*, 31, February-March.

Cain, G.G.: 1976, "The challenge of segmented labour market theories to orthodox theory: A survey", *Journal of Economic Literature*, 14.

Killingsworth, M.R.: 1983, *Labour supply*, Cambridge: Cambridge University Press.

Rosen, S.: 1977, "Human capital: A survey of empirical research", in R. Ehrenberg, ed., *Research in labor economics*, New York: JAI Press.

Rosen, S.: 1985, "Implicit contracts: A survey", *Journal of Economic Literature*, 23, September.

Yellen, J.: 1984, "Efficiency wage models of unemployment", *American Economic Review*, 74, May.

TO ENCOURAGE OR REPRESS?
CORPORATE POLICY AND WHISTLE-BLOWING

Thomas W. Dunfee

Whistle-blowing in its simplest form involves one party accusing another of a breach of an ethical or legal duty. In the context of a corporation, the accusation is directed toward an action attributable to the organisation (target firm) itself. The accusation can be made within the corporation, characterised as internal whistle-blowing, or may be made public outside of the organisation, commonly called external whistle-blowing (De Gcorge, 1986).

Senior corporate management have the option of encouraging, discouraging, or taking a neutral stance in reference to external and internal whistle-blowing by the firms's employees. Over the years, corporations have discouraged external whistle-blowing by employees (Mathews, 1987), and those brave or foolish enough to make public accusations about their employers have paid a high price personally (Chalk, 1988; Kleinfield, 1986). There has been a recent tendency to encourage limited forms of internal whistle-blowing through devices such as corporate ombudsmen and ethics hot lines. A recent survey of 2,000 U.S. firms by the Ethics Resource Center found that 11per cent of the firms have ethics hot lines which typically provide employees with information about firm policies and allow for employee complaints and warnings (Reese, 1989).

The purpose of this essay is to assess this trend and to explore whether encouraging employee internal whistle-blowing is likely to be compatible with the goals and interests of the firm. The factors discussed throughout this paper are assumed to be universal to corporate organisations, and, therefore, not dependent upon the nationality or locus of the firm.

1. Characteristics of external corporate whistle-blowing

External corporate whistle-blowing has been compared to civil disobedience (Elliston, 1982a) and is often discussed as conflicting with duties of loyalty and confidentiality or as counter-pointed to efforts to maintain secrecy (Bok, 1984; Wexler, 1987). Because whistle-blowing is an act of non-conformity which may seen as breaching group norms (Greenberger et al., 1987), it is not surprising that whistle-blowers are often treated as social pariahs or that the typical corporation is unlikely to encourage such activities.

Whistle-blowing is often praised in the abstract and whistle-blowers are treated as heroes by the media. The accusations are perceived as made in the public interest and *ex post* events sometimes vindicate the whistle-blowers. Although some whistle-blowers are unquestionably motivated by a desire to protect the public interest, other less worthy motives may also be common. Some may act in self-defence, revealing what they know when it becomes apparent that if the wrongful corporate activities continue, they may become personally subject to legal sanctions. Others may be motivated by revenge, deciding to reveal damaging things about a manager by whom they feel wronged, or about their firm which they think has mistreated them. Whistle-blowers motivated by revenge or self-defence may be more willing than those motivated solely by concern for the general social welfare to incur personal costs as a consequence of their actions. The reality of the possibility of improper motive must be considered by those responsible for setting corporate policy even though some writers on business ethics question the moral status of whistle-blowers acting for self-serving reasons. (Bowie, 1982: "Those who blow the whistle for revenge, and so on, are not our concern in this discussion." See also De George, 1986, 223).

The question of whether a whistle-blower is morally required to act when he or she possesses information about an impending serious social harm is controversial. Professional codes often describe such obligations in permissive rather than mandatory terms (ABA Model Rule 1.6), and many commentators recognise that a principle of permissibility must dominate (Bowie, 1982) except for extraordinary circumstances involving clear-cut evidence of wrongdoing, which, if made public, will prevent potentially monstrous consequences (De George, 1986, 1981).

Potential whistle-blowers may be subjected to strong peer pressure from within the firm not to go public. They must also exercise personal judgment in evaluating the quality and validity of their evidence and characterising the moral and legal nature of the act which would be the subject of the external whistle-blowing (Bowie, 1982; Greenberger *et al*, 1987). Such formidable hurdles, present in an environment in which going public is generally viewed as optional rather than mandatory activity, support an assumption that most potential whistle-blowers will decide against taking action. Failing to act would be particularly likely whenever a rational actor follows the cost-benefit-oriented decision sequence suggested by Greenberger *et al*. (1987, 530). In that decision process, the prospective whistle-blower considers factors such as the degree of personal responsibility to act, the availability of efficacious actions, and a final, though ill-defined cost-benefit analysis.

These countervailing pressures, presumably faced by most potential whistle-blowers, may weigh greatly against action by those motivated solely by an interest in the general social welfare (Near and Miceli, 1985). H. Margolis has argued that humans tend to have a set of dual preferences: G-preferences pertaining to the group interests, and S-preferences pertaining to self-interest (see also, Dozier and Miceli, 1985). These preferences are not captured in a single utility function, but instead influence behaviour based upon the individual's propensity to act in furtherance of each of the distinct preferences. The relationship of an act of external whistle-blowing to the G-preference is often likely to be unclear, particularly because one can never know with any confidence that corrective action will ultimately be taken. The probable negatives under the S-preference, which may include loss of job or other sanctions, may be much less ambiguous. Miceli and Near found that those who observe wrongdoing, but decide not to act, refrain because they are "unwilling to jeopardize their careers by reporting" the wrongdoing. Whenever it appears that a particular act of external whistle-blowing is incompatible with S-preferences and its fit with G-preferences is unknown, the potential whistle-blower is likely not to act.

On the other hand, prospective whistle-blowers motivated by self-defence, revenge, or possibly even a desire for notoriety, may conclude that action should be taken because all of these interests are captured within the S-preference. When these types of motivations are present, it is easily possible that there is no conflict between S-preferences and G-preferences. Both support taking action. It, therefore, may be reasonable to assume that whistle-blowers will generally, but not always, be motivated at least in part by concern for self-defence, or desires for revenge or self-aggrandisement.

Regardless of motive, and independently of the method of disclosure employed, valid external whistle-blowing should benefit society and may, in certain circumstances, improve the financial position of the target firm. Consider the following case. A chemical firm has illegally disposed of toxic wastes, the malfeasance being disclosed publicly by an employee. The social welfare is improved directly if the activity is still ongoing and further illegal disposals are avoided. In addition, warnings may be provided mitigating unwitting exposure to the material. Finally, legal proceedings can be initiated against the firm enhancing justice through the punishment of wrongdoers (*ipso facto* a social good), and deterring other potential violators through the publicity surrounding a successful prosecution. The only circumstances under which society would not benefit from external whistle-blowing would be when (1) the accuser is wrong and no harm has been perpetrated, or (2) the action occurred in the past, has now stopped, the potential for harm has now dissipated, and there is no potential for deterrence, retribution, or reform, because the capacity to bring legal proceedings has expired. Such limiting circumstances are presumably rare, and, thus on balance, the probabilities should be that society benefits from accurate external whistle-blowing.

The situation with the target firm is quite different. Viewed solely in terms of its financial interests, it would appear that the probabilities are reversed and that generally a target firm will be hurt by external whistle-blowing. Consider again the case of the toxic waste. If the improper disposal never becomes known to outsiders, no legal liability will be incurred. Any external disclosure revealing information that would have otherwise remained concealed can only hurt the firm. Even if the information would have eventually come out, if there is nothing that the firm could do in the interim to lessen its liability, it will have been hurt financially by the information coming out sooner rather than later. This conclusion is based on the assumption that the liability will be substantially the same whenever it is imposed, adjusted for inflation and other relevant factors, and that the corporation, therefore, would benefit from the use of the money during the period that the wrong-doing is not publicly known.

On the other hand, a circumstance in which the target firm can benefit from external disclosure is when the problem is a continuing one, *e.g.* more toxic waste is being improperly disposed of on a regular basis, and the revelation causes the firm to take action reducing its potential future liability. Assuming the information would have eventually come out, and when finally disclosed the liability would have been much greater, then the target firm benefits from earlier external disclosure. The alternatives, depending upon the ability of the target firm to act to lessen future liability and the probability that the information would eventually become known are diagrammed in Fig. 1.

As pictured in Figure 1, valid external whistle-blowing is likely to hurt the firm in most circumstances, and the harms caused are likely to be greater than the benefits gained. It is not, therefore, very surprising that firms discourage and punish external whistle-blowing. And this is true, even though the whistle-blowing is valid in the sense of accurately disclosing a real wrong.

Not all whistle-blowing will be valid. Some will involve false accusations or will seriously mischaracterise the harm. This may particularly be likely when a whistle-blower is acting on the basis of improper motives.

Invalid external whistle-blowing based upon incorrect facts or improper assessment of the consequences or character of the alleged wrong, can hurt the target firm. Even though no legal liability is eventually imposed, there may be substantial costs incurred by the

	Not discoverable by outsiders except by the wistle-blowing (W-B)	Would have been discovered at a later time anyway
Can mitigate damage	W-B hurts --	W-B helps +
Cannot mitigate damage	W-B hurts --	W-B hurts -

Figure 1: Impact of valid external disclosure on the target firm

target firm including loss of reputation resulting from the false charges and the direct expenses of defending against any unsubstantiated legal claims.

2. The pros and cons of internal corporate whistle-blowing

Internal corporate whistle-blowing involves disclosures and warnings within the firm about illegal or unethical actions. Internal whistle-blowing may take place through formal channels designed for such actions, or may occur through the general management structure of the firm. Because employees are seen as having an important obligation of loyalty to the firm, many commentators argue that disclosures should first be made internally (Bowie, 1982), unless such a disclosure appears to be futile and might ultimately compromise the ability of the employee to make an external disclosure. Whistle-blowing may often involve a multi-step procedure in which the dissident employee gradually escalates from an internal disclosure to a direct superior, through higher levels in the firm, and then when all else fails to outsiders. There are, of course, other options available including quitting the job or making a protest for the record (Nielsen, 1987).

Internal disclosure appears on first impression to have many advantages. It provides a venting opportunity for employees, and allows a corresponding opportunity for the corporation to respond to the employees' concerns. Successful responses by the corporation reduce the chances that false accusations will be made to outsiders, or that employees will act out of malice, revenge or self-defence. Most importantly, when legitimate problems are disclosed, it provides the firm with an opportunity to take remedial steps which simultaneously protect its reputation and enhance the public welfare. Returning to our familiar example, a firm, learning early on that some employees are improperly disposing of toxic waste, could act decisively to stop the practice, warn those who might be harmed, and begin efforts to clean up the site.

Presumably in most cases an initial act of internal whistle-blowing would preclude a subsequent act of external revelation (Miceli and Near, 1984). In view of the costs associated with external whistle-blowing one would predict that firms would be more receptive to encouraging internal disclosures (Mathews, 1987), which have been described as "more often than not a form of corporate loyalty" (De George, 1986, 222).

Yet, there appears to have been only limited encouragement of internal whistle-blowing, mostly recent in origin and due in part to outside pressures. And, even more surprising, organisations frequently retaliate against *inside* whistle-blowers (Near and Miceli, 1986). In the next paragraphs, we will briefly evaluate reasons why firms might not be receptive to a programme designed to encourage internal whistle-blowing.

2.1 Increased internal whistle-blowing may compromise necessary confidentiality

An expected result from a formal system of internal whistle-blowing would be increased internal revelations concerning activities of the firm. In order for the system to be effective, satisfying responses must be given to the internal whistle-blowers. The process of questioning and responding engendered by an internal whistle-blowing system may limit the ability of the firm to maintain important confidentiality. For example, a defence contractor working on a secret new weapon system may receive warnings about lax engineering practices affecting the safety of the weapon for users. It may be impossible to investigate the allegations fully and simultaneously maintain the valid need for secrecy. Management may fear that once it encourages internal whistle-blowing, any failure to respond will damage employee morale and cause management to appear insincere.

Interestingly, the defence industry in the United States has been at the forefront in implementing ethics hot lines, primarily as a consequence of the Defence Industry Initiatives on Business Ethics and Conduct, an agreement among the largest firms to implement various steps pertaining to ethics. Principle 4 of the Initiatives provides that "Each company will create a free and open atmosphere that allows and encourages employees to report violations of its code to the company without fear of retribution for such reporting" (Dunfee *et al.*, 1989). Their experience is some indication that a properly designed system can be responsive to the needs for confidentiality while providing genuine venting opportunities for employees.

2.2 Systematised internal whistle-blowing may lead to a restricted flow of information reflecting defensive tactics that reduce transactional efficiency within the firm

There is always a danger that formal encouragement of internal whistle-blowing may create an atmosphere in which employees criticise others for the basic way in which their jobs are being performed. In such an environment, employees may become conservative and risk-adverse, carefully managing any information about themselves to minimise any chances they will be challenged or censured. It is easy to see how such an environment could quickly become very damaging to the firm, stifling the creativity and risk-taking essential to business success. Whether or not such an atmosphere evolves would be influenced by the type of internal whistle-blowing system employed, the manner in which it is administered and environmental factors such as the culture of the firm.

2.3 Setting up a formal system for internal whistle-blowing may support an inference that senior management suspects major wrongdoing within the firm

Whistle-blowing is intimately tied into the reputation of the firm. The very act of accusation involved in external whistle-blowing is likely to inflict some damage on the reputation of the firm regardless of the validity of the charges brought. Internal whistle-blowing which reveals correctable harms should generally prevent a significant loss of reputation.

But, can the institution of a formal system for internal whistle-blowing cause a negative impact on a firm's reputation? For that to happen, outsiders would have to interpret the act of setting up an ethics hot line or similar internal whistle-blowing device as an attempt to uncover suspected wrongdoing. Unless there are rumours of wrongdoing circulating about the firm, such a reaction would seem unlikely. Instead, it seems plausible that the act of establishing a system whereby employees can express concerns internally would be favourably interpreted. In an industry where most firms are setting up internal whistle-blowing systems, firms that fail to act might be viewed negatively, perhaps due to a perception that their resistance to the industry trend could be based on fear of learning something best left secret. Although this issue is something or a two-edged sword, it appears most likely that a firm would not incur a reputation loss from implementing a system of internal whistle-blowing.

2.4 Corporate leaders who believe they have an effective management system in place may think that a formal system for internal whistle-blowing would be redundant that relevant information would come out anyway

Business corporations are dependent upon the efficient transmission of enormous quantities of information. As a consequence, they have extensive systems in place to insure that the necessary flow of information occurs. An internal whistle-blowing system may be perceived as artificial, imposed upon the normal, natural systems.

The ultimate question, though, is whether or not the information expected to flow through the internal whistle-blowing system would be conveyed through the standard systems. Because internal whistle-blowing involves accusations, there is reason to believe that certain types of warnings will not be made through usual channels. The information may pertain to the whistle-blower's superior or to others involved in the standard channels, thus increasing the chances of retaliation and reducing the chances the internal whistle-blowing would bring about necessary reforms. Information that could negatively affect the whistle-blower's superiors will only be revealed if some alternative source is available outside of the basic management hierarchy. In firms without a formal internal whistle-blowing system, prospective whistle-blowers may turn to either the law or human resources departments.

Ultimately, whether or not the existing system can handle such information is dependent upon the particular corporate culture and organisational design factors. Lawyers, performing a specialised staff function, are often not well positioned to bring about necessary changes in operating policy. In addition, lawyers may be subjected to professional constraints to honour confidentiality, further reducing their ability to undertake corrective actions. Human resources staff may similarly be poorly situated to affect corporate policy. There appear to be inherent limitations in the standard alternatives for transmitting information, thereby justifying the implementation of a formalised system allowing for internal whistle-blowing.

2.5 A formal internal whistle-blowing system may create an environment of "tattling" in which the system is abused for settling personal scores instead of its intended purpose

Employees may be unhappy with some aspect of their job and may attempt to use the internal whistle-blowing system to resolve personal problems. For example, an employee may not like the way that he or she has been treated in the firms's evaluation process and may somehow translate a below average wage increase into an 'unethical' action. Or employees may be jealous of a successful colleague and see the internal whistle-blowing system as a means of retaliating.

Complaints based upon pettiness and improper motives may bog down the system and simultaneously create an environment of distrust and back stabbing. This concern is not unique to internal whistle-blowing, there is always such potential in any information system. The key is to inform employees clearly concerning the purpose of the internal whistle-blowing system and to monitor its use to make sure it is not abused. Such potential abuses are controllable, and when controlled, allow the system to achieve its desired goals.

The fact that someone using the internal whistle-blowing system may act on the basis of an improper motive does not detract from the value of the warning to the firm. Any increase in the social welfare resulting from corrective actions by the target firm will be the same regardless of the motive of the whistle-blower. The potential victims of the toxic wastes in the example used earlier will be protected just as much by a revenge seeking whistle-blower as by a more saintly disclosure.

2.6 A formal internal whistle-blowing system may be costly to administer, particularly if it is abused by employees

In a large company with lots of employees it may be expensive to set up an effective internal whistle-blowing system. The system would need to be designed to handle a potentially large number of calls, and there should be sufficient staff available to respond properly to the information received. There would also be costs associated with communicating the initiation of the system, its purpose, and how to use it properly.

Although every internal whistle-blowing system will involve costs, they must be balanced against the benefits to be derived. Benefits would encompass liability costs prevented, reputation loss prevented, and, perhaps, happier, more productive employees. The benefits to be obtained from the operation of a formal system of internal whistle-blowing, although hard to measure precisely, should generally exceed comfortably the costs directly associated with such a programme.

3. Implementation of an internal whistle-blowing system

An efficient internal whistle-blowing system can (1) lessen the reputation and liability costs associated with external whistle-blowing; (2) provide information allowing reduction in social costs associated with harmful actions of the firm; (3) allow employees an opportunity to vent concerns not likely to be raised through the standard information channels; and (4) provide useful information about employee attitudes and business operations. Although internal whistle-blowing can be subject to abuse, particularly when employees act on the basis of improper motives, the main problems, which are essentially administrative, can be mitigated through the proper design of the internal whistle-blowing system.

There are many options available for structuring an internal whistle-blowing system. They include (1) *ethics hot lines* where employees are given a phone number to call to obtain advice or lodge a complaint or voice a concern; (2) *corporate ombudsmen,* executives with responsibility for receiving and investigating complaints and warnings, and whose function is publicised throughout the firm; (3) and *ethics committee of managers* whose function is to set policy, receive complaints/warnings and take appropriate action; (4) an *ethics committee of the board of directors* concerned with general policy and available to investigate charges of major wrongdoing; or (5) special responsibilities of the *corporate law or human resources departments* who are designated to receive and respond to complaints and warnings.

The following characteristics are essential for an effective and reliable internal whistle-blowing system.

3.1 The system must appear to employees to be strictly confidential

An internal whistle-blowing system will only be effective when employees trust it and are willing to use it whenever they have serious concerns. In order for this to occur, the system must not only be confidential, but must appear to be confidential. Any breaches in confidentiality are likely to be quickly communicated among employees and result in the ineffectiveness of the system. Confidentiality can be emphasized through devices such as a national phone number that can be called from anywhere without callers disclosing their identities or through the use of written forms that can be used anonymously. Assurances against retaliation, standing alone, are not likely to be believed (Miceli and Near, 1984). Complete confidentiality is necessary to sustain a viable internal whistle-blowing system. Imposition of strict confidentiality sets up a system of anonymous internal whistle-blowing. Although anonymous whistle-blowing can be questioned on grounds of fairness and effectiveness, it is not *ipso facto* condemnable (Elliston, 1982b). Instead, the system should have checks built into it to mitigate against the potential abuses of anonymity. For example, all facts alleged by anonymous whistle-blowers must be independently confirmed by investigators.

3.2 Those responsible for investigating complaints must have sufficient authority to conduct adequate investigations and to bring about appropriate reforms

A formal internal whistle-blowing system will not be effective if it is widely perceived as a sham. Some employees and outsiders may be suspicious of any new internal whistle-blowing system, which may be viewed as a public relations gambit rather than a sincere attempt to allow for genuine input about corporate problem areas. The most effective counter-point to sceptics is to demonstrate in fact that the system works and that those responsible have adequate authority. Feedback to those invoking the system is important, and should be as substantive as possible. A description of a full, efficient investigation, followed-up by appropriate action, is likely to encourage future use of the system.

3.3 The internal whistle-blowing system must be flexible in all dimensions

The system should be open to all employees, because it is impossible to predict who might possess critically important information about corporate wrongdoing. Further, if just a few groups are seen as responsible for oversight of the operations of the firm (*e.g.* auditors, lawyers, safety engineers), that may discourage those who actually have more knowledge and better access from taking steps to protect the firm's interests. Ideally, there should either be alternative routes for raising concerns, or the system should be independent of all operations. So long as any party in the internal whistle-blowing system may have an interest in the challenged activity, the system is not likely to be effective.

3.4 The purposes of the internal whistle-blowing system must be clearly conveyed to all parties

The only way in which an internal whistle-blowing system can achieve its primary mission is for all parties to understand its function. Otherwise there is the danger that the system will be used as a forum for other types of disputes.

4. Summary

The distinction between internal and external whistle-blowing is important. The latter generally harms the firm while the former has the potential for benefiting the firm through reduction of liability and reputation costs and through better relationships with employees. In spite of this important difference between the two forms of whistle-blowing, firms have traditionally discouraged both. Concerns about inside whistle-blowing include its impact on confidentiality, the possibility of improper motives on the part of those making disclosures, and the potential negative impact of an environment supporting internal whistle-blowing on the operations and reputation of the firm.

The standard objections to encouragement of internal whistle-blowing either don't cancel out the value to be gained from such activity or can be controlled by proper design and administration. Confidentiality, which means that one may disclose anonymously, is essential to the operation of an effective system.

References

American Bar Association: 1983, *Model Rules of Professional Conduct* (amended in 1987, 1989).

Bok, S.: 1984, *Secrets,* New York: Vintage Press.

Bowie, N.: 1982, *Business Ethics*, Englewood Cliffs, N. J: Prentice Hall.

Chalk, R.: 1988, "Making the World Safe for Whistle-blowers",*Technology Review*, January, 48-57.

De George, R.T. : 1981, "Ethical Responsibilities of Engineers in Large Organizations", *Business and Professional Ethics Journal* , 1, 1-14.

De George, R. T.: 1986, *Business Ethics*, Second Edition, New York: Macmillan, Chapter 11.

Dozier, J.B. and M.P. Miceli: 1985, "Potential Predictors of Whistle-Blowing: A Prosocial Behavior Perspective", *Academy of Management Review*, 10, 823-836.

Dunfee, T.W., F.F. Gibson, J.O. Blackburn, D. Whitman, F.W. McCarty, and B.A. Brennan: 1989, *Modern Business Law*, Second Edition, New York: Random House. (Initiatives reprinted at pages 137-139).

Elliston , F.A.: 1982a, "Civil Disobedience and Whistleblowing: A Comparative Appraisal of Two Forms of Dissent", *Journal of Business Ethics*, 1, 23-28.

Elliston, F.A.: 1982b, "Anonymity and Whistleblowing", *Journal of Business Ethics*, 1, 167-177.

Elliston, F.A.: 1982c, "Anonymous Whistleblowing", *Business and Professional Ethics Journal*, 1, 39-58.

Greenberger, D.B., M.P. Miceli and D.J. Cohen: 1987, "Oppositionists and Group Norms: The Reciprocal Influence of Whistle-blowers and Co-workers", *Journal of Business Ethics*, 6, 527-542.

Jansen, E. and M.A. von Glinow: 1985, "Ethical Ambivalence and Organizational Reward Systems", *Academy of Management Review*, 10, 814-822.

Jensen, J.W.: 1987, "Ethical Tension Points in Whistle-blowing", *Journal of Business Ethics*, 6, 321-328.

Kleinfield, N.R.: 1986, "The Whistle Blowers' Morning After", *The New York Times*, (November 9), Section 3: Business, p. 1 *et seq.*

Margolis, H.: 1982, *Selfishness, Altruism and Rationality*, Chicago: The University of Chicago Press.

Mathews, M.C.: 1987, "Whistle-blowing: Acts of Courage are Often Discouraged", *Business and Society Review*, Fall, 40-44.

Miceli, M.P. and J.P. Near: 1984, "The Relationship Among Beliefs, Organizational Position, and Whistle-Blowing Status: A Discriminant Analysis", *Academy of Management Journal*, 27, 687-705.

Near, J.P. and M.P. Miceli: 1985, "Organizational Dissidence: The Case of Whistle-blowing", *Journal of Business Ethics*, 4, 1-16.

Near, J.P. and M.P. Miceli: 1986, "Retaliation Against Whistle-Blowers: Predictors and Effects", *Journal of Applied Psychology*, 71, 137-145.

Nielsen, R.P.: 1987, "What Can Managers Do About Unethical Management", *Journal of Business Ethics*, 6, 309-320.

Reese, P.: 1989, Conversation with Patricia Reese, Director of Finance and Administration of the Ethics Resource Center, Washington, DC (April 13).

Wexler, M.N.: 1987, "Conjectures on the Dynamics of Secrecy and the Secrets Business", *Journal of Business Ethics*, 6, 469-480.

THE RESPONSIBILITY OF INDIVIDUALS FOR A COMPANY DISASTER: THE CASE OF THE ZEEBRUGGE CAR FERRY

Colin Boyd

On 6th March 1987 the British vessel *Herald of Free Enterprise*, the pride of the Townsend Thoresen ferry fleet, sank outside the Belgian port of Zeebrugge with the loss of 188 lives. Only luck prevented the loss of all 539 on board. The ship had sailed with its bow doors open, and the sea had flooded in when the ship built up speed.

At first sight, the disaster was caused by neglect by three employees on the ship. The assistant bosun, who was supposed to shut the doors, overslept, and thus failed to shut them. The First Officer, who had been involved with loading vehicles, waited until he thought he saw the assistant bosun coming towards the door controls, and then left to go to the bridge. The Captain, who should have overall responsibility for ensuring the ship set sail in a safe condition, did not check to see that doors had been closed.

At the Court of Investigation into the sinking, it became apparent that cause of the disaster went far beyond the neglect of three employees on one particular evening. There were a number of contributory factors, all of which had previously been known to the management and directors of the company or brought to their attention by front-line operating managers. Requests to correct various deficiencies which contributed to the disaster had consistently been ignored or rejected.

The Report of the Court of Investigation[1] details the workings of the company as it headed for disaster. The manner of the management of Townsend Thoresen prior to the sinking raises a wide variety of ethical issues, especially in relation to the roles and responsibilities of boards of directors. To what degree should managers and directors be held responsible for this kind of disaster, and how should society handle their lack of social responsibility if they are defined to be accountable?

The capsize of *mv Herald of Free Enterprise*

The *Herald of Free Enterprise*, like her sister ships *Pride of Free Enterprise* and *Spirit of Free Enterprise*, was a modern roll-on/roll-off (ro-ro) passenger/vehicle ferry designed

---

[1]*Mv Herald of Free Enterprise, Report No. 8074 Formal Investigation*, London: Her Majesty's Stationary Office, 1987. ISBN 0-11-550828-7.

for use on the high volume short Dover-Calais ferry route. She could accelerate rapidly to her service speed of 22 knots. She was certificated to carry a maximum total of 1400 persons.

At 433 feet long and 7,950 gross tons, the *Herald* was of record size at her launching in 1980 and was one of the prides of the 22 ship Townsend Thoresen fleet. She had two main vehicle decks, and at Dover and Calais double-deck ramps connected to the ferry, alloving simultaneous vehicle access to both decks. At Zeebrugge there was only a single level access ramp which did not allow simultaneous deck loading, and thus ferry turn-round time was longer at this port. Also, this ramp could not quite reach the upper vehicle deck, and water ballast was pumped into tanks in the bow of the *Herald* to facilitate loading.

When the *Herald* left Zeebrugge on 6th March 1987 not all the water had been pumped out of the bow ballast tanks, causing her to be some three feet down at the bow. Mr. Stanley, the assistant bosun, was responsible for closing the bow doors. He had opened the doors on arrival at Zeebrugge, and then supervised some maintenance and cleaning activities. He was released from this work and went to his cabin.

He fall asleep and was not awakened by the "harbour stations" public address call alerting crew to take their assigned positions for departure from the dock. The Chief Officer, Mr. Leslie Sabel, stated that he remained on the car deck until he saw - or thought he saw - Mr. Stanley threading his way through the parked cars towards the door control panel. He then went to the bridge, his assigned position.

The *Herald* backed out of the berth stern first. By the time the *Herald* had swung around the bow was in darkness and the open bow doors were not obvious to the ship's Master, Captain David Lewry. As the ship increased speed, a bow wave began to build up under her prow. At 15 knots, with the bow down 2-3 feet lower than normal, water began to break over the main car deck through the open doors at the rate of 200 tons per minute.

In common with other ro-ro vessels, the *Herald's* main vehicle deck had no subdividing bulkheads. If water entered the deck it could flow from end to end or from side to side with ease. The flood of water through the bow doors quickly caused the vessel to become unstable. The *Herald* listed 30° to port almost instantaneously. Large quantities of water continued to pour in and fill the port wing of the vehicle deck, eventually causing a capsize to port.

The Herald settled on the sea bed at 7.05 p.m. local time on 6th March 1987 at slightly more than 90°, with the starboard half of her hull above water. There was a light easterly breeze and the sea was calm. The ship had a crew of 80, and carried 459 passengers, 81 cars, 3 buses and 47 trucks.

Following the capsize a heroic search and rescue operation was mounted. At least 150 passengers and 38 members of the crew lost their lives, most inside the ship from hypothermia in the frigid water. Many others were injured. The death toll was the worst for a British vessel in peacetime since the sinking of the *Titanic* in 1912.

Under the 1894 Merchant Shipping Act, a Court of Formal Investigation of the capsize of the *Herald of Free Enterprise* was held in London between 27th April and 12th June 1987. The proccedings of the Court were subject to intense public scrutiny, as was the subsequent Coroner's Inquest into the deaths of the 188 victims.

The Report of the Court of Investigation concluded by naming the three ship-board employees as contributing to the disaster, and while it also blamed the company in general it did not single out any other individuals within the company as having contributed to the disaster. The Inquest jury returned a verdict of unlawful killing, which implied that a crime had been committed. A police investigation into the circumstances surrounding the disaster was then initiatied, and has yet to be completed.

Factors contributing to the disaster

Aside from the specific events on board the ship on the evening of 6th March 1987, the Report of the Court of Investigation identified a number of bachground factors which may have had a bearing on the disaster. These are described below:

- *Crew and officer shift rotations:*
  The officers were required to work 12 hours on and not less than 24 hours off. In contrast, each crew was on board ship for 24 hours and then had 48 hours ashore. Thus 3 crews intersected 5 different sets of officers, frustrating the development of stable working relationships.

- *Elimination of one officer on the Zeebrugge run:*
  The Zeebrugge route was longer than other ferry routes for the vessel. The company took the opportunity to reduce the number of officers from four to three on this route because the longer sailing time gave the officers more time to relax.

- *Rotation of temporary deck officers and trainees:*
  The vessel alternated between the Zeebrugge route and the other shorter ferry routes. Temporary officers were added and subtracted according to the route taken. Additionally, the *Herald* was used as a training vessel for new officers, adding to the rotation of officers. During the period from 1st September to 28th January 1987 a total of 36 deck officers had been attached to the ship. A series of complaints to management addressed this issue: "The result has been a serious loss of continuity. Shipboard maintenance, safety gear checks, crew training and the overall smooth running of the vessel have all suffered..."

- *Order requiring loading officer to be in two places at once:*
  On the Zeebrugge run there was a reduced number of officers, and the loading officer's task was more complex because of the connection of a double-deck ship to the single-level loading ramp. The company's standing orders had not been modified as a result of reducing the number of officers on the route. The consequence was that the loading officer was required to be on the car-deck supervising door closure at the same time as he was required to be on the bridge over-seeing the ship's departure from the dock. Written complaints about this conflict had been sent to senior management.

- *Commercial pressure to sail early:*
  The sense of urgency to sail at the earliest possible moment was exemplified by a memo sent to shore managers: "...put pressure on the first (loading) officer if you don't think he is moving fast enough... Let's put the record straight, sailing late out of Zeebrugge isn't on. It's 15 minutes early for us."

- *The negative reporting system:*
  Captain Lewry assumed that the doors were closed because he did not receive a report that contradicted this assumption. This negative system of reporting (as opposed to a positive reporting system which required confirmation of closure before assuming the doors to be closed) was the normal approved operating procedure for the company.

- *Lack of reference to door closure in standing orders:*
The orders entitled "Ship's standing orders" issued by the Company made no reference to the opening and closing the bow and stern doors.

- *Five prior instances of sailing with doors open:*
Before this disaster there had been no less than five occasions when one of the Company's ships had proceeded to sea with bow or stern doors open. Some of these incidents were known to management, who had not drawn them to the attention of other Masters.

- *Management of Townsend Thoresen:*
The Report states that "...a full investigation into the circumstances of the disaster leads inexorably to the conclusion that the underlying or cardinal faults lay higher up in the Company. The Board of Directors did not appreciate their responsibility for the safe management of their ships. The directors did not have any proper comprehension of what their duties were. All concerned in management, from the members of the Board of Directors down to the junior superintendents, were guilty of fault in that all must be regarded as sharing reponsibility for the failure of management. From top to bottom the body corporate was infected with the disease of sloppiness..."

- *Lack of job descriptions:*
In a meeting of Senior Masters with management, a request was made to provide job descriptions for ship's officers. A senior manager said that, although he was still considering writing definitions of these different roles, he felt "it was more preferable not to define the roles but to allow them to evolve". The Report described this as "an abject abdication of responsibility. It demonstrates an inability or unwillingness to give clear orders. Clear instructions are the foundation of a safe system of operation."

- *Responsibility for safety:*
When asked "Who was responsible?" a director replied "Well in truth, nobody, though there ought to have been". The Report said that "The Board of Directors must accept a heavy responsibility for their lamentable lack of directions. Individually and collectively they lacked a sense of responsibility. This left a vacuum at the centre."

- *No meetings for two and a half years:*
The Report noted that shore management took very little notice of what were told by the Masters. There was one period of two and a half years during which there was no formal meeting between Management and Senior Masters. The real complaint was that the shore management did not listen to the complaints or suggestions or wishes of the ship-board managers, the Masters.

- *Passenger overloading:*
The Masters had sent a series of complaints over a period of time to senior managers about the overloading of passengers on ferries. One wrote that "This total is way over the life saving capacity of the vessel. The fine on the Master for this offence is £50,000 and probably confiscation of certificate. May I please know what steps the company intend to take to protect my career from mistakes of this nature?". The

Report concluded that management made no proper or sincere effort to solve the problem.

- *Request for door warring lights:*
Subsequent to a 1983 incident when a ship sailed with open bow and stern doors, a Master wrote asking for warning lights to be installed on the bridge to show the status of the bow and stern doors. The memorandum circulated amongst managers, who wrote the following comments: - "Do they need an indicator to tell them whether the deck store-keeper is awake and sober? My goodness!!" - "Nice but don't we already pay someone?" - "Assume the guy who shuts the doors tells the bridge if there is a problem." - "Nice!" A subsequent request for warning lights produced this written reply: "I cannot see the purpose or the need for the stern door to be monitored on the bridge, as the seaman in charge of closing the doors is standing by the control panel watching them close."

- *Report of internal inquiry into prior sinking:*
Following the loss of the passenger ferry *European Gateway* in 1982, Townsend Thoresen instituted an investigation into passenger safety. Senior management received a report which began: "The Company and ships' Masters could be considered negligent on the following points, particularly when some are the result of 'commercial interests': (a) the ship's draught[1] is not read before sailing, and the draught entered into the Official Log Book is completely erroneous; (b) It is not standard practice to inform the Master of his passenger figure before sailing; (c) The tonnage of cargo is not declared to the Master before sailing; (d) Full speed is maintained in dense fog."

- *Inability to read draughts:*
A vessel's draught could only be read from the shore by inspecting the water-line measured against the draught depth marking on the hull. Requests to install automatic draught recorders on the bridge were ignored. The Court was told that no attempt was made to read the draughts of ships on a regular basis or indeed at all in regular service. Fictitious figures were thus entered in the Official Log which took no account of actual cargo weight or the weight of any trimming water ballast in the bow of the ship.

- *Excess weight of the ship:*
Research undertaken for the Court revealed that the *Pride of Free Enterprise* and *Spirit of Free Enterprise* each weight about 300 tons more than previously thought. The origin of most of this excess weighted was a mystery. The *Herald* was probably 300 tons overweight also.

- *Excess freight tonnage:*
Loading miscalculations arose from the estimates of the tonnage of freight vehicles on the ship. No weigh scales were used, as the tonnage was calculated by using

---

[1] A ship's draught is the depth of a loaded vessel in the water, taken from the level of the water-line to the lowest point of the hull. Section 68 (2) of the Merchant Shipping Act 1970 makes it a legal requirement for a Master to know the draught of his ship and to enter this in the official log book each time the ship puts to sea.

drivers' declarations of vehicle weights. Experiments revealed that these were frequently false. An average ferry-load of trucks was found to weigh 13 per cent more than the sum of drivers' declarations.

- *Water ballast and the resultant instability of the ship:*
In order to dock in Zeebrugge and unload both vehicle decks via the single-deck ramp, the bow of the *Herald* had to be sunk three feet down by pumping water into tanks in the bow. Complaints were made about the effects of the weight of this water ballast on the ship's handling. At full speed, or even reduced speed, the bow wave came three quarters of the way up the bow door. The ship did not manoeuvre well either. Masters complained that the ship's damage stability could be affected by the combination of unknown freight overloading coupled with the bow being trimmed down by four feet by water ballast.

- *Rejection of request for high capacity ballast pump:*
One Chief Engineer made repeated requests to management to install a high capacity ballast pump which could pump all the bow tanks' water ballast out of the ship quickly prior to departure from the dock. The existing pump took 90 minutes to empty the tanks and thus the ship could not get back on an even keel until it was well out to sea. The new pump would cost £25,000. This cost was regarded by the Company as prohibitive, and the requests were rejected.

Other revelant factors

In 1982 the Townsend Thoresen ferry *European Gateway* capsized with the loss of six lives after a collision with a competitor's ship in the approaches to the port of Harwich. The speed of the capsize drew speculation on the lack of stability of ro-ro ferries when water enters the main vehicle deck. Like the *Herald* after her, the *European Gateway* came to rest on her side half-submerged in shallow water, narrowly avoiding a deep water sinking with heavy loss of life.

According to Lloyd's Register in London, over 30 accidents to ro-ro ferries had involved loss of life. The worst previous British accident was in 1953, when the *Princess Victoria* sank in the Irish Sea killing 134. The world's worst disaster was in 1981, when 431 died on an Indonesian ferry which caught fire and sank in the Java Sea. In roughly two-thirds of the cases, the capsize took less than 5 minutes. The Report of the Court of Investigation raised serious questions about the inherent inability of ro-ro vessels to sustain damage and remain afloat long enough for passengers and crew to escape. The Report recommended that research be undertaken into various design changes which would improve ro-ro ferry damage survival.

The disaster took place against a threatening industry background. The cross-channel passenger travel market had reached maturity, although some further growth in freight traffic was expected. The industry was consolidating in this mature market, and cuts in unit costs were vigorously pursued in several ways; by the reduction of crew levels; via the deployment of larger vessels; and through the speeding up of vessel turn-round times in port.

The Channel Tunnel poses an extreme threat to the ferry industry, and provides a strong impetus to this process, especially the struggle for cost leadership. The tunnel may be considered to be *the* classic threat of a substitute product or service, one which is all the more classic because of the slow gestation and birth of the substitute and the long lead time for strategic response from the threatened industry (see, for example, Porter,

1980). Subsequent to the disaster, a series of strikes over threatened reductions in crew levels in the industry provided evidence of the intense pressure to reduce costs in the face of the anticipated subsitute.

Two final relevant facts are of interest. First, the Court of Investigation found that no laws had been broken when the *Herald of Free Enterprise* sailed with its bow doors open. There were no government regulations which covered door operation on vessels fitted with such doors. Second, 35 days before the disaster the company which operated the vessel was taken over by P&O (The Peninsular and Oriental Steam Navigation Company).

Ethical issues raised by the disaster

The central ethical issue of the disaster is the degree to which managers and directors should be defined as being responsible for the disaster. The Report of the Court of Investigation revealed that the board of directors had failed to identify safety as a policy issue and had consequently failed to assign responsibility for safety. This absence of planning resulted in an astonishing degree of apathy, antagonism almost, toward safety across all level of shore management.

This attitude was most obvious in those managers in Townsend Thoresen who rejected the various requests on safety issues made by their subordinates. Should the middle managers be blamed for their rejection of these requests, or should blame be fixed higher up at director level for the collective failure to define policy and assign responsibilities?

The Court of Investigation appeared to let director and managers off the hook by failing to name any shore personnel as responsible for the disaster. It is ironic, but perhaps the very lack of definition of responsibilities and policies within the Company, which contributed to the disaster, may have saved the directors. The diffusion of responsibility may have caused the inability to provide a focus for blame within the company.

All the directors subsequently lost their positions, but to date no penalty has been imposed on any individual director or manager. Should they be penalized in some way? The current police investigation may of course clarify the situation, for it is possible that criminal prosecutions for manslaughter may be brought against the company and/or individuals.

This raises the question of the degree to which the law should play a role in the definition of ethical corporate behaviour. If the law has a role to play, then what kinds of punishments should be imposed for corporate wrong-doing and to whom should the punishments apply? In situations such as the Zeebrugge car ferry disaster the imposition of a fine on a corporation would seem to be a punishment on shareholders or customers rather than on the managers involved. But a corporation cannot be sent to jail, and so if any punishments beyond financial penalties are envisaged then they must be imposed on individuals.

The notion of manslaugther by a corporation is a fascinating one. Society has only recently begun to contemplate this concept; which at one time seemed as ludicrous as the concept that a corporation could commit bigamy. However, society's attitude is rapidly evolving: in the United States on June 14th 1985 an Illinois court found three executives of Film Recovery Systems Inc. guilty of murder of a company employee, and found the company guilty of involuntary manslaughter and fourteen counts of reckless conduct.

The company recovered silver from used film, and utilised cyanides in the process. They had failed to install fume hoods, despite knowing that other companies in the industry regarded these as essential to the health of employees. An employee, who had asked to be moved to another job, died at his work station from inhaling lethal gases. The executives were each sentenced to 25 years in jail. This was the first known instance of a successful prosecution of senior managers for homicide in the United States.[1]

It may yet be that the Zeebrugge case will produce precedent-setting criminal prosecutions.[2] The plethora of recent tragedies such as the Bhopal Disaster, the King's Cross London Transport fire, and the Piper Alpha North Sea oil-rig fire may have produced an attitude in society that directors and managers cannot hide behind the corporate shield in defense of their actions, but must be held personally accountable. If it takes place, such an evolution of attitude to the responsibilities and roles of management would have far-reaching effects.

A number of other ethical issues are raised by the disaster. These include:

- *The need for and role of government regulation and safety inspection services*
  The Zeebrugge disaster reinforces the necessity for government involvement in the regulation of safety in a wide variety of industries. One difficulty is the conflict that arises when the government department responsible for the promotion of an industry is also responsible for policing safety in that industry. The strict enforcement of safety regulations may be improved by the setting up of policing bodies separate from the industry "parent" agencies.

- *The trade-off between conveniencie and safety implicit in the design of roll-on/roll-off ferries*
  The design of the *Herald of Free Enterprise* , in common with other ro-ro ships, may be thought to have been inherently unsafe. The Report devoted a large number of pages to the question of ship design, and recommended actions such as government evaluation of transverse bulkheads for ro-ro vehicle decks. There is a direct conflict between commercial convenience and safety here.

- *The degree to which the purchaser assumes the moral responsibility for the purchased company after a takeover*
  If I buy another company it is easy to see that I assume responsibility for the legal liabilities of that firm the instant that the purchase takes place; but when do I assume the moral responsibility for that firm's actions? How and when does this transfer to the new owner? If the sinking of the *Herald* took place one day after P&O acquired Townsend Thoresen, then it may be acceptable to argue that no blame should attach to P&O. But what if the sinking had taken place one year after the acquisition; would not P&O then be held to have assumed full responsibility? The actual elapsed time was 35 days. Was this long enough for P&O to be held to have some moral responsibility?

---

[1] For details of this case read "Corporations Can Kill Too: After Film Recovery, Are Individuals Accountable For Corporate Crimes?", *Loyola of Los Angeles Law Review,* 1986, 19, 1411, 1427-28, and also "Corporate Criminal Liability for Homicide: The Need to Punish Both the Corporate Entity and its Officers", *Dickinson Law Review,* Fall 1987, 19, 193-222.

[2] The U.K. law in relation to the Zeebrugge case is discussed in a short article by Lord Wedderburn (1987).

- *The censure of a manager who was acting in accord with company custom and practice, and is castigated for not managing according to a higher absolute standard*
Captain Lewry's position is of particular interest because of this defence that he was following company custom and practice, that the company orders did not refer to door closure, and that management previously knew of open doors and had failed to change operating methods as a result. The Report criticized him for not managing according to a higher professional standard. Is the criticism valid? The question here is whether the Report's view are specific to the Master of a ship, or whether the views apply to all managers. If the views are generic, then we must expect all managers to operate to some normative standard of responsible duty even if, and especially if, the employer has a particular set of operating procedures and customs which deviate from this standard.[1]

- *A subordinate's difficulties in communicating safety concern to superiors*
An important ethical issue revealed by the Court of Investigation is that of how an employee should behave if employed by a careless company. In alerting superiors to problems there may be a natural tendency to wish to protect one's own position by leaving an audit-trail of written documentation, contributing to bureaucratic inefficiencies. The existence of the wealth of written memos in the Zeebrugge case may be evidence of this phenomenon. One problem with this approach was revealed at the Court of Investigation when a manager stated that he ignored a subordinate's memos because if the complaint had been serious he would have done more than write a memo.

- *The role played by the environmental and competitive pressures in shaping managerial attitudes in declining or threatened industries*
It may be argued that the inherent pressures of the ferry industry's commercial environment, especially given the threat of the Channel Tunnel, naturally conspired against safety, and that the disaster was a consequence of these pressures. Is safety sacrificed in such an environment? Do cash cows graze in unsafe pastures? The recent press coverage of US airlines suggests that society suspects degraded safety levels in industries subject to intense competitive pressures.

Conclusion

The Zeebrugge car ferry disaster, in common with a number of other recent industrial and transport disasters, has focussed the world's attention on corporate conduct. There has been general disbelief at the apparently irresponsible nature of many of the management practices revealed in the subsequent enquires into these disasters. Pressure for stronger government regulation and for more direct forms of punishment of negligent managers can only grow if the world of business does not take to steps to reform its attitude towards safety.

For each firm the most effective way of implementing a safety awareness programme must be through the adoption of a value system by the board that places a priority on

---

[1] For classroom purposes the case study "Peter Green's First Day" (Harvard Business School case 380-186) is an excellent vehicle to enable discussion of this issue.

matters affecting safety, defines responsibilities for these issues, and establishes a system to monitor safety performance. Safety and other issues related to social responsibility should be treated as equivalent to other components of commercial strategy, worthy of board-level review and incorporated fully into the corporate value system. The ideal is the opposite of Townsend Thoresen.

In all probability a company which is complacent on safety issues is probably complacent in the general management of its affairs. The terrifying thought is just how many firms exist today which are being managed with the same lackadaisical attitude to safety as revealed by the Zeebrugge car ferry disaster? There are probably more than we would care to imagine.

References

"Corporations Can Kill Too: After Film Recovery, Are Individuals Accountable For Corporate Crimes?", *Loyola of Los Angeles Law Review*, 1986, 19, 1427-28.

"Corporate Criminal Liability for Homicide : The Need to Punish Both the Corporate Entity and its Officers", *Dickinson Law Review*, 1987, 92, 193-222.

Porter, M.E.: 1980, *Competitive Strategy* , Glencoe, Ill.: Free Press.

Wedderburn, Lord: 1987, "Can a Company Be Criminal?", *Times* (October 10), 10.

Part III

Men and Women in Corporations:
Repression, Competition or Co-operation?

INTRODUCTORY REMARKS

Georges Enderle

If we try to understand the topic "People in Corporations" more concretely, we are inevitably faced with the question who are the people we are speaking of: *basically, they are men and women*. Today, at the end of the twentieth century, we can no longer take human beings to be synonymous with men or sexless beings. The gender difference penetrates all dimensions of personal and social life. Without doubt, there is a growing awareness of this reality and deep-rooted, hitherto often hidden and repressed differences and conflicts are becoming visible. Provocative feminist and anti-feminist statements, positions and movements of multifarious forms bear witness to this revolutionary change in our society, and, also on the theoretical level, the gender difference is more and more reflected upon and analysed. It goes without saying that business ethics - if oriented to fundamental and urgent problems of our societies - cannot pretend to be unaffected by this revolutionary change; rather, I am pleading, it should engage firmly with this ongoing debate.

The aim of Part III cannot be to take stock of the full range of aspects of "Men and Women in Corporations" nor to draw a detailed utopian picture of how this relationship should be shaped, without taking into account the constraints of society today. Rather, I would simply like to recall some major characteristics of the present situation and to reflect upon the meaning of three types of relationships between men and women: repression, competition and co-operation.

I think it is fair to say that (1) the daily facts of life for a large majority of women are tough work/family conflicts growing out of the *double burden of job and family responsibilities*. Today, it is still extremely difficult for women (not for men) to combine both realities of human life, to engage in professional work and to have a family. Usually, the woman has to opt for the one and against the other, and this decision has far-reaching consequences for the rest of her life and even, in anticipation, in her preparation for working life.

(2) Although, in most European countries, *schooling and training opportunities* are, in principle, more or less equivalent for boys and girls, they often are, in reality, quite different, to the disadvantage of the female sex.

(3) In addition, even if there are equal opportunities for young men and women starting their work life, women will "normally" have to face more difficulties and hindrances in pursuing their careers than men, and they have still to *fight for an equal chance at job advancement*. Moreover, differently from men, women must deal with *subtle and not-so-subtle sexual harassment* to a varying degree according to the socio-cultural context.

(4) There is undeniable evidence that women (and minorities) are still *under-represented in top management positions* although the percentage might be a little higher in North America than in Europe, and in Scandinavian than in Latin countries. The "sound barrier" seems to be at about five percent - a limit which can only be transcended in exceptional cases. (Of course, to be more precise, this figure must also be seen in relation to the proportion of females in the work-force and the extent of part-time work by women.

One major task of business ethics is *to clarify the concepts we use in our debates*. For real communication and understanding is only possible if it is guided by continuous efforts on the part of the partners in the dialogue to clarify and explain what they mean as clearly as possible. To this end, I would like to sketch briefly the meaning of the three words "repression", "competition" and "co-operation" (beginning with the definitions set out in the Macmillan Contemporary Dictionary) which characterise different types of relationship between women and men:

- *Repress* means to hold back, to keep under control or in check, to put down, to prevent the natural development or expression of somebody or something.

  Repression not only denies equal opportunity to men and women, but also involves the notions of power and powerlessness, dominance, violence, machismo, and the violation of human dignity.

- *Compete* signifies to contend with another or others for or as if for a prize, to strive against a rival or rivals, to overcome a rival; it suggests a reward or prize.

  Competition refers to sports (athletics competition, football game) and to the market-place. The rules are the same for all participating in the competition; there are some fairness conditions and sometimes different categories of competitors. Most important is to win the prize against rivals. Giving one's best is taken to be a high motivational factor. Simultaneously, what results from the competition, is also the best for the common good - at least according to the harmony axiom, *i. e.*, for example, the "invisible hand" theory.

- *Co-operate* means to work or act with another or others for a common purpose, to unite in action, being willing to work together with others, with women and men.

  Hence, co-operation emphasises less the individual's aim and more the common purpose. The relationship is not characterised by rivalry, the rivals being outside the individual's interest sphere. Rather, the partners of co-operation are within a common sphere; there is complementarity, the one does not substitute for the other.

These conceptual reflections may serve as a screening device which can help us understand, in a clearer and more differentiated way, the gender reality not only on a practical, day-to-day level, but also on the theoretical and philosophical level. It is on that latter level that *Brenda Almond* treats the basic question whether there exist both a male and a female ethics. She answers it in the affirmative and sketches some female ethical perspectives which are of great relevance for the shaping of the modern corporation. *José Aguiló*'s contribution starts by analysing major gender problems and attitudes in the Spanish context. To produce some decisive change in the present situation he puts much hope in demographic evolution. It should, he argues, be supported and continued by corporate ethical policy and practice which, in contrast to Brenda Almond's standpoint, he takes as based on a gender-neutral anthropology. *Monique R. Siegel* takes up the policy orientation and asks more concretely how to include women in corporate decision-making. For this purpose she makes a wide range of practical suggestions concerning the personal, corporate and societal level of action.

MALE OR FEMALE ETHICS FOR CORPORATIONS?

Brenda Almond

This question has, implicit within it, another: Is there in fact some significant difference, as far as ethics is concerned, between male and female? *Do men and women face different moral problems?* Or do they, perhaps, encounter similar problems but *answer them differently?* The question as posed already answers these questions in the affirmative. Only if there *are* significant differences between male and female as far as ethics is concerned does it make sense to ask the question: Which sort of ethics is the most appropriate for business, for the corporation?

In the two other contributions to this Part, Monique Siegel and José Aguilá will talk practically about the problems women face in aiming for positions of influence in business, and also about the contribution they might be able to make if they reach those positions. On these questions it is worth mentioning that at least one famous analysis of moral development, to which I will make more detailed reference in a moment, places women at the role-conforming level - something that would make them better workers, but poorer managers. I will return to this suggestion later, but I will not confront these practical questions head on. Instead, I see it as my role to raise some preliminary questions and to consider the theoretical background to these debates.

So if I may begin at the beginning, the role of ethics in public affairs is to seek to offer answers to the question: What *ought* we to do? This is in contrast to looking for answers to questions like "How should we go achieving this or that?" As it happens, this poses an immediate problem in relation to the ethics of business or management because in these spheres achieving objectives is in fact the name of the game.

But for better or worse, my task is not to discuss except tangentially this wider question, but to step to one side and consider the "ought" question specifically in relation to gender. I could take this to be a question about the *treatment* of women in the corporate world, and ask "Are there ethical constraints governing the treatment of women in the corporation irrespective of what is, commercially speaking, being aimed at?"

Now while this is a question that could be applied at the level of top management, it could equally be taken as a more general question about the role of women in the work-force, and perhaps in the end about the social roles of women *and* men in society generally. In its wider aspects, it would require consideration of how the roles of women and men as spouses, as parents, as members of communities, can be integrated with the demands of a corporate or industrial role. For such an enquiry a good deal of sociological information would be required, and solutions in the form of crèches, flexi-hours, job-sharing and, for part-time work, proportionately equal status, pay and pension-rights would need to be considered.

I will take it that the gender "ought" question *should* be answered in terms which recognise the need for those who work for a firm to fulfil their personal as well as their occupational role. But apart from this brief recognition of the issue, I would prefer, for the purposes of this contribution, to return to my original question: "Is there a male and a female ethics?" There are two aspects to this: *First*, it is necessary to ask: Do the moral ideals of male and female diverge? That is to say, does the moral outlook people have depend in some causally-related way on whether they are male or female? And *secondly*, are moral ideals themselves gender-relative? To put these two points in another way: Do women *think* differently about morality from the way in which men think about it? And would they be *justified* in thinking differently? Is there a genuinely alternative moral perspective based on gender?

To illustrate these questions more concretely, I should like to tell you a story which I originally included in my article on ethics and gender in the book "Feminist Perspectives in Philosophy" (Almond, 1988). It is a true story and concerns a visit I made to an old friend - a fellow philosophy student - who had made his career as a tax inspector.

We were discussing the case of a headmaster who had reported his pupils to the police for criminal behaviour, and I expressed the opinion that, since a headmaster is *in loco parentis* (i.e. in the place of the parents), he should have dealt with his pupils himself, privately and without publicity - as would, I suggested, a loving parent. My friend expressed moral outrage at this suggestion, saying that this was not his conception of what a parent should do, and adding that he, as a parent and husband, would have no hesitation in reporting the criminal actions of his child, or indeed his wife, particularly if he saw no signs of either remorse or an intention to reform. He added that people who work for the tax authorities are coached in the matter of the known duplicity of women, and their willingness to lie to protect members of their family. At this point, my friend's wife expressed moral outrage at the discovery that her husband would, without compunction, report her misdeeds, or those of her daughter, to the authorities, and I was left with a sense of having stumbled upon a set of basic moral presumptions which are held in common by one sex, and entirely inverted in the case of the other - a looking-glass reversal of priorities and values.

Kohlberg's sequence of stages of emerging moral judgement

As it happens, of course, this conclusion conforms to the observations of Freud, who believed that women have less sense of justice than men and are more often influenced in their judgements by feelings of affection or hostility. It conforms, too, to some more recent observations of Piaget, Kohlberg and Gilligan.

Lawrence Kohlberg's empirical work on moral development follows, as far as its basic stance is concerned, the structure and assumptions of Jean Piaget, who has demonstrated apparently invariant sequences of change, not only in relation to moral development, but in other areas, too. The underlying assumption is that there is a necessary maturation of cognitive processes, just as there is of physical or motor processes. Just as every normal human child first learns to crawl, then to stand and then to walk - and the motivation and capacity to do these things comes from within the child, and is not artificially imposed from outside - so, *the moral development theorists hold, there is a necessary sequence of stages of emerging moral judgement.* Their empirical research is directed to establishing what these stages are, and to describing the circumstances surrounding the transitions.

Kohlberg's stages of moral development are usually described as a *progression from lower to higher* - itself an inbuilt and at first unrecognised value-judgement. The early or lower stages that he has identified are first, a stage in which children's thinking is rooted in obedience to adults, fear of punishment and acceptance of authority; then a stage of an essentially self-interested acceptance, for the sake of reciprocity, of a principle of fairness between peers; and then a further stage of seeking approval and desiring to be well thought of by one's community or group. Later comes a stage of respect for justice: recognition of the importance of *rules* for community living, followed by an awareness of the *universality* of some of these rules and their embodiment in principles of individual human rights applying across varying cultures and societies. Kohlberg speculated on the existence of a seventh stage in which the universal human perspective is replaced by a holistic cosmic perspective which might have a religious or even a pantheistic orientation. (The six stages are set out in Kohlberg, 1981, 409-412).

All this is *framed in gender-neutral terms*, but researchers have become aware of difficulties in finding women who can be placed by this classification in the "higher stages" of moral development. Women's answers to the questionnaires by which assignments to "stages" are made show them to be *more heavily represented in the early stages of development* rather the later. Women desire to please. Women rebel against impersonal principles of morality which, when rigorously applied, ignore individual pleas for sympathetic concessions, for mercy rather than justice.

Gilligan's different approach

Carol Gilligan's research, which focused on the distinctively female moral dilemma of an abortion-decision, suggested that what was emerging here was *not a moral deficiency of women but a "different voice" on morality*. The findings of the male researchers, she claims, are dogged by what she calls the problem of women "whose sexuality remains more diffuse, whose perception of self is so much more tenaciously embedded in relationships with others and whose moral dilemmas hold them in a mode of judgement that is insistently contextual." (Gilligan, 1977, 482) While she concedes the broad outline of the developmental model - a model which proceeds from an egocentric through a societal to a universal perspective, she sees this development taking place, in the case of women, within a special moral conception. The nature of this moral conception is recognised by a distinctive use of a particular vocabulary: *a vocabulary of selfishness and responsibility, of morality as an obligation to exercise care and avoid hurt*.

The particular sequence of moral development revealed by Gilligan's research is described by her in this way: first, as in Kohlberg's findings, a stage of focus on the self; then, a second level of development in which the notion of responsibility is used to balance the claims of self against the claims of other people. This stage brings a notion of the good as caring for others; it involves a protective care for the dependent and unequal. It is succeeded by a third stage at which the tension between conformity and care, selfishness and responsibility, is dissipated by a self which, in Gilligan's words "becomes the arbiter of an independent judgement that now subsumes both conventions and individual needs under the moral principle of non-violence" (Gilligan, 1977, 492).

Gilligan sees this as a morality of responsibility that stands apart from the morality of rights underlying Kohlberg's conception. In it, a positive conception of caring contrasts with the purely negative policy of non-interference suggested by an emphasis on rights.

What is missing from the latter, and its omission is deliberate rather than accidental, is *the detail and texture that comes with knowledge of particular people and particular circumstances*. Kohlberg's research is based on questionnaires which demand a response to hypothetical and imaginary situations in which concrete detail is necessarily omitted. Gilligan points out that Kohlberg thus *divests his moral actors of the history and psychology of their individual lives*. Many women, confronted by Kohlbergian questionnaires, ask for, or contribute out of their own imagination, concrete detail which might help them resolve the moral dilemma with which they are presented. They are told that this sort of question or embellishment is inappropriate. Kohlberg's dilemmas are not about real people - they can't be if the aim of the research is to discover objective principles of justice.

Gilligan mentions here the anonymous woman whose non-legalistic thinking enabled Solomon to display his legendary wisdom. She contrasts that woman's sacrifice of self and principle for the life of her child with the willingness of Abraham to sacrifice his son for principle and personal integrity.

Applications in the corporate sphere

If Gilligan is correct in judging women to be more concerned in their ethical thinking with *relationships* and intuitive response to situations than with principles, this has interesting applications in the corporate sphere for, as Patrick Maclagan and Peter Sedgwick have remarked: "Relations with others - staff, colleagues, customers, suppliers - raise what are among the most frequently encountered ethical issues for managers." (Maclagan *et al.*, 1989, 2)

Gilligan's critique of conventional ethical theory, which fits with that of other feminist writers on this topic, suggests that women may be particularly well-adapted to managerial decision-making, where sensitivity to individuals, a grasp of detail and a *contextual* assessment of situations produce the best results.

Kohlberg's analysis, as I said at the beginning, appears to offer only the alternatives of uncritical conformity to other people's requirements (and to place women overwhelmingly in this ethical mode), or else a principle-bound approach (distinctive largely of men) which may ignore the highly-specific demands of some situations, the needs of particular individuals and the wider implications of particular actions.

While conceding that there may be more scope in Kohlberg's theory to accommodate the points made by his feminist critics, I would suggest that there *is* a contrast here which is illuminating to this issue. In conclusion, then, I should like to sketch out *what such a contrast might suggest in practice:*

- First of all, an ethical perspective of the kind that, following Gilligan and other feminists, could be described as *"female"* would, I believe, be *more sensitive to the environmental effects of corporate policy*. This is because it would ensure that decisions about what to do would not be considered narrowly on an immediate and short-term basis, but rather with awareness of and sensitivity to the *wider context*.
- Secondly, it would be *more attentive to the personal and individual aspects of corporate policy*. Would this sort of ethical sensitivity, for example, be consistent with arranging for an ageing executive to arrive and find his or her possessions packed for collection as a mark of dismissal with immediate effect?
- Thirdly, the notion of *responsibility for others* which is central to this ethical perspective would be likely to provide a *counter-balance to narrow considerations of cost-effectiveness* so affecting for example, decisions as to whether to include an optional but not costless, safety-feature in a product.

In some ways I believe that the ethical approach sketched out in recent feminist writings is *one peculiarly adapted to the management of families or households* - in other words, of other persons who are recognised as individuals, are respected for themselves, and whose welfare and interests are cared for by the person making whatever ethical judgement is at issue. To the extent that this is so, then an approach has been identified which transfers interestingly and usefully to the corporate sphere.

So, a female ethics for the corporation? My answer is yes. But with an important qualification. This is that contrasts are inevitably drawn by way of caricature. They are bound, then to be in some respects artificial. In this case, for instance, there are undoubtedly men with the kind of ethical sensitivity I have described, and women totally lacking in it. An ethical apartheid for men and women, then, is not a possibility. But neither is it desirable. In the end, what we all, women *and* men, must do, is to use our complementary insights and intuitions to produce an effective ethical perspective for the very different corporate world that the age of high technology and global inter-dependency has generated for us and our successors.

References

Almond, B.: 1988, "Women's Right: Reflections on Ethics and Gender", in Griffiths, M. and M. Whitford (eds.), *Feminist Perspectives in Philosophy*, London: Macmillan, 42-57.

Gilligan, C.: 1977, "In a Different Voice: Women's Conceptions of Self and Morality", *Harvard Education Review*, 47, 481-517. A revised version of this paper was subsequently published in Gilligan (1982).

Gilligan, C.: 1982, *In a Different Voice: Psychological Theory and Women's Development*, Cambridge, Mass.: Harvard University Press.

Kohlberg, L.: 1981, *Essays on Moral Development*, vol. 1: *The Philosophy of Moral Development*, San Francisco: Harper and Row, chs. 4 and 9.

Maclagan, P. and P. Sedgwick: 1989, "Business Ethics Takes Off", *MBA Review*, 1, 2, June.

DEMOGRAPHIC PRESSURE IN FAVOUR OF THE PROMOTION OF WOMEN

José Aguilá

Particularly in the Latin countries, the subject of "men and women in corporations" is a delicate one, not only when one tries to give a real picture of the present situation in Spanish corporations, but also - and even more - when one undertakes to indicate some perspectives and to make some recommendations for promoting women in corporations. Nevertheless, I will try to treat it in three steps: (1) to characterise briefly some main problems, (2) to inquire into the attitudes involved, and (3) to indicate some ways to promote women in corporations.

Gender problems in Spanish corporations

A real case will illustrate the *psycho-sociological gender differences* which are rooted in long traditions and influenced by strong expectations. It is a true story based on my experience as a management consultant.

During an in-depth-interview, a female executive of one of the major Spanish corporations gave me her illustrative experience of the relations between men and women at work in a Latin environment. Having an executive position, she attended all the executive meetings her company held. One of their objectives was to discuss the problems which the company faced and to deal with them and find solutions. This lady had a very creative attitude, but she did not succeed in getting her ideas accepted. Worried by her failures and after deep reflection, she changed her strategy. She continued to give good ideas, but before each presentation she began with the following introduction: "As Mr. So-and-So said, I think that the solution to our problem is ..." By using this trick, she was able to raise her ratio of acceptance of her ideas to the level of her male colleagues.

This actual Spanish story shows us the reality of the subtle and not so subtle inter-gender barriers in Latin corporations. But underlying the psycho-sociological differences, there are *the physiological differences* connected with maternity and all its consequences: pregnancy, childbirth, physical recuperation, psychological adjustment, nursing, child rearing, etc. The effect of maternity on women's professional career is dramatic, as is shown by the more than double turnover in management positions of women, compared to men. For the company, it is a painful experience when they train women executives who acquire more and more competences by moving up the management ladder, and then lose them by career interruption. This means in economic terms that the costs of employing women in management positions are greater than the costs of employing men.

Male and female attitudes

As practitioner I can observe on the spot the respective attitudes of men and women which are directly related to traditional assumptions about their roles. Generally, in Latin countries, men are expected to be aggressive, competitive, reliant, risk-taking, physically strong, while women are expected to be supportive, nurturing, intuitive, sensitive, communicative, etc. Women are trained from childhood to expect their husbands to take care of them, while men are educated to provide dependable financial support for their families.

The men's attitudes towards women are admiration, resentment, confusion, scepticism, anxiety, nostalgia, etc. Therefore, it is easy to conclude that the male perception of women in management positions is at best ambivalent.

Women's attitudes can be divided into three groups: (1) The *Job-First Women* for whom their jobs provide their main motivation. (2) The *Job and Family Women* who are guided by balanced motivations. (3) The *Family and Job Women* for whom their jobs serve as a mere financial help. Because this typology defines three distinct approaches, it follows that solutions for one group are not solutions at all for the other two groups.

How to promote women in the corporations?
By demographic good luck and continuous personal effort

When we take these briefly sketched gender problems and traditional attitudes into consideration, we cannot but state that they will provide little help if any for the promotion of women in the corporations. But I am convinced that the present demographic evolution is going to change our perception of gender relations deeply. In Spain, we are seeing a major drop in the birth rate. While, in 1961, there were 21 live births per 1000 inhabitants, in 1987, the rate has dropped to 11.6 live births per 1000 inhabitants, i. e. about 45 per cent. Therefore, its impact on the labour market will be such that, over the next decade, the majority of new entrants in the work-force will be women. Moreover, the gap between supply and demand in first class personnel will grow dramatically and with it, the competition for professional talent.

My view may seem cynical, but I have no doubt that the demographic gap will be the major ally for women's promotion in the corporations. To be sure, *success is a mix of preparation and good luck* and for me, I believe that, in this context, demographics means good luck. So let us ask about the other component for success: How can we arrange the work environment in order to arrange women in the corporations?

In the arrangement of the work environment, *ethics is like a hinge* between values, corporate responsibilities, effectiveness and leadership. And underlying this approach, there is *the basic philosophy that we are not dealing with "men" nor "women" but with human beings*.

In order to implement this strategy, the philosophical base has to be developed with administrative tools. For this purpose, the study "Corporate Ethics: A Prime Asset", published by the Business Roundtable (1988), makes valuable suggestions. It describes ethical policy and practice in ten companies widely thought of as both economically successful and ethical, and identifies eight influential elements to substain the desired level of ethical performance.

These elements are:

1. Continuity of values in the leadership of successive chief executive officers.
2. Development of a tradition of integrity in the promulgation of standards in all areas where quality is essential.
3. Written statements of belief and policy, perhaps in the form of a credo or code, and in critical cases requiring annual signed statements signifying compliance.
4. Education and training in the meaning of policy and the seriousness of intent.
5. Consideration of ethical performance and interest in community affairs, and in performance evaluation and compensation.
6. Open decision-making in which differences of opinion are welcomed and the relevance of ethical standards to proposals is discussed.
7. A control system, fortified by audit, to supplement trust with broad surveillance.
8. Strict and public punishment of identified violations of law or policy.

In conclusion, I should like to quote a statement based on my experience as a president of the European Recruitment Consultants Group of FEACO (Federation of European Management Consulting Associations): "The present trend of global business is of demographics in favour of the promotion of women on the corporate ladder. Our mission as those responsible for major management consulting firms is to help this trend and by no means hinder it."

References

The Business Roundtable: 1988, *Corporate Ethics: A Prime Business Asset*, New York: The Business Roundtable.

HOW TO INCLUDE WOMEN IN CORPORATE DECISION-MAKING

Monique R. Siegel

When dealing with the issue "Men and Women in Corporations" we encounter two major difficulties. For one thing, we are not talking simply about incidents or situations that call for ethical decision-making, but rather about a state of affairs that has to be changed: *corporate culture*. As we all know, it is tremendously difficult to replace a set of values practised over a long time with a new one - especially if it has been practised with considerable profit. Change brings unrest, and who needs that?

For another, we are obviously dealing with a *nonentity*, because evidently women are not (yet) considered serious partners in the corporate scene, neither a quantity nor a quality to be reckoned with. I suppose this is mainly due to the fact that it has not (yet) dawned on corporations how great women's potential is to increase the bottom line.

There was an article in *The Jerusalem Post* in October 1988, called "US corporations stress need for ethics". As is nearly always the case with such "real life" reporting, only men were interviewed, only men were quoted, and naturally it was a man who wrote the article. But, above all, the language is telling because he quotes the chairman of an international industrial firm who said: "What we're trying to do is build up the individual, making *him* feel like *he* counts and therefore *he* participates and does better the things that *he* ought to do." (The accentuation of the pronouns is mine.) This is common practice: it would not occur to such a man to say "he/she", let alone "she" by itself.

Another example: In the book *Ethics in Practice* (1989) published by the *Harvard Business Review* (HBR), I went through the table of contents to see how many women were included and I finally found one - on page 243 of a 296-page book! Naturally, I read her article first - a practical, usable one, as a matter of fact - and then thumbed through the book from back to front. I became increasingly annoyed at the absence of any reference to women in the corporate scene. In addition, I became confused as I came across an article which seemed to have been written in the fifties, because the author referred to the "forty years that Lenin's ideas..." etc. Puzzled, I now turned to the foreword which explained that this book contained a variety of articles on the subject of ethics published over a number of years by the HBR. At the end of the foreword, there was the following "Editor's Note":

> "An obvious feature of the book should be acknowledged and placed in context. Some articles included in this book were written before researchers, writers, and editors began to take into consideration the role of women in management. These articles have been included because their insights far outweigh their anachronistic qualities. Nevertheless, the archaic use of the

> masculine gender and the assumption that a manager is necessarily male are regrettable. The editor and the publisher hope outdated assumptions about gender will not undermine otherwise cogent and relevant essays." (Andrews, 1989, 11)

Does not this statement prove that up to now women have obviously not been part of the "ethical scene"? However, women *are* part of the corporate world - and thus of the ethical scene as well. Their quantity has increased considerably in recent years, and many of them are concerned with ensuring that they are also a quality to be counted on. What can be done, then, to include them in corporate decision-making? I propose taking action on three levels: personal, societal and corporate.

Actions to include women in corporate decision-making:
(1) on the personal level

The easiest one is obviously the personal/individual level, because it involves only one person at a time. I admit that I am now arguing my case for the benefit of the next generation. As all of those who have children know, education begins at home, and ethics do, too. This means:

- living by the principle of equality in the home,
- role modelling what you would expect society - or the corporation as a microcosm of society - to do or to be,
- pointing out other role models,
- studying the lives and achievements of great women in history and learning from them. There are many valid lessons to be learned (see Siegel, 1989).

The value-system which will provide guidelines for later life is instilled at home. This does not, of course, offer much help to the woman who is currently fighting her hierarchical battle. What should one advise her to do? A few basics for her daily fight for survival might be:

- accepting responsibility,
- having the courage to make mistakes, despite the fact that every mistake a woman makes is being looked at through the magnifying glass and attributed to her gender as a whole,
- not trying to be "Super Woman",
- getting rid of the "No. 1 female sickness": the guilty conscience,
- not trying to be everything to everybody - this is a sure recipe for failure,
- instead, trying to remember that women usually bring personal integrity and loyalty to their jobs and that professional competence coupled with vision, clear objectives and human concern can take them as far as any man, and will make an enriching contribution to corporate cultures.

Also, it helps to have or develop a good sense of humour. She will need it when, for example, she is looking for guidelines and comes across advice such as this: "Look like a lady, think like a man, and work like a horse!"

One of the most important DON'Ts: Don't ever, ever try to become "one of the boys"! A woman is hardly ever more ridiculous than when she is trying to emulate her male colleagues. Being one of the boys is one game that "the boys" are better at - so leave it to them!

(2) on the societal level

As far as education is concerned, society can do the same as we can do as individuals at home. In the words of Robert Fulghum: "Most of what I really need to know about how to live, and what to do, and how to be, I learned in kindergarten. Wisdom was not at the top of the graduate school mountain, but there in the sandbox. These are the things I learned: Share everything. Play fair. Don't hit people. Put things back where you found them. Clean up your own mess. Don't take things that aren't yours. Say you're sorry when you hurt somebody. Wash your hands before you eat." Kindergarten, school, university and - very important - the business school can help intensify the values that were/are taught at home.

But important as this may be, the crucial issue on a societal level is that of procreation or, put it in plain words, the fact that women get pregnant. This serves as a convenient excuse for corporations not to hire or promote women, not to help them advance. Is it not absurd, when one reflects that there is a next generation? Women have been performing this noble task ever since the beginning of mankind. Society, however, instead of being grateful and rewarding them for it, has penalised women by excluding them from almost all decision-making levels.

If we are going to change this, then *the issue of child-bearing and -rearing must become a societal issue* rather than a corporate or, worse, an individual one. Women who want to have children should have them - without any detriment to their professional careers. Women who do not want children should expect to find total acceptance in society for this decision and should never be told that they have "missed their true calling". Society should teach and practise *the notion of options* - the very essence of the concept of freedom. The issue of child-bearing and child-rearing is too important to be left to men - thus, it *has* to be taken away from the corporate level.

Finally, on the societal level, one could turn to *the media* for additional help: The media can easily throw in their weight when it comes to role modelling or to catering to women as decision-makers in consumer decisions of which roughly 80 per cent are made by women. The media should report on women of achievement, not on so-called women's issues, and women in the media should bring to bear their influence when it comes to designing programmes - as has successfully been done in commercial television.

(3) on the corporate level

For any change on the corporate level, there are two rules for the start:

1. It is the chief executive officer who has to devise the programme and then *live* it.
2. Corporations must stop thinking of ethical issues as something that can be delegated to women, such as the newly created job of communications officer, or the personnel department - now often fittingly renamed something like "Human Resources Development" - or the Public-Relations department. ("If she's got pretty legs she might sell the explanation of the next environmental disaster better to the media than a man might do...") Women, on the other hand, must stop accepting such jobs and thus being considered single-handedly responsible for corporate ethics.

Beyond this, however, things are not so spectacular, but rather banal and very pragmatic. The biggest obstacle for the corporate woman are the *men in middle management*. Understandably so. We are not talking here of a thick crust of villainous males ganging up on female colleagues, but again of *a set of values instilled during their formative years*. Most of the men who are in middle management today - those aged, say, 40-55 - were raised to have as their main objective an income high enough to support a family (in style). There are still a number of European countries where it is considered a blemish on the "head of the household", if the husband "allows" his wife to go to work. Does this not imply that he does not make any money to support his family? These men were not prepared for today's "facts of life" as they are represented in most corporations, they are not (yet) ready to accept women in the corporation as peers. Thus, the obstacles here are not necessarily based on unwillingness, but rather on *inability*. This is the main reason why a corporation that tries to establish a partnership-oriented corporate culture has to have an all-encompassing programme, devised and role-modelled by the chief executive officer.

Apart from the most basic ethical considerations such as *equal pay, equal opportunity, equal chances for training or travelling,* there are *more subtle ones* that demonstrate to insiders and outsiders that the ethical issue of gender discrimination has been successfully dealt with. This should include:

-   All texts - memos, letters, invitations, instructions, etc. - make explicit use of both pronouns: He/she, his/her, him/her, etc. In languages such as German or the romance languages this may become cumbersome, but until we invent a new language that is gender neutral, attention has to be paid to this issue.
-   Every public appearance or statement of the corporation should be considered a chance to prove to the public that equal rights are part of corporate policy. Thus, for example, the corporation should be represented as often as possible by a high-ranking woman.
-   Customers/clients have to be shown that women are equal partners in the corporation. No outsider should ever get a chance to question the authority or position of a female when she appears somewhere as representative of her company.
-   Internal affairs, such as a corporate anniversary celebration or a committee on issues of substance, are a chance to demonstrate this attitude within: Key positions at such occasions should be held as frequently by women as by men.
-   Women inside the corporation should neither be treated as birds of paradise or precious exotic plants, nor should their qualifications be questioned. Internally, the thinking and acting pattern should be: "May the best person win!" This would also mean eliminating the "glass ceiling".

Finally - and this is *the crucial issue on the corporate level* - corporate policy must make it possible for women

-   to become pregnant without feeling guilty about it,
-   to keep a foot in the door during the family phase,
-   to have the option of returning to the corporation on acceptable terms.

It must further provide ways for women *and* men

-   to take parental leave (women *or* men here),
-   to practise job-sharing, work flexible hours at flexible places, whenever and wherever possible.

Men frequently try to discard such considerations as "women's issues", as "mountains made of mole hills", as - worst of all - God-given facts. "After all, Nature made you that way", they say. Maybe they should try to follow the pattern suggested by Laura Nash in her essay "Ethics without the sermon" (Nash in Andrews, 1981). In her "Twelve Questions for Examining the Ethics of a Business Decision", the first three might be helpful here:

1. Have you defined the problem accurately?
2. How would you define the problem if you stood on the other side of the fence?
3. How did this situation occur in the first place?

The chief executive officer might be well-advised to ask himself question no. 11: "What is the symbolic potential of your action if understood? If misunderstood?"

The value of a credo

As one can easily see, the responsibilities abound on all three levels. What might help on the corporate level, though, is what more and more corporations are adopting: a corporate credo. A number of firms these days submit themselves to soul-searching on their attitudes towards ethics and procede to create a credo that the individual employee is expected to adhere to. While this is commendable and should prove to be of great significance - if it is re-examined at least once a year, followed by a renewed pledge to adhere to it -, there is an additional factor that speaks in its favour. As Laura Nash puts it:

> "Articulating the corporation's values and objectives provides a reference point for group inquiry and implementation. Ethical codes, however, when drawn up by the legal department, do not always offer a realistic and full representation of management's beliefs. The most important ethical inquiry for management may be the very formulation of such a statement, for the process of articulation is as useful as the value agreed on." (Nash 1989, 256)

Now, apart from maybe feeling good about it, what is in it for the corporation? The answer is quite obvious - and is a case in point that ethics are so frequently smart business. *The demographic changes in Western industrial countries,* caused by the decline of birth rates, will make women the "No. 1 human resource" in the decade to come. By the year 2000, there will be 25 - 40 per cent fewer people entering the work force. This has to be seen in the light of the fact that we keep creating jobs - mostly in the high-tech area - that call for qualified and motivated people. The young people who will be entering the work force in the years to come operate in a seller's market: They can choose to whom they want to offer their coveted skills, know-how and enthusiasm. According to John Naisbitt and his partner Patricia Aburdene, co-authors of "Re-inventing the Corporation" (1985), this is the trend for the future:

> "To attract the best women and the best men (who want to work for a fair company), companies will want to earn a reputation as a comparable worth employer - and maybe even advertise themselves as such." (Naisbitt *et al.,* 1985, 262)

In view of this development of the work force, it is a matter of survival to create corporate cultures which allow women to be integrated with all their different views, thinking patterns, and sets of values - instead of forcing them to assimilate to an outdated set of rules and rituals which have already been recognised as counter-productive. This will, however, only be successful when men can be convinced that women do not want to take power away from them, but rather that they want to share responsibilities.

References

Andrews, K.R. (ed.): 1989, *Ethics in Practice: Managing the Moral Corporation,* New York: Doubleday.
Naisbitt, J. and P. Aburdene: 1985, *Re-inventing the Corporation,* New York: Warner Books.
Nash, L.L.: 1989, "Ethics without the Sermon", in: Andrews, K.R. (ed.): 1989.
Siegel, M.R.: 1989, *Frauenkarrieren zwischen Tradition und Innovation. Führungsfrauen der Geschichte,* Stuttgart: Poeschel.

Part IV

The Ethical Role of the Top Manager

WHO OR WHAT IS THE "BOSS"?
AUTHORITY WITHOUT AUTHORITARIANISM

Sara Morrison

Recent happenings in British commercial circles, be they incompetence or avarice inspired crime, *have* shaken the system of corporate management in the United Kingdom. Closer attention to best practice now seems inevitable, as well as necessary for public confidence, and therefore for good business. The evidence may be elusive but ethical thinking seems needed to inspire and motivate most levels of industry and commerce.

The rapidly growing volume of studies and writings about business ethics has focussed lucidly on the ways in which companies deal with the outside world of governments, customers, regulators and media specialists. Whether it is a matter of a company's dealings with, say, much criticised regimes, or the practices which assist in the winning of contracts, or the handling of adverse features of products - in all these cases, it is the *outward-looking factors* between a company and the other interested parties in a country or community, that are involved.

However, the ethics of operation *inside* a company, and how it is managed, will also need to be considered, if a company is to keep in step with any code of reputable practice which it fosters in its dealings with the outside world, because it is vital that managers, and indeed all employees, are clear about the basis on which they are to do business. There is probably little room in real life for Milton Friedman's market purity, despite Montesquieu's *dictum* that "liberty is the right to do whatever the law permits". Montesquieu wrote that in 1748, and I have to say that circumstances today are very different. Legality as a shield is defensible in many cases, but, in others, can be entirely too relaxed.

Not only may laws in a land be themselves outmoded in terms of behaviour with which one would care to be associated, but the international nature of large-scale business creates an effect in which a company's actions in one country are judged in many others using different standards of what is acceptable behaviour.

What then is the concept of *"the boss"* in this context? And how do we achieve authority without unacceptable, indeed unworkable, authoritarianism? It seems to me that a contemporary company must develop standards to which it adheres; install a method of transmitting those standards through its managers to all those who may face ethical dilemmas - and that increasingly means quite a lot of a company's employees - and evolve a way of supporting those who find themselves in the ethical front line.

So two interlocking themes now: The support of managers who carry the prime operational responsibility for the company's reputation and second, the company's treatment of its employees in the businesses and places in which it requires them to work. Top management has the duty to *lead* in both these respects.

Supporting managers

The first requirement is support for managers in the *varied* ethical circumstances in which many of them find themselves as they compete in international markets - often against suppliers from other nations who have their own, some might say, *less* than ethical standards.

Even leaving international competitors aside, there are four considerations which have to be reconciled. The first is the standard of behaviour expected in one's own country by one's laws, one's government, shareholders and the media. The second is the company's own standards of behaviour in its own dealings in the world at large. The third is the legal and political framework which exists in the territory in which the company is operating. And the fourth concerns the actual practices which are normal where one is seeking to do business.

Clearly, most of these considerations fit well together. Honesty sees to that, and between many countries there is a harmony of practices which fits also with a company's overall principles of operation.

Nevertheless, the world is not composed of a single culture and ways of doing business outside "home" can be a culture shock to the unprepared - particularly when the enticing nature of a project is coupled to what appear beguiling short cuts. Managers are exposed to a tempting snare. They want to achieve profitable results; they may see it as a career decision, and yet are rightly wary of the trap of temptation. They also have to consider what may amount to good manners in the context of the national culture in which they are operating.

A guiding principle here is that any contract or operation should only be undertaken that will sustain, and preferably add to, the company's *long-term* reputation. Good practice requires that managers only do business on that basis, and that means that, not only must they work to good practice in their various markets; they must also meet the absolute standards of the company.

Where dilemmas arise, managers must be required to refer to the top management of their particular business. The ultimate responsibility has to rest with senior people. It would be intolerable to tell managers to succeed and then to abandon them just when they need a judgement and proper support. Hence, it is essential that they know that this support will be forthcoming and equally essential that the top management will be well represented by *them* - the business's managers - in sometimes difficult circumstances.

As it isn't practical, or desirable, for the most senior management of a company to spend all its time on such matters, it is vital to ensure that front line, indeed, *all* line managers, have the necessary guidelines, and are of the required calibre in terms of good sense; that they are capable of making well-informed judgements in line with the company's standards; and that they act with due prudence in their dealings with suppliers, customers and employees.

The company's treatment of its employees

What, finally, about the treatment of employees wherever, and however, they find themselves working? It might seem tempting to rest on the policy of just meeting the standards of the host country in which the work is being undertaken. But that would miss several key factors.

The first is that the *long-term* reputation of a company in a country, as in a smaller community, depends on it being an honourable citizen and assisting in the development of *better* standards than the average. Typically this will not just mean providing welfare items such as good medical treatment and proper regard of safety, but can include the training and skills development of the local employees.

Secondly, it is incumbent on a company to minimise the possibility that an accidental "love them and leave them" climate will prevail, in which key personnel from the home country bring in their expertise, and then later leave, with the local personnel having gained little more than minimum knowledge to keep the show on the road, and certainly not enough to keep upgrading their own abilities.

That would be short-sighted on expedient grounds, let alone on ethical grounds. Most nations - the wealthiest as well as the less advanced - now see that their future prosperity is intimately linked to their ability to add more value to the endeavours of their workforces. Without claiming that it is for companies alone to educate the world's working populations, there is an ethical dimension, a duty if you like, to raise the capabilities of all the employees that one can.

Clearly this can be problematical for a company whose top management is determined to maintain its own authority, which may be efficient, benign, successful, and so on. It may also fall short of these standards, but, either way, a consequence of the need of most companies for ever better skills is that those people who possess them have more freedom of choice and, usually, an increasing desire to exercise their own judgement, have more autonomy, and be in control of their own working lives.

The expedient ground for wanting to train local personnel, certainly for a technically sophisticated company, is that the more capable are the people in a territory, the more likely is it that *future* technological contracts will become feasible there.

So, a further consideration is how best to handle matters in any large *decentralised* company. There is always a basic dilemma: If a company wants to secure *highest* common denominator behaviour and co-ordinate *control* of standards of practices, then it must centralise all relevant decisions; if, on the other hand, it wants to *encourage* local control and more satisfaction or autonomy for individual managers, whether for reasons of different local conditions or because it sees decentralisation as better in itself, then inevitably there will be some divergence in the way that different parts of a large company behave from time to time. They will, by definition, be out of the centre's *complete* control.

It follows that what a company seeks for its businesses, is to train people in, and expose them to, the guiding principles which they are expected to uphold in their work and in their connections to local cultures. There must also be the candid recognition that the idea of a uniform standard of behaviour and achievement, across what may be many businesses operating in many countries over many years, is a counsel of excellence, beyond what most of us can reach given human nature's imperfections.

What matters is that the inevitable failures are not only quickly recoverd, but that the organisation learns and transmits the lessons to all its links, so that the maximum positive effect can be gained from what, left to fester, could become a diminishing experience.

Top management, be it the boss or the board, has an unavoidable role in the setting and demonstrating of what standards of behaviour are legitimate. Employees gauge the actions as well as the views of their top managements. What is called "the language of signs" is important; that is: What do the signals from *them, the top management,* tell us, the employees, about the way they want *us* to behave?

From time to time, this may require top management not so much to relax normal pressures for the achievement of business, but, in cases where it appears that the business can only be won by adopting or at least acquiescing in, practices which fall outside the code of proper behaviour, at least to ensure that there is no *casual* slip in standards.

In some predicaments it requires effort by all concerned to analyse the essentials of the problem, as openly as competitive and confidential restraints allow, to find an acceptable way round or through the dilemma. This means setting as a management objective the principle that, as far as possible, no manager should feel *un*supported during whrought decision processes, whatever their outcome.

Of course, a case - often an appealing case - can be found for marginal exceptions to be made for business reasons, occasionally on the self-deluding grounds that what is feared to be true is really not so and is unlikely to recur, or because it can be shown that it is a "one off" special instance, and therefore less worrying. But the example that this sets can too easily become a signal to the rest of the company, and has to be considered in that light, and *not* as an isolated incident - whatever the attractions at the time.

The essence of all this is that guiding principles, training and communication within a company are vital, and that authoritarian managements will increasingly find themselves off-balance, as they attempt to respond to changing opinions about what constitutes ethical behaviour - largely because they may, by definition, have autocratically left their employees out of the process of managing, or even facing key ethical questions.

In any increasingly complex world, it is ever more impractical to exclude employees from influencing decision-making and the process which decides how the company will make decisions *and on what grounds*. The reason is not a romantic notion of democracy at work - assuming that a big public company could be run as a kind of local worker co-operative - but is to be found in the fact that the technical expertise and service levels which are now required are creating the conditions in which more and more employees are in touch with the customers, metaphorically or literally, and the interface between organisations, between manufacturers and their product users, is becoming more diffuse, more varied, more complicated and therefore less open or accessible to centralised or top management control.

I see no perfect assurance, or insurance, where behaviour is concerned, but what is obviously needed is for leaders who have authority, but are not authoritarian, to orchestrate a clear, simple understanding of the company's standards and practices, if it is to survive into the next century, not only as a company which is confident and profitable in the business context, but also as an honourable and regarded corporate citizen. Of course, survival or success, and with that employee progress, will ultimately depend above all, and as ever, upon creativity, and upon satisfying customers with quality goods and services at competitive costs.

Attracting and retaining people of the necessary calibre to achieve business objectives may not depend in any exact way on the company's internal or outward ethical behaviour. But, only a foolhardy, or blind boss or board would completely ignore the question of what is likely to attract tomorrow's employees, or have no regard for what might repel or hinder the recruiting of people with talent and expertise. There are not many such people, and yet they will undoubtedly be required by companies which must operate in ever more competitive market places.

It is unnecessary to devote a great deal of time to the question of whether the need to adopt a serious attitude to ethical dilemmas is because it is proper so to do in mature and advanced societies, or simply because business wisdom and self-interest requires companies to enhance quality, standards and values in matters which affect a company's most costly and necessary resource: its people.

Conclusion

I would reply to the question of who or what, practically and ethically, is the boss, by saying that if healthy growth, profit and continuity are laudable objectives, then he, or it, is the pivotal head of the team closest to the design, production and distribution of a company's product in any particular location. The ultimate or responsible company leaders lurk in their boardroom fiduciary lairs, setting the tone and monitoring standards to *enable* creative, productive activity. The hands-on "boss" is whoever does it, or fails to do it.

But, in the end, the world's wealth creators are doomed, and much that we cherish in civilised societies is at risk, if the practical restraints of the work place are ever ignored. So my reasons for putting daunting contemporary ethical issues on the "boss's" agenda, and in their leaders' minds, are not only a belief that it is proper to be as good as circumstances permit, nor that it is acceptable to make hollow excuses for lapsing into behaviour that diminishes standards, but rather that, increasingly, the well regarded companies will be magnets for scarce people with the skills, the broad perspectives, and specialist expertise on which, when all else is said and done, the major companies depend.

It may seem that there is no shortage of people, but most western companies' futures now depend on attracting enough people of the highest calibre. Time may alter the western world's industrial scarcity of key skills and talent, but this cannot be soon; meanwhile cherishing and enhancing the most acceptable aspects of industrial activity, is critical to standards of life for us all, and corporate *ethical* standards are likely to be a part of the "carrot", or safe road, to that end.

"I AM THE BOSS. WHY SHOULD I BE ETHICAL?"

Juan A. Pérez López

The title of this paper is a question which may not be very frequently formulated in an explicit way, but it is frequently there, at the back of our minds, whenever we feel that those people who may not like our actions, are in no position to retaliate.

That is not surprising, because it is only a translation, in colloquial terms, of that very fundamental question about what are the forces which produce the practical acceptance of ethical rules by any given decision-maker.

There are many theoretical analyses of the content of ethical rules, which are those rules, and what is the purpose that they have. These analyses are what we usually call "ethical systems". A particular ethical system is based on the assumption of a final purpose for a decision-maker, a final purpose which underlies any other specific purpose that he may want to achieve at the time of selecting the performance of an action.

Different assumptions about the final purpose - individual happiness, psychological well-being, long-run maximum pleasure, social contribution, and so on - produce different sets of ethical rules. These rules specify the conditions that have to be accomplished by any action of the decision-maker, provided he or she really wants to achieve his or her final purpose - the one assumed by the particular ethical system which those rules come from - while, at the same time, he or she is attempting to achieve another specific purpose.

There has been much argument about the superiority of assuming a particular final purpose rather than any other one. But, on the other hand, it seems that very little attention has been paid to *the logical structure of ethical decision-making*.

What I mean is that, in my opinion, most arguments have been developed starting from an implicit assumption, namely: that *ethical* decisions - those decisions made in order to achieve a *final* purpose, whatever that final purpose might be - were identical with any other kind of decisions - decisions made to achieve *specific* purposes.

A little analysis of the logical structure of ethical decision-making reveals that *that identity is not possible*. No matter what the meaning assigned to final purposes is, any final purpose has a formal property which makes it different from *any* specific purpose. It is a kind of purpose which underlies all possible specific purposes. It is final not in the sense of being the last one to be achieved, which would mean that specific purposes would only be means to achieve an end (final purpose). It is final in the sense of being a higher-level purpose, in the sense of including some set of conditions which make possible the very existence of specific purposes.

So, a decision-making process opened to the application of ethical criteria, whatever they might be, and depending on the specific assumptions made about the content of the final purpose, has to be described, *at least,* by *a framework of the following type:*

A decision-maker who is confronted with the choice of an action in order to achieve some specific purpose, has to evaluate his or her actions from two different points of view:

- The contribution of the action to the achievement of the specific purpose. We will call this property of an action *effectiveness.*
- The contribution of that same action to the achievement of the final purpose of the decision-maker (whatever that final purpose might be). We will call this other property of the action *consistency.*

With those definitions in mind, what we call ethical decision-making can be conceptualised *at least* by its formal properties: it is the making of decisions by a decision-maker whose choice is influenced by the consistency of his or her actions.

The use of that framework is equivalent to the representation of the structure of human decision-making by a model, a model that explains the making of decisions attempting to *solve simultaneously two different problems* with the following formal properties:

(a) They are related to one another. They are not independent: the action meant to solve one of them has consequences which affect the solution of the other.
(b) They are irreducible to one another. Each one of them has its own unit of measurement to evaluate actions, and no common unit can exist; they are incommensurable with one another.

In our case, condition (b) means that it is impossible for a decision-maker to set any specific purpose that might include the final purpose. Condition (a) means that actions are always bi-valued.

With the use of a framework conceptualising problem-solving as an activity of a decision-maker attempting to solve one problem through the choice of an action, the "ethical" aspects of the decision are left outside the conceptualisation. The theories of problem-solving developed on the basis of this framework will have a common characteristic: *any reference to ethical questions* - questions having to do with the achievement of any final purpose - *will be meta-theoretical.* (See, for instance, Simon, 1976).

The formal distinction between specific purposes and final purposes that we have been dealing with, is not a trivial one. It is the formalised equivalent of the question opening these pages. If I - the boss - have the power to act with a high degree of effectiveness to achieve a specific purpose that I want to achieve, why should I sacrifice that level of effectiveness in order to ensure a level of consistency towards the achievement of some final purpose that *you* - the "ethical person" - postulate that I also want, although I do not happen to be aware of it? What makes you think that my specific purpose does not include *everything* that may be *in any way* relevant in order to satisfy my own preferences? Can you see that *for me* what you call "final purpose" is just an abstraction devoid of meaning?

We do not have to quarrel with our hypothetical boss as to whether or not he or she happens to have a final purpose different from whatever specific purpose he or she explicitly wants to achieve for the time being. We have just to keep in mind that he or she is a decision-maker who approaches his or her problem-solving processes *as if* he or she were always solving only one problem. The best we can do is *to show him or her the complete list of conditions that have to be met* in order to reduce human problem-solving processes to the process of solving an isolated problem, or a sequence of independent problems, and, of course, the non-trivial consequences which follow from that reduction, when those conditions are not met. This is the purpose of this paper.

Using our dual-problem framework to help bosses

Much can be learnt about the decision-making processes of human beings through the analysis of particular models of decision-making based on the structure of our dual-problem framework. Of course, in order to perform these analyses, we have to develop some particular model representing the decision-making process that we want to analyze. That is obtained by giving an interpretation of the real problems of a decision-maker in terms of two problems that meet those above-mentioned conditions (a) and (b).

One of the simplest particular models that we can develop may be very useful to answer the question of our hypothetical boss. Being a boss means, by definition, bossing somebody else in order to get something from him or her. That is to say, it means an interaction between an active agent - the boss - and a reactive agent - the subordinate(s) -, both of them decision-makers. The active agent performs an action, which produces some particular reaction of the reactive agent.

Being a boss means something else: it also means that the relation between the active agent and the reactive agent will be maintained through many sequential interactions. They form what we may call an *organisation*.

The specific purpose of the active agent can be represented by the achievement of the "optimal" interaction. And, of course, "optimal" means the one producing the active agent´s maximum satisfaction. That is to say: the effectiveness of an action is measured by the *degree of satisfaction achieved by the active agent while he or she experiences the interaction produced by that action.*

We have to take another step to introduce the problem representing a final purpose. It is a very easy step: it is given with the introduction of the idea of "learning". By learning we understand the changes produced by the experience of interactions in the decision-rules of the agents.

The learning of the agents makes the relation between them - the organisation - a dynamic relationship, a reality whose states change as a consequence of the history produced by past decisions.

The particular state of the decision-rules of the agents determines the *state of the organisation*. And the state of the organisation determines the set of *feasible* interactions. So, the effectiveness of an action also changes, due to its dependence on a reaction which is determined by the decision-rules of the reactive agent.

The model can now represent a problem having the formal properties of a final purpose. *It is the problem of the achievement of the optimal organisational state.* The meaning of "optimal" in this case directly follows from the function itself that organisational states play in the achievement of the specific purpose. *The optimal state will be the one that maximises the set of feasible interactions.*

Any decision made by the active agent starts a particular interaction. This interaction produces some particular learning in both agents. And that means that the organisational state may be changed as well. *The test of consistency provides a way of evaluating those changes that the performance of the action produces in the organisational state.*

On the basis of what we have described so far, we can give very precise meaning to statements about short-run vs. long-run optimisation. For instance: an optimal decision in terms of a given set of alternatives (choosing the most effective action among the set of feasible interactions determined by the organisational state), may not be optimal at all when evaluated in terms of its consistency (changes produced in the organisational state that reduce the set of feasible alternatives for future decisions).

But no statement of that kind is powerful enough to undermine the position of our hypothetical sceptical boss. He or she might say that our definitions of specific purposes and final ones are quite arbitrary. Or he or she might state that his or her specific purposes are defined taking into consideration long-run implications. He or she might also say that his or her choice of an optimal action means the choice of an action that is best for both purposes, producing the optimal organisational state and the most satisfying interaction for him or her.

We might point out to this person the almost unbelievable amount of knowledge that an active agent must have in order to be able to make such a choice. First, he or she has to be able to make accurate predictions about the specific learning that will take place *in the reactive agent* for each possible interaction. And second, this means that he himself or she herself will not have anything to learn from the experiences produced by any interaction with that reactive agent.

Most real decision-makers - who are not only rational but reasonable - will strongly agree that they do not have such powers. And, in fact, we can easily observe that their decisions are made on the basis of two different criteria, frequently in conflict with one another, which look very much like applications of a criterion meant to ensure some degree of effectiveness, and of another criterion meant to ensure some consistency. They conceive interactions with other people as a non-zero-sum game, and the general idea is that "if you like some reaction from other people, give them some action that they also like to get from you". The idea is not a wrong one, and its application produces in quite a few cases an improvement on what we have called the organisational state (the relation between both decision-makers).

This approach is sometimes used in order to defend the practicality of what may be considered "ethical behaviour". The argument runs, more or less, like this: Taking into consideration the value of your actions for other people - the satisfactions or dissatisfactions that your actions may produce for them -, pays off in the long-run. The trouble with this argument is that the long-run may be too far away, that the "prediction" of the positive results may have a very high degree of uncertainty, and the pay-off may not be big enough.

If effectiveness in the achievement of a specific purpose can be measured in economic terms, as it can in the case of business, personal convictions about the certainty of the pay-off, its size, and the immediacy of the long-run, have to be very strong in order to compensate the "opportunity costs" incurred by trying to be ethical. Those personal convictions have to come from outside the economic world (very frequently they come from outside *this* world; they are a by-product of religious faith, and that has solved quite a few problems for mankind).

As a matter of fact, any rigorous analysis of human action - even those analyses which only attempt the explanation of "economic aspects" of human action - seem to demand some "postulate" asserting the existence of non-economic motives - driving forces - in the human actors (see, for instance, Adam Smith, 1976 or, for a contemporary comment, Barnard, 1958).

In most cases, these motives fall into the category of what we are loosely labelling "ethical motives", such as, for example, those motives that originate actions which produce satisfactions in other people. So, we might talk about an "economic man", whose only motives are the maximising of his own satisfactions, and an "ethical man", who seeks his own satisfaction but cares about the satisfactions of other people as well.

The trouble with our hypothetical boss is that he or she is an "economic man", and the only things we have been able to show our boss so far are:

(1) That the satisfactions of other people do have an influence on the evolution of the state of the organisation, and it is this that determines the effectiveness of his or her own actions.

(2) That given the difficulties of knowing *a priori* the influence of actions on the evolution of the organisational state, many reasonable people think that, in the long-run, the only way to make sure that organisational states will always improve, is an unconditional commitment to the application, in any decision which may affect other people, of a policy similar to the "golden rule", the "categorical imperative" and the like.

Our boss might say that the long-run mentioned in (2) above has to be very long because, in his or her own experience - a fairly long one if he or she happens to know history - there are quite a few cases where the application of those policies by one partner did not improve the organisational state at all - cases, that is, in which the decision-rule employed by the other partner did not make for any improvement.

This being the case, it is by no means surprising that some might find the opportunity costs of applying those policies too high. Fundamentally, it seems like a question about uncertainties in the not-so-long-run. On the one hand, there is the probability of improving the organisational state by the application of those policies vs. the cost of applying them. On the other hand, there is the probability of making mistakes due to lack of specific information about the consequences of actions upon the organisational state vs. the immediate savings in costs obtained by simplifying the problem, approaching it as a reduced one (as if the only thing that really mattered were the achievement of the maximum effectiveness possible within the set of feasible actions).

Of course, an ethical man would say that the argument is missing a most important thing: that the satisfactions of other people are important in themselves, and not only because of their instrumentality in achieving the satisfactions of the decision-maker.

That brings into the picture a new dimension. We are dealing with a question where motivation, and not only knowledge, plays a role. Our model can easily help us to explore the issue.

Motivational processes in dual-problem solving

It seems that the only difference between the "ethical man" and the "economic man", provided that both of them are motivated to achieve their own satisfactions, is that their motivations towards the satisfactions of other people are different.

The economic man is motivated to act in order to satisfy other people, but only insofar as those satisfactions are instrumental in achieving his or her own satisfaction. The ethical man seems to be motivated to act in order to satisfy other people, without further considerations.

It is very easy to conceive a mechanism which generates "forces" - *motivations* - bringing about the performance of actions by an agent in order to obtain some satisfaction, *provided that the agent who obtains the satisfactions and performs the actions are one and the same agent*. But in the case of one agent's motivation to perform an action in order to produce satisfactions in a different agent, the problem of the mechanisms needed to explain the process is by no means a trivial one.

To approach the description of the mechanisms explaining decision-making in the latter case, we can start from a very simple fact: a decision-maker has to *evaluate a priori* the consequences that will follow the performance of any action that he could perform in his or her present situation. The choice of a particular action means that that is the action with the highest evaluation (it *does not mean* that it is the action with the highest *value*: most frequently that can only be found *a posteriori*).

So, we can go through the following steps:

(a) The evaluation of an action is made by anticipating the satisfactions that will be achieved by the performance of that action, an anticipation made by the decision-maker at the time of making the decision. So, the decision-maker has to be endowed with a mechanism capable of making these assessments or anticipations (forming *a priori* judgements about future phenomena). The simplest mechanism with that property is what we usually call a memory. Memory generates anticipations on the basis of records produced by past experiences.

(b) The impulse or driving force that leads a decision-maker to perform an action is what we usually call motivation. The motivation to perform an action is generated by the evaluation of that action. So, we can say that motivations are automatically or spontaneously generated by anticipations produced by memory.

(c) Those constructs - a memory producing anticipations on the basis of its records, and the spontaneous motivation generated by those anticipations - can explain perfectly the choice of actions by a decision-maker confronted with the single problem of achieving goals which are mono-valued. What this means is that it is the *satisfaction felt* by a decision-maker, while experiencing a particular interaction that determines *the value of that interaction* for that decision-maker. And the value of interactions is a datum of the problem. Preferences of the decision-maker *about interactions* cannot be changed by experiences.

(d) But, going back to our model, it so happens that our decision-maker, in order to evaluate his or her actions *a priori*, has to look at *three different values of the interaction:*

1. The satisfaction he will get while experiencing it. That is the *extrinsic value* of an interaction.
2. The change it will produce in the organisational state. That is the *organisational value* of an interaction.
3. The satisfaction that the reactive agent will get. That is the *instrumental value* of an interaction.

Of course, the third value is a value for the active agent and a reality that influences his or her future satisfactions only insofar as it is instrumental in achieving both values mentioned in 1. and 2. above. It is clear, then, that we are taking the point of view of the economic man in that the overriding or ultimate purpose is the maximisation of the active agent's satisfactions through interactions with the reactive agent. However, it must be made absolutely clear from the beginning that the *first condition* of achieving that purpose is the optimisation of the organisational state. It is that state which determines the feasibility of interactions and, thereby, the possibility of producing the interaction with the highest extrinsic value.

So, we do not have to worry as to whether or not the concept of motivation has any meaning when applied to the achievement of satisfactions different from those of the decision-maker. We can start from the assumption that a decision-maker has an impulse to maximise his or her own satisfactions. What we have seen is that that impulse cannot be reduced to his or her spontaneous motivation in performing his or her actions. Were his or her decision-rule based only on spontaneous motivation, he or she would only be maximising *a priori anticipated satisfaction.*

The real problem is the description of the mechanisms and processes whereby a decision-maker can modify his or her spontaneous motivation in order to generate an *operative motivation* to perform actions which actually optimise his or her real *a posteriori* satisfaction.

I can only give here a very partial and summarised account of those mechanisms and processes, just to show where those analyses might be arrived at. Doing otherwise would take us too far in the areas of anthropology (applying the constructs needed to explain the making of decisions within a dual-problem framework to the analysis of human action) and ethics (finding decision-making rules which ensure that the decision-maker's learning will always be "positive", that is, will always involve a growth in the ability of the decision-maker to generate operative motivation towards actions that are consistent with the achievement of maximum *a posteriori* satisfactions).

The first point that we have to recognise is that, in order to generate an operative motivation different from the spontaneous motivation, the decision-maker must have a source of information about the value of actions different from the records in his memory due to past experiences.

Of course, that source is easy to identify in human beings: it is what we call "abstract knowledge", "human reason", and so forth. There we have many data which help us to make more or less accurate predictions about the results obtained by performance of actions. The trouble is that those predictions, in quite a few cases, are very "cold" ones. We have no way of *anticipating* the value of those results: we have never experienced the satisfaction produced by the experience of that value.

Abstract predictions by themselves cannot generate spontaneous motivation. So, the decision-maker has to be endowed with some mechanism to make them influential in his decision-making processes. That mechanism is called *virtuality* and it determines, given the information contained in abstract knowledge and the spontaneous motivation, the operative motivation that the decision-maker can generate. Two different dimensions have to be considered in virtuality.

1. Its *intensity*, which is defined by the capacity a decision-maker has to control his or her spontaneous motivation, enforcing the performance of actions due to rational (abstract) motives.
2. Its *rationality*, which is defined by how well the decision-maker uses the abstract information that he or she has in order to set rational motives.

Virtuality is a property of a decision-maker that changes while actions are chosen and performed. The development, whether positive or negative, of both the intensity and rationality depends on how decisions are made by the decision-maker.

Intensity develops by effective implementation of actions chosen for the sake of rational motives. The greater the difficulties posed by spontaneous motivation which have been overcome, the greater the development of that intensity.

The most important aspect of rationality - the only one which really matters from an ethical viewpoint - is that of *its completeness or incompleteness*. Complete rationality means that all the data in abstract knowledge have been taken into consideration by the decision-maker at the time of defining his rational purpose. The *deliberate* omission of data at the time of making decisions generates patterns of behaviour based on incomplete rationality. Whether or not the explicit purpose at hand (the extrinsic value of the interaction) is achieved by the decision-maker, is very important in this context. The worst possible outcome is that success in the achievement of his or her purpose despite deliberate omission of data might reinforce this practice and thus become a habit of the decision-maker when he or she is confronted with similar problems in the future. He or she becomes a victim of instrumental rationality; an expert achiever of some specific purposes at the cost of growing more and more unable to establish satisfying relationships with other human beings.

Complete rationality means using whatever relevant abstract information a decision-maker may have for solving the problem at hand. The most relevant information is the fact that he or she is interacting with other human beings. The most relevant value involved in any process of interaction is what we have called organisational value. So, it seems that whatever information the decision-maker might have about the influence of the interaction on the improvement of the organisational state is information which cannot be deliberately ignored at the time of making the decision. Effective use of that information in decision-making develops both the habit of behaving under norms of complete rationality, and the intensity of virtuality.

We do not have to go very far to find out what constitutes the "perfect" organisational state from the point of view of an active agent. It means an internal state of the reactive agent whereby any possible reaction that he or she could perform will be performed by him or her as a response to merely asking him or her to do so. This internal state means that the reactive agent must be motivated to act on the basis of the value of his or her reactions for the active agent, as if he himself held that value.

Such operative motivation calls for perfect virtuality in the reactive agent. So, the most fundamental value of an action is its contribution towards helping the reactive agent to develop his or her own virtuality. Helping other people to develop their own virtuality is what I call *enlightened altruism* (as opposed to *blind altruism,* which only looks at the satisfaction that the reactive agent may get from the interaction, ignoring those learning processes taking place at a deeper level of reality).

But, the other way around, the most fundamental value of an action performed by a reactive agent also happens to be the way in which it helps the active agent to grow in virtuality. The perfect organisational state is that formed by the relation between two decision-makers who have both achieved perfect virtuality. That state is achieved to the extent to which both decision-makers try to make their decisions motivated by enlightened altruism.

Two points must be stressed here:

-   That the development of virtuality in an agent cannot be produced by *any action* of another agent. Virtuality only grows as a result of the *intentions* motivating an agent's own actions. No external power can produce the development of virtuality.

    When those intentions are "closed" to what we have called enlightened altruism, the decision-maker develops patterns of behaviour based on reduced or incomplete rationality. He or she "learns" to ignore more and more that most important aspect of reality that is the inner response of persons. We cannot go further into the analysis of what happens in the affective life of a person due to that "ignorance".

-   The achievement of a perfect organisational state would produce the maximisation of satisfactions (extrinsic values) as well. That is but another way of saying what most people mean when they agree that a world in which everybody was really moved by the good of the others would be a very nice world indeed. The trouble is that the achievement of that state of affairs - perfect organisational states - does not depend on only one partner. An active agent - the boss - may do whatever is needed from the point of view of his or her own actions to achieve that organisational state and yet fail to achieve it. So, the investment - his or her own sacrifices - may very well be an economic failure: the intentions of the other partner are "closed" to enlightened altruism, so that he or she may even be doing what is required but for other reasons and, in consequence, his or her virtuality may be diminishing.

The investment, however, has been a complete ethical success: that active agent has developed his or her own virtuality. His or her decisions in attempting to build a perfect organisational state have caused his or her "learning" to be motivated by enlightened altruism. He or she becomes an agent with the abilities required to build perfect organisational states with other agents who go in for the same kind of game.

The reason for behaving ethically is, then, the achievement of *motivational learning* by the decision-maker. Why be ethical? Just in order to learn how to develop really satisfying relations with other people. Being ethical means learning to evaluate persons as persons, it means learning to love.

Conclusions

1. The conflict between economics and ethics is not a conflict between self-interest and altruism. It is a conflict between *blind* self-interest and *enlightened* self-interest. But the distinction between both types of self-interest cannot be made according to any *static* decision-making theory (any theory that does not formalise the criteria for evaluating learning produced by the decisions). In those theories, the distinction is meta-theoretical.

2. Motivation to act in order to satisfy blind self-interest is spontaneous. Motivation to act in order to satisfy enlightened self-interest has to be learnt by decision-makers. Ethical rules are those rules for the making of decisions that specify the conditions to be met in order to ensure that the decision-maker achieves that learning.

3. The fundamental ethical policy - which is the basis for developing specific ethical rules - is *enlightened altruism*. It means the motivation to act in order to help other people to learn (that is, to develop their motivation to act in order to satisfy their enlightened self-interest). Acting in order to satisfy other people because of the satisfaction that the decision-maker achieves from observing the satisfactions of other people - *blind altruism* - is a matter which has to do with aesthetics, not with ethics. Such actions are motivated by sentimental values and not by ethical ones.

4. Learning to satisfy enlightened self-interest depends only on the real influence that enlightened altruism, defined and operationalised in   terms of all the information that a person happens to have as abstract   knowledge, has on the decision-making processes of the decision-maker. The higher the influence, the higher the development of the decision-maker's *virtuality*.

5. The purpose of ethical decision-making is not to ensure that the state of the organisation where the decision is made will reach its optimum. That can never be achieved by the decision-maker's actions in themselves, because it depends on the *intentions* of the reactive agent in performing the reaction (whether or not enlightened altruism motivates that performance, and that can never be externally imposed). It has as its purpose to make sure that the decision-maker is learning to interact with any human being as a human being, whoever he or she happens to be, and whatever the nature of their mutual interaction.

References

Barnard, C. I.: 1958, *The Functions of the Executive*, Cambridge, MA: Harvard University Press.
Simon, H.: 1976, *Administrative Behavior*, Third edition, New York: The Free Press.
Smith, A.: 1976, *The Theory of Moral Sentiments*, Oxford: Clarendon Press.

ETHICS AND THE DEFINITION OF BUSINESS STRATEGY

Miquel Bastons

Management and corporate strategy

A classical author compared human behaviour with the movement of an arrow towards a pre-established target (Aristotle, 1970). Although I was not quite sure why, I was bothered by this comparison and moved to analyse it more closely. My unease did not stem from the fact that we were comparing human behaviour with the movement of an inert object. What troubled me intellectually was the supposition implicit in the comparison that within human behaviour we indeed find "pre-established" targets or objectives. Consideration of this point leads us, I believe, to a key topic of management theory, be it the management of one's own life or the management of organisations (Andrews, 1987), that to a large degree is yet unsolved. Is it true that we behave as an arrow moving towards a pre-established target? Is it not rather the case that our effort is oriented not so much towards hitting a target as towards discovering "which" target we have to hit?

Sticking to the field of business, it would seem that we find an affirmative answer to this latter question and that managerial action is not simply understood as an aptitude for applying resources to objectives which are previously proposed. Any manager could confirm that the definition of corporate goals and objectives, the knowledge of *what* goals have to be attained, is the fundamental - and perhaps the most difficult - task facing management.

Since the mid-sixties management science has assumed that decisions made within business do not only deal with the use of means and resources in order to attain goals which were presupposed as "given" beforehand and which were taken to be almost unalterable. It was seen that in practice business managers are "creators of goals" and that therefore not only can they or must they decide concerning the means, but also that they must and can decide upon the ends, and that this, precisely, is the basic and central task of business management.

K.R. Andrews identified these two dimensions in terms of "policy" and "strategy", respectively, as applied to business corporations (Andrews, 1987). He also made it clear that although it also refers to the means, the basic function of strategic definition is precisely that of setting the corporation's objectives and goals, and that reference to ends, precisely, is what makes of it a "managerial" task (Andrews, 1987).

Many years before, Aristotle had pointed out something similar when he indicated that the knowledge which tends to the determination of ends is the one which properly receives the name of "directing". Although an inversion of terms has been brought about, given that what Andrews calls "strategic" Aristotle calls "political", and that what for Andrews is political was, for Aristotle, tactical or strategic (Aristotle, 1970), the coincidence of ideas in both authors is complete. Bearing this in mind, I will from now on refer to both dimensions of management according to Andrews' terminology.

The lack of balance between policies and strategies

Paraphrasing Alejandro Llano, it can then be said that the fundamental problem facing management today is, above all, that of "understanding" that which in fact is being "practiced" (Llano, 1989). It is a matter of replacing intuitive managerial practice, which at times has produced good results, by articulated knowledge which permits better results. In this, in my opinion, we are far removed from having attained an acceptable degree of profundity (Simon, 1957). Many studies on the management of organisations continue to forget what any manager actually does in practice, and those who do not forget it attain, at best , descriptions which at times are quite complete yet superficial.

It is still common to come across clearly unilateral approaches stemming from the higher echelons of management. Management is understood as merely firing at pre-established targets and therefore managers who take this view concentrate on "abilities" - in the end, upon intellectual abilities - in order to encounter and combine the appropriate means. But one is not taught to decide on objectives.

This approach introduces a lack of balance within the organisation which makes it tilt towards the side of its policy dimension - often and immediately towards its most urgent policy dimension - to the detriment of its strategic dimension - which requires a longer term perspective. What I will try to show in this paper is that ethics is essential in order to recover a state of equilibrium.

(a) Business games

The recourse to the *game* as a model or schema in order to comprehend the managerial function has the danger of fostering this unilateral approach to the managerial function. Indeed, we are today faced with a sudden proliferation of works which present it as the basic model for training managers.

At least in part, this should not greatly surprise us, because corporate strategy, which we have defined as the essential activity of management, has at times been explained in terms of the example of military strategy which, in turn, has been inspired by games. It has been influenced by games having an oriental origin, but above all in the "war games" (*Kriegsspiele*) which were at fisrt played by children and which then proved themselves to be most efficient in real war.

The first applications of this model to managerial action date back to the mid-fifties and from then on they have been developed further and are known as *business games*. This development has also received a strong impulse from the *general theory of games*, a discipline of a mathematical nature developed by von Neumann and Morgenstern (Andlinger, 1958; von Neumann and Morgenstern, 1944; Rodríguez Carrasco, 1975).

The application of the game structure to business has to be seen as a reaction against uncertainty within managerial decision-making, which is present in both the policy and strategy levels. On the one hand, we rarely have the guarantee that a certain "policy" or the mobilisation of precise resources will necessarily take us to the attainment of a concrete purpose. But, on the other hand, we also have to count upon uncertainty within the definition of the strategy, given that although we tend to take it for granted that the application of a "policy" will effectively take us to the proposed objective, this does not necessarily come about.

Objectives are not chosen in a state of isolation. They almost always come along with a set of effects which are hard to predict and which can cause us to revoke our original interest in those objectives.This means that decisions on the future destiny of the organisation have necessarily to be made a state of incomplete information. As H. Simon says, the theory of organisation is the theory of a "limited rationality" and its place is the ambit in which human behaviour "tries" to be rational, although this may only be attained in a "limited" way (Simon, 1976). Therefore, all decisions have to count upon the possibility of error.

One possible attitude in the face of the situation of uncertainty affecting decisions on goals is *decisionism*. This consists in converting the "incomplete determination" of the strategy into a complete strategic "indetermination". Another way of responding to this has been to conceive of action as a game. And it consists in placing decision-making within a simulated context.

Simulation is the carrying out of an activity within a fictitious context "as if" it were the real context. This makes possible the mobilisation of means, the application of policies and the development of abilities without having to decide upon a real objective, since the latter is simply irrelevant.

What is most characteristic of a game - let us suppose chess - is that in the game the objectives - for example, the elimination of the King - are already set *a priori* and what is least important is the nature of the objectives. The finality of the game is "outside the game". What is really important is to ascertain what "policies" to apply: given a goal, we have to find the policy, among many alternatives, that will best take us to the attainment of that goal.

A game is a relaxing activity precisely because simulation places the decision on objectives within parentheses and limits itself purely to the question of means. It removes from us the pressure of responsibility for having to decide on our destiny, or that of the organisation we manage, under the uncomfortable risk of error.

Now, for this same reason the recourse to games as a framework for understanding the government of an organisation can introduce imbalances. The application of this schema to business can be most advantageous within training programmes for future managers if it is kept in mind that it is a simulation which must not be confused with real managerial action. Managing a business is not a game. And the difference resides, precisely, in the fact that whereas in a game victory depends exclusively upon efficiency in the use of means and what is of the least import is the outcome, within managerial action in actual practice we have to decide upon the latter and it is upon this decision that success hinges (Andrews, 1987).

(b) The "techniques" of management

Another idea which has taken us off the path towards understanding the strategic function of management is the obsession with the discovery and employment of managerial "techniques". It is often forgotten that technique cannot dictate objectives. What is taken for granted and what is fundamentally achieved is the discovery and mobilisation of resources in order to attain those objectives.

The same occurs here as in the game, but with the difference that in this case there is no longer simulation. A technician cannot seek to produce a fiction, but rather something real, although - as in the game - this arises from something external to the decision-maker, usually from another person. For example, when we seek an architect, we do not expect him to start arguing about whether or not we need to build a house. This decision is made by us and what we expect of him is simply that he tell us *how* to carry out its construction. The technician, as such, is solely concerned with the articulation of means and on principle he refuses to be responsible for decisions made concerning ends. Many specialists take this course of action in order to avoid being responsible, for example, for certain "advances" within fields such as biotechnology or technology for warfare.

But not only does the technician not solve the problem of deciding what has to be done: neither does he carry out what has been decided upon. Not only does the architect not enter into the discussion over whether we should build or not; neither does he personally build the house. His sphere of work is restricted to *knowing how* to build it and to what means have to be used. And this can be solved in terms of logical-formal knowledge without the need for any action whatsoever.

Applying a technical model of government within an organisation gives a one-sided picture of managerial action and it implies, first of all, a theoretical error: confusion between prudence, which is the optimum form of management, and *astuteness*, which is a degenerate form of the former and which consists of an intellectual aptitude for combining and mobilizing means for a proposed objective, no matter what that objective may be.

This kind of shrewdness is an important obstacle in the way of efficient practice because it produces pointless actions. As we are unfortunately able to see in our own time, nothing can be less productive, even on a short-term basis, than a brilliant intelligence placed at the service of perverse ends.

Within managerial practice the question of the destiny of the organisation is never answered, as it is within suggested games or within specialised techniques. However, the task of clarifying the mission, the establishment of plans and the definition of purposes which have to be pursued is, on the contrary, as we have already seen, recognised in practice as the central question to be answered by the organisation.

Within the organisation the order of priorities is therefore exactly the opposite of the one proposed by the mentioned models: strategic definition, which in the latter is irrelevant, is essential for the former, and the combination of policies, which for the latter is basic, is secondary for the former. In fact, when an organisation reaches a certain size, it is habitual to delegate policy decisions to the lower hierarchical echelons. "General" managers are not essentially responsible for executive and technical functions. It could even be unproductive for such matters to be subject to their decision, given the negative by-products which could derive from their lack of specialisation. It is convenient to leave these aspects in the hands of "functional" managers (Andrews, 1987).

The contribution of ethics to strategic definition

If neither managerial "techniques" nor business games question that which is the most important thing within the government of organisations, namely the strategic tracing of objectives, what, then is the adequate conceptual model for coming to grips with this?

Let us first shed some light on what an objective is, properly speaking. Philosophers give a definition which I think is useful and easily admissible: anything to which we can aspire (Aristotle 1970). Evidently, to tend towards or to pursue something presupposes that there are some things which we lack; it assumes that is, that there are needs. For example, human beings have to grow physically, develop themselves psychically, progress intellectually, socially, and so on. An objective, therefore, has to bring together two different conditions: in the first place, it must express a need and, in the second place, it must represent an aspiration. I say that they are two different conditions because the connection between needs and aspirations is not automatic: every need does not necessarily convert itself into an aspiration. An objective arises only when there is an adjustment between the two. Now, in order for this adjustment to come about there necessarily has to be a third element, namely the interests and preferences of the individual: something which I do not possess converts itself into an aspiration and therefore into an objective if I happen to become interested in that thing.

This is well known in commercial departments where it is known that what is important is not so much letting the client "know" that he or she needs the product, but rather that the product will only be converted into an operational objective when the client, apart from knowing about the product, becomes interested in it. In fact, advertising campaigns are fundamentally oriented towards this very fact: the creation of demand.

The same thing can be said about the objectives of an organisation: it is not simply that they have to be known. What happens is that even while recognising them as objectives, we have to be *interested* in them. Whereas success in the application of policies to a large degree depends upon the reception and transmission of objective information, the identification of objectives and the follow-up consisting of setting forth the right strategy are necessarily conditioned by interests, that is, by what is sought. It is interest that converts "that which is known" into an "objective", that which converts a need to an aspiration.

It could be objected to this that, in turn, nothing can be sought unless it is previously known. This is true. But it is no less true that nothing can be known "as a goal or an objective" and, therefore, nothing can be operational, unless that thing is in some way sought. The problem which affects the practical implementation of many so-called objectives within an organisation has a great deal to do with this. It could be that these objectives are not correctly known, but the main problem generally comes from the fact that they are not sought and therefore from the fact that in practice they are not true "objectives". It is as though they did not in fact exist.

The intervention of wanting/seeking and personal preferences means that the definition of a corporation's strategy has a peculiar "logic". It is a matter of a model which does not permit - as do the models of science of technology - to keep a distance vis-a-vis what is known. On the contrary, the manager has to be "involved" with what he knows and, for this very reason, he or she cannot pretend to remain impartial or neutral. An "objective" can be known in a state of indifference. A goal can only be recognised as a goal if I am interested in it.

The influence of personal character, personal preferences or subjective interests with regard to something as important as the government of an organisation is inevitable, yet undoubtedly it arouses certain worries and even fears. There are sufficient examples of the negative effect of the intervention of certain personal tendencies within management in business, to make one suspicious of them.

Now, this does not mean that strategic decisions have to be made in a state of asepsis. That they are not handled by means of universal and necessary logical and rational frameworks does not mean that management functions - the setting of goals - are completely outside our control and that we must abandon them to luck, whim or some strange enlightenment. Apart from being a fiction, this would also be counter-productive.

Not because they unsettle us nor even because we may deny them will the personal character and the particular interests of the decision-maker cease to have an influence in his strategic decision. It would be better, given the fact that managers cannot be but interested in what they are deciding upon, that we should try at least to have them be interested in a correct manner. This is what immediately places the art of managing within the sphere of ethics and it is this that makes of ethics a necessary instance for strategic definition.

As K.R.Andrews has stated,"we have reached the point in which the influence of the leader is owed more to the person than to the role which he represents" (Andrews, 1987). Again here Aristotle corroborates this by indicating that whereas to "be" in an organisation it is good enough to appear to be good, in order to govern that organisation appearance of goodness is not enough; one has to be good in fact.

Ethics is not properly speaking a "science", at least in the usual meaning which we give to the word. There is no science to teach us what is truly interesting. This is something which each and everyone has to learn by becoming engaged, and by becoming ever more engaged. Ethics is, above all, a task.

But this does not mean opening the door to arbitrariness, because it is in our power to educate and model our preferences so as to make them worthy in the discovery of what is deserving. In the same manner in which taste, through repeated acts of drinking vulgar wines, loses the discrimination needed to perceive the quality of top-rate wines, a poorly cultivated will loses its capacity for interesting itself in what is convenient. What to the perverted man "seems" interesting is then pure "appearance": he ignores what is optimum. And this is not the case of an error, but rather of blindness: he cannot see it. This blindness can produce difficulties at the lower or intermediate levels of the organisation - the "functional" levels - but if it affects management - the "general" government of the organisation - the result is catastrophic.

But in the same way in which there are people who are blind to what is best, there are people with preferences whose quality has made them to be, so to speak, extremely intelligent. What to them "seems" to be interesting, even while being erroneous due to the uncertainty which we mentioned earlier on, is yet not merely an "appearance" but rather something which "is" truly interesting. Their subjective aspirations become charged then, thanks to their quality, with a quasi-objective value. They permit those people to discover new opportunities, to propose attractive objectives and to "point out" paths which others can follow. We can readily see that such people are authentic leaders.

Ethics has as its object that of teaching and preparing men and women for achieving an appropriate synthesis between what "can" be done (the knowledge of resources and opportunities) and what we "want" to do (preferences and aspirations), and what we "ought" to do (duties and responsibilities). We know today that management is an activity which is more synthetic than analytic, that today's business manager is not so much a "compiler" of knowledge and abilities as he or she is a person capable of bringing together different perspectives; and that his or her central mission is precisely that of unifying the elements I have described, which also constitute the basic aspects of corporate strategy. Therefore, preparation in ethics is what can most help him or her.

The leader's authority is not based upon inexorable logical arguments, but rather on his capacity for finding syntheses arising from his or her personal ethical quality. The leader does not govern because he or she has a monopoly of wisdom. He or she governs because he or she is the bearer of the most good, which in practice is a matter of being wise, in the best possible way.

In a word, then, human and ethical "education" is what prepares a man or a woman to be able to define a strategy and to provide authentic leadership. This makes the widespread call for the introduction of ethics within business to be considered as something more than just a poetic - and naive - declaration of good intentions. Business managers have to come to realise that it is simply a question of professional efficiency.

References

Andlinger, G. R.: 1958, "Business Games. Play One", *Harvard Business Review*.

Andrews, K.R.: 1987, *The Concept of Strategy*, Homewood, Ill.: Irwin.

Aristotle: 1970, *Etica a Nicomaco*, Madrid: Instituto de Estudios Políticos.

Cohen, J.K. *et al.*: 1960, "The Carnegie Tech Management Game", *Journal of Business*, 33, 4.

Llano, A.: 1989, "La empresa ante la nueva complejidad", *Cuadernos del Seminario Permanente Empresa y Humanismo*, 15.

Rodríguez Carrasco, J. M.: 1975, *Juegos de empresa*, Madrid: Esic.

Simon, H.: 1957, *Administrative Behavior*, New York: MacMillan.

Simon, H.: 1976, *Administrative Behavior*, New York: MacMillan.

von Neumann, J. and O. Morgenstern: 1944, *Theory of Games and Economic Behavior*, Princeton: Princeton University Press.

MANAGEMENT AS THE SYMBOLISATION OF ETHICAL VALUES

Ceferí Soler

The purpose of this paper is to provide an understanding of ethical decision-making in organisations which is important to the development of organisational science. Ethical issues are ever present in uncertain conditions where multiple stakeholders, interests, and values are in conflict and laws are unclear (Trevino, 1986). Managers engage in discretionary decision-making behaviour affecting the lives and well-being of others. Not only do businesses act - they act *rationally*, according to a rational decision-making procedure. These rational actions affect people. Hence their actions can be evaluated from a moral point of view. Managerial decisions and acts can have important social consequences, in the realms of health, safety, welfare of consumers, employees and the community. Managers and corporations are involved in ethical decision-making.

Ethics and decision-making

The term "ethics" denotes the application of values to the decision-making process. Ethics has been described as a set of standards for decision-making. Values may be thought of as the guidance system a manager uses when confronted with choices amongst various options. A value can also be viewed as an explicit or implicit conception of what an individual or group, selecting from amongst available options, regards as desirable ends and means to these ends. *The role of values and ethics* in the decision-making process *can be made explicit* (Harrison, 1975):

(1) *In setting organisational objectives,* it is necessary to make value-judgements regarding the selection of opportunities and improvements that are possible within the constraints of time and resources.
(2) In the development of a *range of relevant options*, value judgements must be made about the various possibilities that emerge from the search activity.
(3) *At the point of choice,* the values of the decision-maker, as well as ethical considerations relevant in the particular context, are significant factors.
(4) *The time-scale and methods used to implement the choice* necessarily involve value-judgements, as well as an awareness of ethical interests.
(5) *In the follow-up and control stage* of the decision-making process, value-judgements are unavoidable in taking corrective action to ensure that the outcome of the implemented choice is compatible with the original objective.

Values and ethics then, pervade the entire process of choice. They are also an integral part of the decision-maker's belief-system, as they are reflected in the way in which he arrives at a choice and then puts it into effect. Decisions are complex sets of value premises which involve choice among these value premises.

Proposition 1:
Ethics provides values, standards, rules and decision criteria that are integral to the effectiveness of the decision-making process in organisations and to the concept of corporate moral social responsibility.

Bounded rationality and decision-making

The concept of rationality

The uncertainty about goals and causal outcomes in organisational decisions leads us to consider constraints on the decision-making process. To do this, it is necessary to examine the concept of rationality in decision-making. An initial conception of rationality relates it to the ability to select means to achieve goals. A more refined definition of this basic notion suggests that a decision is rational if it maximises goal achievement within the limitations of the environment in which it is made. However, this definition is inadequate as it leaves no room for evaluating the "rationality" of the goal which is to be attained through the chosen course of action. For example, *the least cost method* for eliminating an ethnic group, as in the case of Nazi Germany, would be regarded as *rational* given the goal of the elimination of the Jews (Helbrigel and Slocum, 1974). *Rationality must include goals as well as means.* The concept of rationality is most often used in normative (what ought to be) decision models. Whereas the previous definition focuses on the rationality of a given decision to reach some predetermined goal, the concept of rationality often emphasizes the process which should be employed to arrive at decisions. *The essential requirements for rational decision-making* include:

(1) *The search for and assimilation of all information relevant* to the issue;
(2) *The ability to determine preferences* according to some measuring device (usually money rather than ethical values);
(3) The ability to *select the alternative which maximises the decision-maker's utility*. (Here the problem is one of satisfaction versus cognitive dissonance arising from value conflicts).

Bounded rationality

One of the reasons for the conflicts and differences in decisions arrived at by individuals, when confronted with the same information, can be partially explained through the concept of bounded rationality. This principle describes the decision process individuals actually go through, as opposed to the process of rational behaviour. The principle of bounded rationality consists of *several elements:*

- *First*, it asserts that an individual *rarely seeks a single optimum action in considering a decision*. Instead, the individual might establish a very limited range of outcomes that would be satisfactory.

- *Secondly*, bounded rationality assumes that the individual or the organisation undertakes only *a limited search amongst the alternatives* which might be used to obtain the outcome (goals) desired. The attempt to obtain information about *all possible* alternatives could "freeze" the decision-maker.
- The *third* element of bounded rationality holds that *some factors outside the control of the decision-maker will affect the outcome of his or her decisions*. In other words, the state of the future, which is determined by numerous factors, affects the decision outcome.

In sum, bounded rationality represents the idea that a decision-maker has incomplete knowledge, value conflicts, cognitive limitations in information processing, environmental uncertainty and so on in the decision problem.

Proposition 2:
The concept of bounded rationality visualizes the complexity, uncertainty, and subjectivity of the ethical premises in the decision-making process as a major intrinsic constraint that produces a satisficing choice.

According to Daft (1986) the bounded rationality approach to decision-making is often associated with *intuitive decision processes*. In a decision situation of great complexity or ambiguity previous experience and judgement are needed to incorporate intangible elements. (Issack, 1978). The intuitive processes may be associated with both the problem definition and problem solution stages of a decision. A study of management problem identification showed that thirty of thirty-three problems were ambigous and ill-defined (Lyles and Mitroff, 1980). This can happen in decision situations where ethical issues and parameters are complex and ill-defined. The manager may not have been able to "prove" a problem existed but knew intuitively that a certain area needed attention. Intuitive processes are also used in the problem solution stage. A survey found that executives frequently made decisions without explicit reference to the impact on profits or other measurable outcomes of the organisation. Many intangible factors influenced selection of the best alternative. Ethical premises and criteria fall into this category. The factors cannot be quantified in a systematic way so intuition guided the choice of a solution. Managers made a decision based upon what they sensed to be right rather than what they could document with hard data (Stagner, 1969).
   The bounded rationality approach applies to nonprogrammed decision-making of this kind where both goals and outcomes are uncertain. The novel, unclear, complex aspects of nonprogrammed decisions mean that hard data and logical procedures are not available. A study of executive decision-making found that managers simply could not use the rational approach   (Nutt, 1984). The rational approach is limited in the case of decision-making with complex and ambiguous, ill-defined ethical premises and criteria. Another decision model is imperative, one that is bounded by discretion.

200

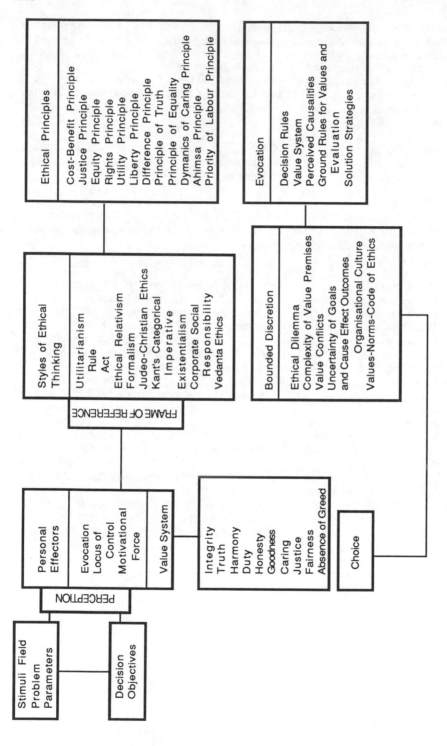

TABLE I: A Bounded Discretionary Model for Ethical Decision-Making

Bounded discretion and ethical decision-making

This model of decision-making integrates the following elements:

(1) *The stimuli or basic data* which define the parameters and major dimensions of the problem, and suggest some preliminary causal analysis,
(2) *the objectives or ends of the decision being sought,*
(3) *the influences bearing on the decision-maker,* including his/her subjective perceptions of the problem and frame of reference as well as the values, motivational force, and locus of control that evoke action.

In fact with reference to the decision-making process, human cognition acts as a kind of filtering system based on imagery that separates the stimulus or cue from resultant action. This imagery is a construct of relationship, experiences, values, emotions. The image is the key element in cognitive behaviour. The decision-maker's choice reflects his or her personality and his or her perceptions of people, roles and organisations as well as his or her values. *The perceptions of the decision-maker are critically important in the search activity,* and the act of cognition with its filtering imagery exerts a marked influence on the comparison and evaluation of alternatives.

The first major effector that is elaborated in the model is the value-system of the decision-maker, which may include, for example, integrity, harmony, justice and so on. The second major effector that is also expanded on in the model is the style of ethical thinking of the decision-maker. Styles of ethical thinking include utilitarianism, Kant's categorial imperative, Judeo-Christian moral imperatives, Vedantic ethics, and so on. From these theoretical perspectives of ethical thinking are derived principles for judging decision outcomes. For example, *utilitarianism is closely associated with a cost-benefit principle* which focuses on the evaluation of the consequences of decision alternatives;*Vedanta supplies the Ahimsa Principle, the principle of non-violence* - physical, psychological, and spiritual - which converges on the dynamics of *caring.* Some principles fall into economic, social, and ethical categories and may have a potential to produce conflict in the choice of the decision alternatives.

While individual behaviour can be understood and predicted by these effectors, the sociological environment in which the decision-maker operates is also critical. Decision-making is also a social event to the extent that facts and values are social phenomena. Values often reflect group norms internalised by other managers. The intrinsic elements of the decision process such as decision rules, perceived causalities, evaluation criteria and solution strategies, most of the variables associated with the decision making process, are often sociological in nature.

The decision-making process is also bounded by organisational or contextual constraints such as perceived environmental uncertainty, organisational culture, organisational values and code of ethics, information uncertainty in the analysis of cause and effect and not only by personal effectors. The choice, the act of selecting an alternative, is a function of the predisposition of the decision-maker, the contextual constraints on the decision-making process, the styles of ethical thinking of the decision-maker, and the intrinsic elements of the decision process.

Proposition 3:
The potential conflict between the influences bearing upon the decision-maker and the contextual constraints on the decision-making process may produce the following outcomes: (a) ethical dilemma, (b) cognitive dissonance, (c) a satisficing alternative, and (d) a change in the organisational culture.

The value-system of the decision-maker and the values of the organisation exert an influence on the process of choice. In the setting of objectives, the values of the organisation must be considered by the decision-maker. The search will reflect the values of the decision-maker as he or she attempts to relate the alternatives surveyed to the objectives of the organisation. In doing this, the decision-maker's frame of reference and value system, conditioned by the values of the organisational culture and objectives, influence the comparison and evaluation of alternatives. At the moment of choice, the same combination of values is salient. With the making of choice, the implementation phase is initiated, and in the process of executing the decision, the values of the organisation take precedence over those of the decision-maker. At all points in the integrated process of decision-making, the values of the decision-maker may conflict with the values of the organisation. In the presence of such conflict, a satisficing choice, made within the bounds of rationality, is directed toward furthering the objectives of the organisation. Another aspect of the conflict is the ethical dilemma which produces cognitive dissonance in the decision-maker if the personal influences are stronger that the contextual factors, particularly the organisational culture illustrated in our model.

Organisational culture, ethics, and decision-making

Culture is a set of key values, beliefs, and understanding that are shared by members of an organisation (Smircich, 1983). Cultures define basic organisational values and communicate to new members the correct way to think and act, and how things ought to be done (Schein, 1984). Culture represents the unwritten, feeling part of the organisation. *The function of culture is to provide members with a sense of identity and to generate a commitment to beliefs and values that are larger than themselves* . Culture also enhances the stability of an organisation and provides members with an understanding that can help them make sense of organisational events and activities (Smircich, 1983). Culture can be a positive force when used to reinforce the goals and strategy of the organisation. Chief executives can influence internal culture so as to make it consistent with corporate strategy. Culture embodies the values employees need to adopt if they are to behave in a way that is consistent with organisational goals. Top executives deal in symbols, ceremonies, and images (Peters, 1978). Managers signal values, beliefs, and goals to employees. Techniques that top managers may use to convey the appropriate values and beliefs are rites and ceremonies, stories, symbols and slogans. Symbols, stories, and ceremonies are techniques to manage organisational culture - something which is hard to shape by conventional means (Pfeffer, 1981). Issuing a written rule or policy, for example, would have almost no impact on the organisation's value system (Daft, 1986).

Even though ethics and culture are closely related, however, the infatuation with culture does not extend to ethics. One reason is that those promoting organisational culture are now competing in a small but quite profitable industry, *organisational culture consultancy*. Introducing ethics into the discussion is perceived as not at all likely to help sales. And those who sell culture, like the managers who buy it, have allowed themselves to become illiterate in the language of ethics. So they ignore it (Pastin, 1986).

But the truth is that the ethical ground rules are the heart of organisational cultures. In fact, if ethics is the heart of organisational culture, then the myths, symbols, rituals, ideologies, and customs, the elements of culture, are the fat around the heart, strangling it and destroying its vitality. Ethics is not only the heart of organisational culture, it is also the fulcrum in culture for producing change. The Adaptive Organisation seeks strong ethics and weak culture. A strong culture puts basic beliefs, attitudes, and ways of doing things beyond question. But unquestionables must be questioned for an organisation to be quick on its feet, strategic, and just plain smart. *Because cultures are rooted in tradition, they reflect what has worked, not what will work.* A bureaucratic culture is more preoccupied with precedents, rules, regulation, and operating procedures rather than ethical standards in decision-making. If culture is an information system, then such rules, precedents, and procedures may contribute to information distortion, omission and filtration in the decision-making process, and disinformation.

Cultures are, by consensus, hard to change. The stronger the culture, the harder it is to change. And most established organisations have strong, if not attractive or "appropriate" cultures. The complaint about organisational culture is that they change too slowly. But the complaint about ethics is that it is changing too fast. ("What happened to the work ethic of integrity, honesty, and hard work?" - Pastin, 1986). This is puzzling since the ethics of an organisation comprises the basic ground rules by which it operates. What is the relation of ethics to culture? Are there strong ethics, weak culture companies? There are, and these companies have the best prospects for sustained success, unimpeded by tragedy.

Ethics is closer to the surface of culture than any other components (myths, ideologies and aesthetics). We use ethics to ensure that others agree with us on the basics and to lock out those whose ideas or values threaten us. When an organisation enforces its ethics, its principles come to the surface. Ethics has another role. Ethics is the forum in which societies, groups, and organisations debate fundamental changes in their ground rules. *Criticism is as much part of ethics as enforcement is.* You can ignore criticism of your aesthetic ("You call that music?"), your ideology ("You can't be serious about voting for him?") and even personality ("You lack drive"). But if someone criticises your ethics, take note (Pastin, 1986). For a culture to persist and serve those who work in it the culture must learn. It must allow challenges to its basic principles in a setting that tolerates some change without threatening to undo the culture. Thus, culture promotes discussion of issues in ethical terms and insists that these discussions are serious. This is functional in that it provides an opportunity for a culture to change while keeping what is valuable in the culture intact.

Proposition 4:
The major means for changing the culture of an organisation is its underlying ethical premises. A dynamic culture will facilitate learning through the decision-making and information systems which convey these ethical premises .

Ground rules for ethical decision-making

Once we have surveyed the alternatives in the decision-making process we must visualise what each alternative offers. There are two parts to this as illustrated in our model. One part is to see what we can say *factually* about each alternative. In order to reach a decision we need to form a view or visualise what is likely to happen if we adopt each alternative. We evaluate each of the projected outcomes. In assessing outcomes there are two major questions: (1) *How much value do I see in each outcome?*, and (2) *what do I have to do to get the outcome I desire?* (Pastin, 1986).

Ground rules for value

Answers to the first question reveal one kind of ground rule, a ground rule for value. In reaching a decision, we rate some outcomes as more desirable than others, as more valuable. Here the factual issues concerning alternatives are important. But once we have considered the facts, what we count as desirable (valuable) and undesirable (not valuable) orders the options. Decisions are complex sets of value-premises and involve a choice among these value-premises.

Ground rules for evaluation

The second question in the process is "What do I have to do to get the desirable outcome?" Answers to this question reveal the second type of ground rule: *ground rules for evaluation*. We often judge one option to be the most desirable yet choose to pursue another because the first would have required us to do things we just do not do. The point is not that the option involves so many risks that we prefer to avoid it in assessing how desirable the option is. Rather there are kinds of actions that we will not take or do not want to take in order to obtain very desirable outcomes. We evaluate these actions as unacceptable using a set of principles, economic, social, and ethical.

Proposition 5:
The more consistent the ground rules for value-premises and evaluation criteria, the more effective the decision-making process will be from an ethical perspective.

At the heart of every decision, and thus of every action resulting from a decision, are ground rules expressing what we value and what we will do to get what we value. "To find your ground rules squeeze the factual assumptions out of your decisions; the ground rules are the residue that drives the decision." The ground rules for the individual are to be found in the value-system and frame of reference of the individual, the code of ethics of the organisation, and the culture of the organisation.

References

Daft, R.: 1986, *Organizational Theory and Design*, St. Paul, Minnesota: West.

Harrison, : 1975, *The Managerial Decision-Making Process*, Boston: Houghton Mifflin.

Helbrigel, D. and F. Slocum: 1974, *Management: A Contingency Approach*. Addison Wesley, 1974.

Issack, T.: 1978, "Intuition: An Ignored Dimension of Management", *Academy of Management Review*.

Lyles, M.A. and I.I. Mitroff: 1980, "Organizational Problem Formulation: An Empirical Study", *Administrative Science Quarterly*, 25, 102-119.

Nutt, P.C.: 1984, "Types of Organizational Decision Processes", *Administrative Science Quarterly*, 29, 414-450.

Pastin, M.: 1986, *The Hard Problems of Management: Gaining the Ethics Edge* , San Francisco: Jossey Bass.

Peters, J.: 1978, "Symbols, Patterns and Setting: An Optimistic Case for Getting Things Done", *Organizational Dynamics*.

Pfeffer, J.: 1981, "Management as Symbolic Action. The Creation and Maintenance of Organizational Paradigms", in L. Cummings and B. Straw (eds.), *Research in Organizational Behaviour*, Greenwick: Jai Press.

Schein, E.: 1984 , "Coming to a New Awareness of Organizational Culture", *Sloan Management Review*, 25, 2, 3-16.

Smircich, L.: 1983, "Concepts of Culture and Organizational Analysis", *Adminstrative Science Quarterly*, 28, 339-358.

Trevino, L.K.: 1986, "Ethical Decision-Making in Organizations: A Person-Situation Interactionist Model", *Academy of Management Review*, 11, 3, 601-617.

VALUES AND TYPES OF ENTREPRENEURS IN SMALL BUSINESS

Erwin Fröhlich

1. Introduction

To avoid the confusion that might be generated by the existence of a variety of levels of values, objectives and facts (see Falise, 1985), the following differentiations and definitions might be helpful:

Level 1: *What should be:* sphere of values, ideals, perfection (abstract, hardly or not be reached)
Level 2: *What is:* sphere of reality, imperfect actual world
Level 3: *What can be:* sphere of objectives, politics (concrete, to be reached by education, codes of ethics, etc.)
Level 4: *What may be:* decline of morale, increasing scandals

This contribution mainly refers to an empirical investigation, i.e. to level 2, carried out by a research group working on a broader project on "Strategic Orientation of Small and Medium Sized Enterprises (STRATOS)".[1]

The research design of this STRATOS project shows the main research questions, which are close to the key-topics of all EBEN conferences: How do the values of entrepreneurs affect performance and success ?

The data on which this project was based include approximately 500 answers of about 1.100 personally interviewed entrepreneurs. These are allotted as equally as possible by means of appropriate stratified samples over eight European countries (A, B, CH, D, F, GB, NL, SF), divided into five size classes (1-9, 10-19, 20-49, 50-99, 100-499 employees) and three sectors (food - for stable market conditions in Europe; electronics - for growing markets; and clothing - for declining markets).

Finally some remarks concerning the underlying theoretical concepts of entrepreneurial values and attitudes: Although in conducting empirical social investigations every researcher will try to find usable well formulated research hypotheses, questions or statements (those which have been tested and proved in former studies) we also put

---

[1] This group consists of I. Bamberger, R. Donckels, E. Fröhlich, E. Gabele, A. Haahti, K. Haake, C. Koning, A. Lehtimaki, J.H. Pichler, H. Pleitner, J. Van der Wilde and A. Weir. One of the more comprehensive publications on the respective project results (in German) is Fröhlich and Pichler (1988).

208

Frame of reference:

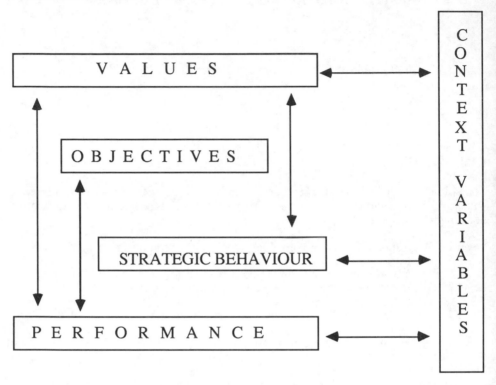

some effort into elaborating a kind of "table of entrepreneurial values", to check if the spectrum of such values is covered comprehensively and that no major gaps were visible. For that purpose we followed an approach of the Austrian philosopher Othmar Spann (1968, 222), designing a matrix with one entrance (horizontal) for his holistic economic theory, bringing in such relevant approaches as stages or levels of economy, priorities among functions or stakeholders, and so on; and a second (vertical) for his concept of applied ethics, with its key-terms: "Order of reperfection"; "imperfect initiate state"; "virtues"; "state of achieved perfection"; etc.

Although this is basically a social-philosophic economic approach, the final foundations of virtues or values - as in most of the moral and philosophic investigations of Christian thinkers in the last twenty centuries - tie into theology.

The last introductory remark is on the small business entrepreneur. STRATOS broadly defines the "small business entrepreneur"[1] as the owner and/or owner-manager of a firm with less than 500 employees.

Entrepreneurs' values are considered to be inherent and fundamental features of their personality. Accordingly, in the context of the project, an attempt has been made to design a value-based typology of the small business entrepreneur by principal characteristics as will be shown in this paper.

2. Delineating entrepreneurial values

In the STRATOS context values are considered guiding principles for the formulation of business objectives and strategies.

The empirical approach to identifying entrepreneurial values consisted, first, in searching for appropriate "value indicators" (based on 85 agreed normative statements) and, second, in measuring agreement or disagreement with these statements using a five-point Likert-scale.

Consequently, specific reference groups or so-called "stakeholders" were identified as being affected by various "value-strata" defined as follows[2]:

"Stakeholders" or reference group	Value strata
The entrepreneur himself/ herself	Entrepreneurial self-awareness and his/her family
Labour force, personnel	Entrepreneur-employee relationship
Manager and supervisor	Principles of organisation
Innovators, researchers	Attitude towards change
Financiers, creditors, suppliers, customers, competitors	Strategic postures
State, society	Entrepreneur and socio-economic environment

Based on the above, the results of comparisons among industries and among size categories can be summarised as follows:

---

[1] Central European usage of the term "Gewerbe" relates to that segment of small business which, by its very nature, is typically personalised and service-oriented; in the STRATOS context, however, "small business" is understood in its broader, more comprehensive meaning as part of industry generally (including "Gewerbe"). This has implications both for the very definition of entrepreneurship and, hence, for the structuring of entrepreneurial values within functionally different settings.

[2] Gabele et al. (1977a); cf. Gabele (1984), 243 ff., and Gabele (1981), 8 ff.; also Gabele and Öchsler (1982), 21 ff., Gabele at al. (1987).

1. The hypothesis is not supported, that entrepreneurial attitudes and behaviour are largely determined by systems-related preconditions or by the market as such.
2. When compared with the more impersonal and systematic patterns of larger enterprises, the variety of results reveals a wide range of entrepreneurial decisions, corresponding to a much broader spectrum of values that is typical for the small business entrepreneur in particular.
3. In depicting specific "value profiles", both similar and dissimilar values emerge, reflecting behavioural attitudes typical for small business in general. Looking at the similar profiles for different industries and size categories, the hypothesis seems to be supported, that differences are relatively small. More pronounced differences resulting from comparisons among countries may be interpreted as reflecting systems-related and cultural characteristics.[1]
4. Most of the descriptive statistics - not only by size and sector of industry, but also by the formal position of entrepreneurs - showed surprisingly small deviations in values and attitudes.

Subsequent statistical analysis led to a "typology" of entrepreneurs, as described in the following.

3. Value-based "types" of entrepreneurs

3.1 Empirical aspects and evidence

Traditional and, in part, well-known typologies of entrepreneurs (dating back to Bacon, Cantillon, etc.) are frequently related to history or sectors of industry: "pre-capitalistic entrepreneurs", "bankers", "traders", etc. More recent approaches (Miles, Snow and others) are primarily associated with strategies: "defenders", "prospectors" and the like. In contrast to these, the typology in the STRATOS-project is strictly based on the 85 value indicators mentioned.

In line with more recent findings of both psychology and physiology of the brain (Ornstein), as well as more comprehensive wholistic approaches (Spann, Heinrich), one could start out with two very basic human dispositions: more intuitive, and more analytical.

As a first step, correlation analysis[2] resulted in a classification of four groups of values which at that stage, however, could not readily be associated with identifiable "types" of entrepreneurs either by countries or by size or class or sectors of industry.

Using cluster-analysis[3] hypotheses were tested in a second step by "tearing down" overall sample results from ten to four value-based clusters of types of entrepreneurs as a typology[4] proving to be least ambiguous and well substantiated by the empirical data which support the following findings :

1. The identification of four "types" of entrepreneurs to be classified by distinct "values

---

[1] Cf. Institut für Gewerbeforschung (1986); also Fröhlich and Pichler (1988).

[2] Spearman correlation coefficients of the value indicators produced more plausible results than factor of component analyses for the types of entrepreneurial behaviour referred to.

[3] Based on SAS, FASTCLUS: additional advice on relevant statistical methods and testing provided by P. Hackl, University of Economics, and by J. Millendorfer, Studia, both Vienna.

[4] (footnote 4 in page 211)

and attitudes" and reflecting the following distribution (per cent of the whole sample):

the most frequent type: cluster 4 - 33%
cluster 1 - 28%
cluster 3 - 24%
the least frequent type: cluster 2 - 15%

2.   Types of entrepreneurs classified by value indicators show greater differences than if classified by sector of industry, size of firm or any other characteristic. Distinctions among them have to be explained before attributing differences in value patterns to the types of entrepreneurs as a basis for analysing their weaknesses, strengths and potentials.

3.2 Theoretical aspects

In assuming that the very basis of an individual's specific or "typical" characteristics lies in the sphere of intellectual attitudes (as, e.g., more intuitive or more analytical), two kinds of "prototypes" emerged. With respect to entrepreneurial attitudes and behaviour, this could be translated into a basic distinction between the more *"dynamic-creative"* or the more *"administrative-executive"* type of entrepreneur.

As a result, four typical behavioural patterns could be arrived at by associating each of these basic features with strong or weak characteristics and their respective combinations:

Dynamic-creative	Administrative-executive	"Type"	
strong (+)	strong (+)	"Allrounder"	A (28%)
strong (+)	weak (-)	"Pioneer"	P (33%)
weak (-)	strong (+)	"Organiser"	O (24%)
weak (-)	weak (-)	"Routineer"	R (15%)

Type "A" (two strengths) can be described as the versatile, universally responsive and adaptive entrepreneur - an "allrounder"; a kind of Sombart's industrial Mr. Microcosm, acting, for example, as his or her own designer, accountant, salesman and foreman. Frequently, however, such versatility entails also mediocrity in all those activities. This might explain, why this type seemed to have just the second-best chances for survival.

(footnote 4 page 210 cont.)

SAS, FASTCLUS procedure
cluster summary

cluster number	frequency	rms std dev	max distance seed to obs.	nearest cluster	centroid distance
1	312	0.932463	14.4374	4	3.65105
2	175	1.01245	15.5964	1	4.36576
3	273	1.00883	15.8974	1	4.26821
4	371	0.964737	14.5796	1	3.65105

Type "P" is dynamic-creative, suggesting someone like Schumpeter's "innovator", a "pioneer" being generally little averse to risk.

Type "O" is largely administratively oriented - the "executive" entrepreneur - applying his or her rational, analytical and organising strengths with empathy; the typical "organiser".

Finally, the least spectacular type "R" - if a risk-taker at all - generally represents the cautious entrepreneur - the classical "routineer". By criteria of success or "survival", he or she is expected to be the one with diminished chances in the long run - something that is, in fact, supported by the analysis.

For illustration, an analogy can be drawn with the traditional distinction of four types of human temperament. The "allrounder" corresponds to the "choleric", the "pioneer" to the "sanguine", the "organiser" to the "melancholic" and the "routineer" to the "phlegmatic" type (the last again being the one with lesser chances of survival, especially in a competitive business environment).

4. Structural characteristics of value-based "types" of entrepreneurs

4.1 Age and sex

When characterised by age or sex, the theory that the "pioneer" is associated with youth, seems to be supported by the empirical data, as he or she is represented in the age-group up to 45 above average, but below average in the group 46 and older (deviation in each case between 2 and 5%).

Perhaps not surprisingly, the "organiser" is overrepresented in the age-group 46 and older.

Interestingly, women entrepreneurs are strongly represented in "allrounders" and "routineers", but least in "pioneers".

4.2 Professional background and income

Attempts to correlate professional background, income and type of entrepreneurs produced results which by and large might have been expected: the "pioneer", for example, does not have a distinctly higher income than the other types. This presumably reflects a greater exposure to risk with a corresponding higher rate of failure. If anything, higher incomes tend to be associated with more and longer training, higher skill levels and business experience in general. Professional know-how and adequate education obviously are not readily compensated with on-the-job-training or merely traditional "experience" (as might be the case, e.g., with the typical "routineer").

4.3 The role of the entrepreneur in business creation, in re-organisation and succession

Among self-employed entrepreneurs or entrepreneur-managers particularly the "pioneer" seems least likely to have his or her own capital at risk, but - rather typical perhaps in his or her role as a moderniser or innovator - tends to rely more on outside funding by third parties.

With regard to the crucial problem of succession and carrying on with the business - especially in the case of family enterprises - the following aspects are characteristic:

1. Wherever succession within the family is assured, the management styles of the typical "organiser" are predominately that of the "allrounder" and "routineer"; the dynamic-creative "pioneer" seems to be atypical.
2. Classical family ownership, with the owner's own capital as the basis of capitalisation, is quite evidently not the form most conducive to risk-prone activities of innovation and modernisation.
3. A high degree of uncertainty seems to be associated with business succession (remaining an unsettled issue for 56% of the entrepreneurs interviewed); partly this reflects inadequate strategic foresight and planning, partly also a generally less developed forward-looking attitude associated with a lack of self-awareness and a certain degree of insecurity or even pessimism.

On the whole, however, over 80% of those interviewed appeared to have a fairly clear idea of who is to take over "if they had an accident tomorrow" - in other words, in case of an emergency; typically, therefore, long-term strategy is lacking. (In taking the sample as a whole, covering all "types" of entrepreneurs, only about half of the career opportunities offered by succession are reserved or meant for members of the family; succession to higher managerial positions figures most strongly in pioneering type enterprises.)

4.4 Environmental conditions: the socio-economic framework

One of the central aspects is the question of whether, or to what extent, small business entrepreneurs are generally conditioned by common value concepts in the context of, for example, business objectives, strategies and criteria of success as altogether superseding national, regional or cultural boundaries.

While the overriding importance of national, cultural or systems-related and socio-economic influences is hardly to be denied, the empirical findings tend to underline that behaviour-based "type-forming" characteristics clearly outrank these aspects.

4.5 Dynamic aspects by industry

Identified "types" of entrepreneurs are represented at all stages of a firm's life-cycle in the three sectors of industry investigated. Yet, in a typical growth industry such as, *e.g.* electronics, the "pioneer" is to be found more frequently than the "organiser" or the "routineer". Thus, relative representation of entrepreneurial types reflects an interrelation between growth and/or stability orientation in the different sectors: the "routineer" and the "organiser" being indicative of stability, the "pioneer" more of dynamic change and growth.

4.6 Size of business and pattern of demand

Results of relating size categories to types of entrepreneurs tend to support both Sombart's well-known concept of the industrial Mr. Microcosmos as exemplified by the small business entrepreneur in particular (the typical "allrounder") and Schumpeter's concept of the "moderniser" or creative "innovator" (the "pioneer"). While representation of the latter appears to be generally more closely associated with growth and size, both the "organiser" and the "routineer" are fairly evenly distributed throughout the various size categories.

A common assumption concerning "small business" is that one of its particular characteristics is catering to personalised and differentiated demand. It is not surprising, therefore, that the "pioneer" and "allrounder" seem to correspond best to a conception of business as requiring a high degree of adaptability and flexibility, while the "organiser" typically tends to be more traditionally product-oriented and less responsive to differentiated customer needs.

4.7 Aspects of competitive behaviour

When discussing "competition", particularly in regard to small business, it is usually price competition which is referred to. In the context of this project, an attempt has been made to probe more deeply into potential relations between value-based "types" of entrepreneurs and their respective attitude to, and intensity of, competitive behaviour. By comparison, the "organiser" and "routineer" seem to be relatively better conditioned for coping with "strong" competitive pressure, especially if it is to be countered by economising and/or rationalising existing cost structures, while avoiding riskier and more creative or innovative responses, which are more typical of the "pioneer" and the "allrounder".

As regards ethical implications, the analysis reveals that rising competitive pressure tends to reinforce disagreement with the statement: "A manager should consider ethical principles in his or her behaviour".

4.8 Government interference

Government intervention and bureaucratic interference in the context of a competitive economic system and business environment is generally assumed to be detrimental to the innovative drive and motivation, characteristic of entrepreneurial behaviour. The typical small business entrepreneur, as being especially exposed to competition, may therefore be affected most. This is particularly the case for the "allrounder" and the "pioneer", as will be shown, while the "organiser" proves to be more adaptive in coping with interventionistic tendencies and the "routineer" even might welcome them.

Among the eight countries included in the analysis, Austria ranks highest in regard to government influence, regulative interference and "business guidance"; it is therefore not too surprising, that here the "organiser" is more commonly represented than other types.

5. Entrepreneurial "types" and success criteria

5.1 Objective performance criteria

In respect of indicators such as cash-flow, profit or sales as criteria for "success", the "routineer" - again perhaps not suprising - clearly ranks behind the other types. Cash-flow as a percentage of turnover in "routineer"-firms only reaches about a third to a half as compared to "pioneer"-, "allrounder"- or "organiser"-firms. (65% of those identified as "routineers" have an inadequate cash-flow of less than 2% of turnover, while the proportion of "allrounders" and "pioneers" with a comparably low figure is 27% and 28%, respectively.)

In translating this into criteria of overall performance, the "allrounder" on the whole emerges as the top-ranking "successful" type, followed by the "pioneer", the "organiser" (taking a kind of "middle" position) and finally the "routineer". This corresponds to the frequency distribution of entrepreneurial types based on the overall empirical sample and, thus, can also be taken as an indicator for evaluating longer term perspectives of eventual business survival.

The "allrounder", being top by criteria of success, is supported by his or her very characteristics of being most versatile and having strong dynamic-creative as well as administrative-executive talents. By comparison, the "pioneer" is more one-sided in respect of both.

5.2 Subjective criteria of performance

In terms of subjective success criteria, as perceived by individual respondents, the "organiser" shows a generally high level of satisfaction, especially in the achievement of family-based entrepreneurial goals, on which great importance is being laid.

In contrast and quite typically for, particularly, the "organiser", satisfaction in the achievement of family-based objectives ranks lower with the "pioneer" and the "allrounder" (clearly ranking below, for instance, in such aspects as achievement of an attractive life-style or high income).

Therefore not surprisingly, the less successful "pioneer", in relation to his or her ambitions, shows the lowest levels of satisfaction (below those of the moderately successful "routineer"). In particular, this applies to the objectives of productivity, goodwill and the image of firm, competitiveness and product quality, economic and financial independence, and, finally, to the achievement of creative or innovative aspirations (rated as being "very important" by more than 50% of "pioneers" as compared to only about 30% of other types).

Furthermore, the typical "pioneer" lags behind in organisational achievements, such as overall rationalisation measures, cost reduction or concentration on market-shares. Here the "organiser" typically shows the best results.

6. Values and attitudes of successful entrepreneurs:
A complementary approach of relating values to "types" of entrepreneurs

In relating given "value indicators" to, e.g. "corrected cash-flow" (i.e., taking into account the opportunity cost of self-employed managers) as a typical criterion for small enterprises, the following conclusions can be drawn (related again to the "value-strata" as initially defined):

6.1 Entrepreneurial self-awareness

Moral or ethical considerations do not constitute an impediment to successful entrepreneurship and management. On the contrary, they prove to be a catalyst for business success and performance.

This is supported by the results arrived at by cross-tabulating the possible (five) answers to the value indicator "A manager should consider ethical principles (e.g., related to his or her religion) in his or her behaviour" with assumed (three) ranges or levels of cash-flow: The following table shows the percentage of respondents within a given range of cash-flow agreeing or disagreeing with the above statement.

Percentage spread across ranges of cash-flow[1]

	cash-flow as per centage turnover			
	< 2%	2-5%	> 5%	n
strongly disagree	43.59	17.95	38.46	39
disagree	47.86	17.95	34.19	117
no opinion	34.26	22.22	43.52	108
agree	32.61	23.74	43.65	417
strongly agree	36.36	25.25	38.38	99

6.2 Employee relationships

Successful entrepreneurs (as measured by the criterion "cash-flow" mentioned) do not necessarily pay higher salaries, but rather support the principle of equal pay for equal work.

This is derived from the following two value indicators: "Firms should adopt a high wage policy", and "A firm should start from the principle of equal pay for equal work even when this raises costs". Both successful and less successful entrepreneurs disagreed more or less equally (about 45 per cent) with a high wage policy; however, 57 per cent of the successful entrepreneurs agreed to the concept of equal pay for equal work - as against 47 per cent of the unsuccessful ones.

Successful entrepreneurs tend to enhance employee participation in decision-making. This is based on the value indicator: "Those who carry out day-to-day decisions should have a hand in making them", and on corresponding questions with respect to "Management of Human Resources", especially in regard to workers' rights, employee information, consultation and participation in decision-making. 66 per cent of the least successful entrepreneurs tend to inform, or consult with, their workers over and above what is legally required, while 85 per cent of the most successful ones do so.

6.3 Principles of organisation

Successful entrepreneurs, on the whole, are aware of the importance of organisational principles and tend to support hierarchical structures.

The respective value indicator: "Even at the risk of the management being considered unco-operative by the staff, clear hierarchical relationships should be established" was responded to positively by the majority of "profit-making" entrepreneurs (48 per cent as against 42 per cent of "losers"); a further 22 per cent of the "losers" (as against 18 per centof "profit makers") were "undecided" or "without opinion".

---

[1] Corrections have been made by calculating opportunity cost for owner-managers if they were not on the payroll of the firm.

6.4 Attitude towards change

Successful entrepreneurs aim at properly balancing established and proven business principles against more progressively oriented innovations thought to be conducive to overall business conduct.

Among the value indicators (nine) aimed at measuring "willingness to change", the statement "Innovation involves too much risk", in particular, produced notable differences by ranges of cash-flow as referred to: 74 per cent of successful entrepreneurs "disagreed" as compared with only 60 per cent of the "losers"; it is, however, revealing also that successful entrepreneurs are quite risk-conscious when it comes to innovations - something that clearly imposes limits on willingness to change.

6.5 Strategic posture

Entrepreneurs catering to differentiated customer needs are more or less equally successful, though generally less exposed to risk than firms with more standardised products or product lines.

Specific variables analysed in this particular context related to questions on overall demand patterns as for instance: Were customer needs "very differentiated", "very much the same" (standardised) or "mixed"? When cross-tabulated again by levels of cash-flow as defined, entrepreneurs catering to very differentiated needs proved more frequently successful (47 per cent) than unsuccessful (28 per cent); with regard to remaining patterns, successful and unsuccessful cases were equally distributed.

Successful entrepreneurs, furthermore, are generally quite aware of their own strengths as well as weaknesses, thereby limiting risks and potential business failures.

This results from a combination of interrelated variables as follows: the identified (four) "types" of entrepreneurs; Ansoff's (four) product-market strategies; and levels of business success as measured by (three) ranges of cash-flow ratios referred to above.

Respective cross tabulation reveals correlations, at the higher cash-flow end, between "diversification strategy" (new products/new markets) and "pioneers" and, at the lower end, between "market penetration strategy" (old products/old markets) and "routineers".

In stressing "co-operation" as business strategy, successful entrepreneurs outranked less successful ones by favouring the statement: "Professional bodies and similar organisations should only provide assistance to their members" (78 by 72 per cent respectively), while less frequently supporting the view: "Professional bodies and similar organisations should work as pressure groups to defend the common interest of their members" (54 to 66 per cent).

6.6 The socio-economic environment

By comparison, successful entrepreneurs seem to be less inclined purposely to evade - or outright neglect - legal provisions and other formal obligations.

The respective value indicator in this case "One should not blame firms if they get around the law sometimes" was disagreed with by successful entrepreneurs more frequently (41 per cent) than by the less successful (33 per cent).

Based on these findings, one may conclude that pursuit of value concepts, as more specifically reflected in the context of small business "entrepreneurial culture", proves to be linked with economic success and performance, with business survival or failure. Entrepreneurial values are thus indeed being translated into concrete business objectives and strategies; in the case of the small business entrepreneur in a seemingly more direct way than otherwise.

7. Summary

Unlike conceptualisations of "prototypes" of entrepreneurs to be found elsewhere, the "typology" presented here is based entirely on values and attitudes as defined and analysed by way of 85 specified "value indicators" within the framework of the STRATOS-project.

In starting out from two basically defined entrepreneurial dispositions: more intuitive or dynamic-creative, and more analytical or administrative-executive and associating these with both "strong" and "weak" characteristics, four principal entrepreneurial "types" were derived: the "allrounder", the "pioneer", the "organiser" and the "routineer".

In terms of objective performance criteria (as measured by ranges or levels of cash-flow ratios) the "allrounder" emerges as altogether the most successful type, followed by the "pioneer" and the "organiser"; the "routineer" finally being the least successful one.

As to subjective success factors, achievement of family-related entrepreneurial goals ranks highest in the case of the "organiser", while for the "pioneer" and the "allrounder" income, an attractive life-style and similar attributes take precedence.

In relating given success criteria to specific strategies (Ansoff), their respective predominance again tends to correspond with the entrepreneurial types as identified. Thus, the "pioneer" and the "allrounder" more distinctly relate to innovative strategies such as diversification and market promotion, while the "routineer", by contrast, does relatively best in market penetration and the "organiser" in product development.

Response to differing systems-related and overall environmental conditions is also reflected in "types" of entrepreneurial behaviour: thereby both the innovative "pioneer" and the versatile "allrounder" turn out to be more willing and able to cope with changing environmental conditions.

Finally, value-based dispositions on the whole, and moral or ethical considerations more specifically, as can be demonstrated, are not hampering but rather fostering entrepreneurial success and performance which constitute an inherent element of "entrepreneurial culture" in the context of small business generally.

References

Falise, M.S.: 1985, "Opening Speech", Symposium on Church and Economy, Rome, November.

Fröhlich, E. and H.J. Pichler: 1988, *Werte und Typen mittelständischer Unternehmer*, Institut für Gewerbeforschung, Berlin.

Gabele, E.: 1981, "Erfolgsfaktoren in kleinen und mittleren Unternehmen. Ein vergleichende europäische Studie", *Forschungsbericht*, Bamberg.

Gabele, E.: 1984, "Die Messung von Werten in Unternehmen. Ein empirischer Versuch", in H. Klages, and P. Kmieciak (eds.), *Wertwandel und gesellschaftlicher Wandel*, Third edition, Frankfurt and New York.

Gabele, E., W. Kirsch and J. Treffert: 1977a, *Werte von Führungskräften der deutschen Wirtschaft. Eine empirische Analyse*, Munich.

Gabele, E., P. Kupsch, and W.A. Öchsler: 1987, *Führung mittelständischer Unternehmen*, Bamberg.

Gabele, E., and W.A. Öchsler: 1982, *Führungsgrundsätze und Führungsmodelle*. Bamberg.

Institut für Gewerbeforschung (Ifg): 1986, *Werthaltung und Strategien in Klein- und Mittelbetrieben, STRATOS-Report*, Vienna.

Spann, O.: 1968, *Gesellschaftsphilosophie*, vol. 11 of O. Spann, *Gesamtausgabe*, Second edition.

EXECUTIVE DECISIONS AND VALUES[1]

John H. Barnett and Marvin J. Karson

Introduction

Research in values and business decisions has necessarily encompassed a breadth of variables. A survey of both current and seminal research literature suggests that factors such as gender, age, organisational level, and role influence decisions involving relationships, methods and results, and ethics.

Gender and relationships

Observers suggest that women are more concerned with relationships than men. Communion, the view of oneself in relation to others, has been defined as a feminine trait, as opposed to the masculine trait of agency, seeing oneself as an individual (Bakan, 1966). Due to the different socialisation pressures on boys and girls (Barry *et al.*, 1957; Bardwick, 1971; Bem and Bem, 1971; Maccoby and Jacklin, 1974), it seems that feminine personality comes to define itself in terms of communion with other people more than masculine personality does (Chodorow, 1974). The conclusion that women see relationships as more significant in their lives than men do is supported by several other studies (Erikson, 1968; Carlson, 1971; Miller, 1976; Kanter, 1977, 1987; Hodgson and Watson, 1987).

In interviews, it was found that women tended to define their identities in terms of the relationships they were involved in and the resposibilities they had to other people (Gilligan, 1982). Men, on the other hand, described themselves with characteristics such as "intelligent" and "logical," and did not mention relationships as integral parts of their personalities.

Even the moral orientation of women is more toward relationships. Women act on a level where "Good behavior is that which pleases or helps others and is approved by them" (Kohlberg and Kramer, 1969). Men, however, come to accept moral rules and principles as separate from the relationships in which they are involved.

---

[1] The authors wish to gratefully acknowledge the assistance of Laura S. Sweeney and Blue Cross-Blue Shield of New Hampshire in this research project.

This research investigates whether gender has an impact on relationships decisions made in a business environment. Specifically, response to relationship scenarios is examined by the gender of the respondent. The first null hypothesis being tested is:

Hypothesis 1: There is no difference between men and women on decisions involving relationships.

Gender and methods versus results

Research suggest that women are primarily concerned with the method used to accomplish a task, while men are more interested in the result of a task. This difference results from socialisation pressures. Women have been socialised to take part in the personal development of others. This is done by focusing on the methods that will help others in their development. Men, on the other hand, "...have been socialised to value having an impact, to express primarily task-oriented or instrumental behavior" (Sargent, 1981).

This difference in orientation can be seen in the way men and women develop a strategy for career advancement. Women concentrate on the planning aspect, finding the best possible method for achieving a career goal. In contrast, men tend to look at the final gain of a strategy, focussing on the bottom-line results (Henning and Jardim, 1977).

Group problem-solving studies also suggest this gender difference in approaches to tasks. Wood *et al.* (1985) found that women performed better than men on tasks involving a discussion method and consensus, while men performed better than women on a problem requiring a number of solutions. Other studies support the suggestion that women are more methods-oriented, while men are more concerned with the results of a task (Rotter and Portugal, 1969; Baird, 1976).

This study tests whether gender affects a decision involving a methods versus results option. Response to a scenario is used to test a second null hypothesis:

Hypothesis 2: There is no difference between men and women on decisions involving a methods/results issue.

Ethics and age

The literature suggests that age is a factor in determining values, as younger managers tend to assign less importance to trust and honour, and more importance to money and advancement, than older executives (England, 1978). Senior managers are interested in personal growth and an enjoyable work experience, unlike younger managers concerned primarily with achievement (Johnson *et al.* 1986). Response to ethical decision scenarios is analysed by career stage of the respondent, as career stage is used as a surrogate for age. The third null hypothesis being tested is:

Hypothesis 3: Career stage has no effect on decisions involving business ethics.

Ethics and level

Organisational level affects the personal values of managers. Johnson *et al.* (1986) found that top-management executives include integrity as an important quality for successful job performance, while entry-level managers are not as concerned with this factor. Managers are influenced by the behaviour of superiors (Baumhart, 1961; Brenner and Molander, 1977). Goals set by superiors may be difficult for managers at the lower end of the hierarchy to achieve, and may cause these subordinates to feel pressure to compromise personal values in order to achieve and may cause these subordinates to feel pressure to compromise personal values in order to achieve company standards (Carroll, 1975, 1978; Posner and Schmidt, 1984). This research assesses the effect level has on ethical decisions. Response to ethical decision scenarios is used to test a fourth null hypothesis:

Hypothesis 4: Organisational level has no effect on decisions involving business ethics.

Ethics and role

Role in an organisation also has some effect on ethical decision-making. Toffler (1986) sees the concepts of role and responsibility as having critical effects on a manager's ability to act in an ethical dilemma. Participants in this study described their role in the company as either quantitative, qualitative, executive and/or administrative. Response to ethical decision scenarios is used to test a fifth null hypothesis:

Hypothesis 5: Role has no effect on decisions involving business ethics.

Ethics and gender

Gender was analysed as a factor in business ethics in a study which found that women acted less ethically in a situation where guilt would not be discovered than they acted in more public situations (Barnett and Karson, 1987). This study analyses the effect gender has on ethical decisions, and response to ethical decision scenarios is used to test a sixth null hypothesis:

Hypothesis 6: Gender has no effect on decisions involving business ethics.

Research design

This research project asked participants to rank their own personal values by indicating a level of interest in both methods versus results and in ethical versus economic matters. Further, this research studied participants' occupational role, stage of their career, organisational level, and gender, as well as collecting data on sex role (Bem,1977).

Finally, a series of business decision scenarios required participants to make either-or decisions in ten vignettes. The reseach classified responses to these vignettes as ethical or economic, relational or non-relational, or methods or results.

The Promotion

The first vignette dealt with the importance of relationships. It stated:

You are the head of the sales department of a small computer firm. Your sales co-ordinator has recently retired, and needs to be replaced. The most qualified candidate is X, and you are confident that X would do an excellent job. Promoting X, however, means removing X from the sales team X has worked with for twelve years. The team has been co-operative and friendly over the years. X is both the peacemaker and the motivator of the team, but you feel that X would do a good job in the new position. You would:

_____ A. Promote X
_____ B. Not promote X

Promoting X was determined to be the non-relational act, versus the relational act of preserving a consensus.

The Child Employee

The third vignette also involved relationship values. This scenario stated:

You are self-employed, and some close friends of yours have asked that you hire their child to work for you as an office assistant for the summer. You do so, and give the child a variety of tasks to do. You soon find, however, that the child is not particularly motivated, and has a tendency to make mistakes on even the most simple tasks. You would like to let the child go, but you know that this would cause problems between you and your friends, who see their child as quite talented and ambitious. You would:

_____ A. Let the child go
_____ B. Keep the child for the summer

Keeping the child was deemd the relational act, versus dismissing the child.

The Team

The tenth vignette presented a methods versus results choice. It asked:

You are the coach of a Little League baseball team for children ages 9 to 15. Your team is doing exceptionally well this year, and is currently in first place. It is the eighth inning of a close game between your team and another good team, and some of your less skilled players have not yet been put in the game. There is no league rule that says every player must play every game, but you know that each of these children wants to play . This is an important game that your team wants to win. You would:

_____ A. Put the less skilled players in the game
_____ B. Not put the less skilled players in the game

Putting the less skilled players in the game was determined to be the methods decision, versus the results decision of not using less skilled players.

Seven other vignettes measured ethical versus economic action.

The Marketing Plan

The second vignette presented this scenario:

> You are a newly-appointed marketing director attending a trade association meeting. The marketing director of your chief competitor is carrying a stack of copies of the competitor's marketing plan for next year. After the competitor has gone you discover that he has dropped one of the copies. Would you:
>
> _____ A. Contact your competitor and return the plan unread
> _____ B. Read the plan

Returning the plan unread was determined to the ethical action, while reading the plan was economic.

The Personal Injury Case

The fourth vignette stated:

> You are the new director and major shareholder of a large corporation. The corporation is currently being sued by a customer claiming the customer has received a personal injury. While going through your predecessor's personal files, which only you will see, you find some information supporting the customer's personal injury claim. There is a large sum of money at stake, and you are presently in good shape to win the case. Would you:
>
> _____ A. Reveal the information
> _____ B. Not reveal the information

Revealing the information was determined to be the ethical action, versus the economic action of not revealing information in the file.

The Expense Refund

The fifth vignette asked:

> While on a business trip prepaid by your company you are snowed in at the Boston Airport. The airport provides you a bus ride to Portland, Maine for $25, returning to you the $100 plane fare. The delay means you reach home several hours later than expected. Would you:
>
> _____ A. Include the $75 refund on your expense report
> _____ B. Not include the $75 refund on your expense report

The ethical action was to include the refund, while not including the refund was an economic act.

The Buyout

The buyout scenario stated:

> Two firms, an investment banking group and a large firm highly experienced in the machine tool industry, are in a fight to acquire a small high-tech machine tool firm that is in grave financial trouble. The large machine tool corporation has offered 2% more money to the shareholders of the small corporation. Also, if the investment banking firm acquires the small unit, it will be only for resale again in the near future, or whenever the time and the price for resale is right. Thus, the investment banking group, who has no expertise in the running of the machine toll industry, will not replace senior management. Many senior managers are your good friends. The other large machine tool firm, however, is likely to improve operations and cut down costs, including pruning down top personnel by 25% to 75%. As the president would you approve the takeover by:
>
> _____ A. The investment banking group
> _____ B. The large machine tool company

Protecting your job and your friends' jobs by selling to investment bankers was determined as the economic action; getting the highest value for shareholders was the ethical act.

The Overheard Telephone Message

The seventh vignette presented the following scenario:

> As you leave your office for an extremely important sales meeting with a major potential new customer, you overhear the swichboard operator saying, "If X call in, please see that X calls home, as X's spouse says there is a mini-crisis." You are to meet with X at the customer's office, and the two of you are to make the sales presentation. X's participation is critical. X is quite nervous and often gives a bad impression if distracted. Would you:
>
> _____ A. Relay the information to X before the sales meeting
> _____ B. Not relay the information to X before the sales meeting

Relaying the message was the ethical action, while the economic act was not relaying X's message.

The Photocopier

The eigth vignette asked:

You have recently resigned from your position as a sales consultant for a photocopier firm, and you will be leaving in several weeks. A customer is interested in purchasing a used copy machine, and you have a recent model which the customer feels would meet company needs. You stand to make a good commission on the deal. However, you know that the customer could purchase a brand new copier from your firm for the
same amount of money during a special rebate period. The commission on the new product, however, is substantially less than on the used machine. You would:

_____ A. Inform the customer about the special rebate
_____ B. Not inform the customer about the special rebate

Not informing the customer was deemed the economic act, versus the ethical action of telling the customer about the special rebate.

The Dock

The ninth vignette stated:

You are a real estate broker in the Lakes region. Times have been tough during the recession, but you now have a prospect for a shorefront home that will pay you $10,000 in commissions. The property has no boat dock. You overheard the buyers discuss where they would have a new dock built. They have not addresed the problem with you at all, but you know it is important to them. You also know that on this particular lake it is almost impossible to get approval for a new dock from the state licensing authority. No new permits have been allowed for two years. Would you discuss the dock problem with your clients?

_____ A. Yes
_____ B. No

Revealing the dock problem was determined to be the ethical action, while not discussing the problem was the economic act.

Methodology

A New Hampshire insurance company co-operated in this research by distributing a confidential questionnaire to its 1,100 salaried employees. The questionnaire included the ten vignettes, the Bem Sex Role Inventory (Bem, 1977) and questions as to organisation level, career stage, role, gender, and the level of interest (1 to 7 scale) in ethics, economics, methods and results.

The returned questionnaire resulted in a sample of $N = 513$ respondents. The sample, of course, is not a random sample from a well-framed population, and thus in this sense the research is exploratory, with statistical results being descriptive of the sample for this company and not necessarily inferential. The research uses methodologies that could produce inferential results under a random sampling procedure, and that here help develop models that may be subjected to further empirical data research.

Ethical versus economic actions were predetermined for five of the scenarios replicated from an earlier study (Barnett and Karson, 1987), while the ethical versus economic, relational versus non-relational, and methods versus results actions were determined by the unanimous consensus of the business, business ethics, and economics faculties at a New England university.

Loglinear logit analysis and the scenarios

Analysis of the scenario data used loglinear logit models to study the multidimensional contingency tables (Goodman, 1971; Feinberg, 1980; Fingleton, 1984). The actual statistical analysis for a given scenario was done in three interrelated stages.

The first stage involved a variable selection procedure that was intended to determine the important explanatory variables best able to model the response. The best fitting model, of course, involves all seven potential explanatory variables and could include as many as 128 effects. Nonetheless, this saturated model is typically over specified and not parsimonious. For each scenario we seek as few variables as necessary to obtain a statistically well-fitting model that is subject-matter meaningful and that will address the appropriate research hypothesis.

The second stage selected the best-fitting loglinear logit model in terms of main effects and interaction effects of the variables selected.

In the third stage, the effects were estimated. These analyses used the BMDP4F computing program (Dixon, 1985).

Discussion

Table 1 below summarises for each scenario the main effects and interaction effects that appear in the best model. The ethics-economics scenarios are listed in sequence of percentage acting ethically.

Gender was an important main effect in 6 of the 10 scenarios; it was unimportant in two ethics-economics scenarios where most (83.2% in the buyout) people were ethical and in the overheard telephone message where only 64.5% acted ethically.

Methods-results was the most frequent main effect, being important in 7 of the 10 scenarios. It was unimportant only in the promotion case, where no factor was important and where 96% of the respondents made the same decision, and in the buyout and expense scenarios. In these buyout and expense refund vignettes minimal amounts of money were involved.

Bem score was significant in four scenarios, and it was the only significant effect in the buyout. Sex-role and not gender was most important in this decision choosing between shareholders' wealth and one's own job and those of friends. Bem sex-role was the only main effect to be of singular importance.

Stage was important in three scenarios and role in two. Level was never significant.

Table 2 below presents data on the seven ethical-economic scenarios arrayed by the overall percentage acting ethically, 90.1% for photocopier to 44.1% for the marketing plan. This table shows the distribution of the percentages of respondents acting ethically by Bem group and within Bem group by stage. For example, in the buyout 427 of the 513 respondents, or 83.2% acted ethically. In addition, there were 97 respondents in the feminine Bem group, 71 in the near feminine group, and so on, in the study; of the 97 in the feminine Bem group, 42 were early stage, 32 middle, and 23 late. In the buyout

TABLE I

Summary by Scenario

MAIN EFFECT

	Level	Gender	Bem	Methods Results	Ethics Economics	Stage	Role	INTERACTIONS
ELATIONSHIPS omotion 6.1% Non relational)								
ild Employee 0.2% Non relational)		x	x	x			x	Gender and Bem Gender and Role
ETHODS-RESULTS am 5.1% Methods)		x	x	x				Gender and Bem;Methods Results and Bem; Gender and Bemand Methods-Results
THICS-ECONOMICS otocopier 0.1% Ethical)		x		x		x		Gender and Methods-Results: Gender and Stage; Stage and Methods-Results; the three-way interactions
ayout 3.2% Ethical)			x					
ock 8.0% Ethical)				x	x			Methods-Results and Ethics-Economics
rsonal Injury Case 6.8% Ethical)		x			x	x		
xpense Refund 1.3% Ethical)		x				x		Gender and Stage
elephone Message 4.5% Ethical)				x		x		Stage and Methods- Results
arketing Plan 4.1% Ethical		x	x	x			x	Gender and Methods- Results; Bem and Role
--								
otal Factor Count.	0	6	4	7	2	3	2	

scenario 83.5% of the 97 in the feminine Bem group acted ethically and of the 42 early stage respondents in the feminine Bem group, 78.6% acted ethically.

This table suggests several things. First, there is an interesting pattern in the progression from scenario to scenario if we consider the nature of the affected party. That is, the highest ethical behaviour comes in a scenario (photocopier) involving a customer and a little money, and the next highest ethical behaviour in a scenario (buyout) involving shareholders. Less ethical behaviour is then encountered with a customer and a significant amount of money, an injured person, one's employer, a co-worker, and finally a competitor, who gets the least ethical treatment in the marketing plan scenario.

Secondly, within the five Bem groups, the general pattern of decreasing ethical percentages holds as one moves from left to right in the table with three important exceptions, highlighted by asterisks.

Feminine and near feminine (*) responded more ethically than others in the personal injury case. Does this higher ethical behaviour have something to do with the stereotypical female trait of nurturing?

Masculine and near masculine (**) responded more ethically than others in the overheard telephone message about a co-worker's mini-crisis at home. Is this a suggestion that males are more sensitive to problems of a spouse at home, even though gender was not a significant effect in the analysis?

Feminine and near feminine (***) are not as extreme in the non-ethical act with the competitor's marketing plan, except for middle stage feminine. Do middle stage females internalise business objectives more than early and later stage females?

The near feminine group (****) acts more ethically (91.5%) in the buyout.

Finally, the effect of stage is clear. It was an important main effect in three scenarios. Later groups in total are more ethical than early groups in all scenarios. The middle group varies its behaviour with the big dollar customer dock sale, the co-worker's telephone message, and the competitor's marketing plan.

Part of this middle group variation can be traced to the less ethical behaviour of the large group that is in the middle stage Bem androgynous group. We might speculate about identity crises for mid-career and androgynous groups, a speculation further suggested by the middle near masculine group.

The middle near masculine groups act less ethically than the early near masculine groups in five of the seven scenarios. This near masculine group is actually composed of 57 respondents of whom 34 are females. Only 23 of the 57 near masculine are males.

In only four of the 35 Bem group examples is the increasingly ethical behaviour as we move from early to mid to later stage reversed; three of these four reversals occur with the female-dominated near masculine group with the personal injury case, co-worker telephone message, and the marketing plan. (The other increasingly ethical behaviour reversal occurs with near feminine and the expense refund.)

Summary and conclusions

The first null hypothesis that there is no difference between men and women on decisions involving relationships was accepted in the promotion scenario, but was rejected in the child employee relationship where gender had a significant effect on the probability of dismissing the child employee.

The second null hypothesis that there is no difference between men and women on decisions involving a methods-results issue was rejected in the team scenario, where gender had a significant effect on the probability of putting less skilled substitutes into a critical game.

TABLE 2

Summary of Ethical-Economic Scenarios

	Photocopier		Buyout		Dock		Injury Case		Expense Refund		Telephone Message		Marketing Plan	
	#	%	#	%	#	%	#	%	#	%	#	%	#	%
Total Ethical	462	90.1	427	83.2	400	78.0	394	76.8	366	71.3	331	64.5	226	44.1
FEMININE 97		91.8		83.5		79.4		82.5*		76.3		69.1		56.7
E 42		88.1		78.6		83.3		76.2		69.0		66.7		61.9***
M 32		93.7		87.5		75.0		87.5		78.1		75.0		46.9
L 23		95.7		87.0		78.3		87.0		87.0		65.2		60.9***
NEAR FIMININE 71		88.7		91.5****		77.5		84.5*		73.2		59.2***		60.6
E 32		84.4		87.5		78.1		78.1		75.0		59.4		56.2
M 32		93.7		93.8		75.0		87.5		71.9		53.1		62.5
L 7		85.7		100.0		85.7		100.0		71.4		85.7		71.4
ANDROGYNOUS 208		89.4		78.4		77.9		75.0		70.2		59.1		38.9
E 69		84.1		76.8		79.7		71.0		65.2		59.4		37.7
M 112		90.2		78.4		75.9		75.9		71.4		54.4		36.6
L 27		100.0		88.1		81.5		81.5		77.8		77.8		51.9
NEAR MASCL. 57		93.3		91.2		80.7		73.7		70.2		75.4**		36.8
E 22		95.5		86.4		90.9		77.3		54.5		81.8		40.1
M 29		89.7		96.6		72.4		72.4		75.9		72.4		34.5
L 6		100.0		83.3		83.3		66.7		100.0		66.7		33.0
MASCULINE 80		88.8		82.5		75.0		70.0		67.5		70.0**		32.5
E 27		82.5		70.4		66.7		66.7		59.3		70.4		25.9
M 42		92.9		88.1		80.9		73.0		73.8		69.0		38.1
L11		90.9		90.9		72.7		72.7		63.6		72.7		27.3

Note: Asterisks explained in text pages 29-30

The third null hypothesis that career stage has no effect on decisions involving business ethics was accepted in four of the seven ethics-economics scenarios. The hypothesis was rejected in three scenarios, the photocopier, the expense refund, and the telephone message, where stage had a significant effect on the ratios of probable ethical versus economic action.

The fourth null hypothesis that organisational level had no effect on decisions involving business ethics was accepted. Level had no effect on the seven scenario ratios of probable acts.The fifth null hypothesis that role had no effect on decisions involving business ethics was accepted in six scenarios and rejected only in the marketing plan scenario where role had a significant effect.

The sixth and last null hypothesis that gender had no effect on decisions involving business ethics was rejected in four scenarios (photocopier, personal injury, expense refund, and marketing plan) where gender had a significant effect. The null hypothesis could not be rejected for the buyout, dock and telephone message scenarios.

In addition to our hypotheses findings, this research presents four suggestions and conclusions relative to this sample regarding (1) situational relativity, (2) gender stereotypes, (3) career stage, and (4) future research efforts in measures of decision-making variables, scenarios and the nature of the affected party, and in the decision behaviour of middle, centrist, or "non-polar" groups.

Situational Relativity

There was no consistency of behaviour across all scenarios. In a promotion scenario, 96% acted against relationships while only 60% did so in the child employee scenario. Further, the nature of the parties affected by the behaviour seemed an important aspect of the scenarios in total. Respondents acted less ethically as the scenarios changed from customer and stockholder to co-worker and competitor.

Decision responses in these scenarios thus seemed to support the argument of ethical relativists that ethics are situationally specific (Sumner, 1907; De George, 1986).

Gender stereotypes

Analysts of managerial action and the role of gender often stress the difference between male and female executives. Our study concludes that gender had a significant effect in only six of the ten scenarios. The Bem sex-role inventory had an effect in only four of the ten scenarios and in two of these the gender by Bem score interaction was significant. A more frequent significant effect was the methods-results orientation score, an unsophisticated measure, significant in seven of the ten scenarios.

Not only is gender not the most frequent significant effect, but stereotypical gender characteristics were not consistent or coherent. There was no set of "rules" of male or female behaviour. While most females acted more ethically than males in the personal injury - and thus presumably nurturing-case, near masculine males did not fire the friends' child while near masculine females did. Within the Bem classifications near masculine and near feminine kept the child and the androgynous and feminine groups ignored relationship and fired the child.

Career Stage

Career stage had an important effect. For example, early career stage respondents acted significantly less ethically in the expense refund. Later stages were generally more ethical in all scenarios.

Career stage was viewed as a surrogate for age in this research. We can speculate as to the relationship between increasing age, and increasing career stage, as increasing factors in explaining higher percentages of respondents acting ethically. Age/career stage may be viewed as causal; it could also be that each career stage, or each age, is representative of differing ethical values and that the higher ethical percentage in the later stages and lower ethics in the early stage reflect increasingly lower ethical standards in current times.

Future research

An unsophisticated measure of a variable in decision-making, methods-results orientation, resulted in the most frequent main effect, significant in seven of the ten scenarios. Future researchers might refine this measure. One aspect of interest is the setting of the scenario. In the personal injury case, the results group acted more ethically than the methods group, while the equal group acted least ethically. Although 63% of the respondents classified themselves as results-oriented, 65% chose the methods (versus results) option in the Little League team scenario. Additional attention should be focused on the interactions with methods-results. The ethical-methods group acts more ethically than the ethical-equal and ethical-results groups in the dock scenario, but the ethical-equal group acts less ethically than the ethical-results group or the equal group. Early stage male methods are more ethical than early stage female methods in the photocopier option, while early stage male results are less ethical than early stage female results in the same scenario.

Future research efforts might further explore the effect of the third party - customer, shareholder, injured party, employer, co-worker, and competitor - in ethical versus economic decision making. Scenarios might be developed to contain a spectrum of third parties based upon a hypothesised degree of importance, and these multiple scenarios might include relational and methods-results decisions as well as ethical-economic outcomes.

Finally, the middle and centrist groups, those that did not fall into the extremes, the "non-polar" respondents, made interesting and often inconsistent decisions. The middle stage group acted in atypical fashion in the dock, telephone message, and marketing plan scenarios.

Future researchers might study the centrist groups, the level of commitment, and decisions. One might inquire if the equally ethical and economic group, the equally methods and results group, the androgynous and/or middle career groups make atypical and inconsistent decisions because values have not been thought out or are still being formed. A hypothesis that ethical values are relatively neutral initially and are then formed during the business career is suggested in the data about the level of certainty respondents used to characterise themselves.

This value formation could lead to most significant conclusions for management development specialists. Many observers of business see recent notorious breaches of business ethics standards not as acts of immoral or evil executives, but as decisions made in an ethical vacuum; executives had not considered ethical implications. Ethics did not play a part in those managerial decisions, because ethical values had not yet been formed, presenting a major challenge and opportunity for management educators.

References

Baird, J.E., Jr.: 1976, "Sex differences in task and social-emotional behaviour", *Basic and Applied Social Psychology*, 3, 109-139.

Bakan, D.: 1966, *The duality of human existence*, Chicago: Rand McNally.

Bardwick, J.M.: 1971, *Psychology of women*, New York: Harper and Row .

Barnett, J.H. and M.J. Karson: 1987, "Personal values and business decisions: An exploratory investigation", *Journal of Business Ethics*, 6, 371-382.

Barry, H., M.K. Bacon and I. L. Child: 1957, " A cross-cultural survey of some sex differences in socialisation", *Journal of Abnormal and Social Psychology*, 55, 327-332.

Baumhart, R.C.: 1961, "How ethical are businessmen?", *Harvard Business Review*, 39, 156-176.

Bem, S.L. and D.J. Bem: 1971, "Case study of an unconscious ideology: Training the woman to know her place", in D.J. Bem (ed.), *Beliefs, attitudes and human affairs*, Belmont, Cal.: Brooks/Cole.

Bem, S.L.: 1977, "Bem sex-role inventory (BSRI)", in J.E. Jones and J.W. Pfeiffer (eds.), *The 1977 annual handbook for group facilitators*. San Diego: University Associates.

Brenner, S. and E. Molander: 1977, "Is the ethics of business changing?", *Harvard Business Review*, 55, 57-71.

Carlson, R.: 1971, "Sex differences in ego functioning: Exploratory studies of agency and communion", *Journal of Consulting and Clinical Psychology*, 37, 261-277.

Carroll, A.B.: 1975, "Management ethics - A post-Watergate view", *Business Horizons*, 18, 2, 75-80.

Carroll, A.B.: 1978, "Linking business ethics to behaviour in organisations", *Advanced Management Journal*, 43, 3, 4-11.

Chorodow. N.: 1974, "Family structure and feminine personality", in M.Z. Rosaldo and L. Lamphere (eds.), *Woman Culture and Society*, Stanford: Stanford University Press.

De George, R. T.:1986, *Business ethics* , Second edition, New York: Macmillan.

Dixon, W.:1985, *B.M.D.P. statistical software* , Berkely: University of California Press.

England, G.W.: 1978, "Managers and their value system: A five-country comparative study", *Columbia Journal of World Business*, 13, 2, 35-44.

Erikson, E.H.: 1968, *Identity: youth and crisis*, New York: W.W.Norton.

Feinberg, S.E.: 1980, *The analysis of cross-classified categorical data*, Cambridge: MIT Press.

Fingleton, B.: 1984, *Models of category counts*, Cambridge: Cambridge University Press.

Gilligan, C.: 1982, *In a different voice*, Cambridge: Harvard University Press.

Goodman, L.A.: 1971, "The analysis of multidimensional contingency tables: Stepwise procedures and direct estimation methods for building models for multiple classifications", *Technometrics*, 13, 33-62.

Hennig, M. and A. Jardim: 1977, *The managerial woman*, Garden City, NY: Anchor Press/Doubleday.

Hodgson, R.C. and E.D. Watson: 1987, "Gender-integrated management teams", *Business Quaterly*, 52, 68-72.

Johnson, R. A., J.P. Neelankavil and A. Jadhav: 1986, "Developing the executive resource", *Business Horizons*, 29, 33.

Kanter, R. M.: 1977, *Men and women of the corporation*, New York: Basic Books.

Kanter, R. M.: 1987 , "Men and women of the corporation revisited", *Management Review*, 76, March, 14-16.

Kohlberg, L. and R. Kramer: 1969, "Continuities and discontinuities in childhood and adult moral development", *Human Development*, 12, 93-120.

Maccoby, E. and C. Jacklin: 1974, *The psychology of sex differences*, Stanford: Stanford University Press.

Miller, J.B.: 1976, *Toward a new psychology of women*, Boston: Beacon Press.

Posner, B.Z. and W.H. Schmidt: 1984, "Values and the American Manager: An update", *California Management Review*, 26, 3, 202-216.

Rotter, G.S. and S.H. Portugal: 1969, "Group and individual effects in problem-solving", *Journal of Applied Psychology*, 53, 338-341.

Sargent. A.:1981, *The androgynous manager*, New York: AMACOM.

Summer, W.G.: 1907, *Folkways*, Boston: Ginn and Company.

Toffler, B.L.: 1986, *Tough choices*, New York: John Wiley and Sons.

Wood, W., D. Polek and C. Aiken: 1985, "Sex differences in group task performance", *Journal of Personality and Social Psychology*, 48, 1, 63-71.

Outlook

Some Perspectives

SPHERES AND LIMITS OF ETHICAL RESPONSIBILITIES IN AND OF THE CORPORATION

Jack Mahoney

What is the *raison d'être* of the business corporation? My reaction to this central question is to think that its answer depends on who is asking it: the manager, the employee, the consumer, the share-holder, society or government. There are many possible points of view from which to look at the purpose of the business corporation. From the ethical point of view I should like to begin by applying a phrase of the American psychologist Gordon Allport in a different context and describe the corporation as desirably *"a community of reflection"*.

It was Aristotle who remarked that the unexamined life is not worthy of a human being. And this I would apply not only to individuals, but also to groups of human beings, as a mark of their human maturity. The first step, then, I suggest, in understanding the ethical responsibilities of the corporation is to get it to think seriously about itself.

Sooner or later in this process the traditional questions will arise about *the relationships between individuals and groups,* as two poles of human identity and activity. The permanent danger, of course, is that the relationship can become polarised, so that one of these elements, the individual or the collectivity, dominates, and leads to either individualism or collectivism. Within the context of the corporation this raises questions as to whether the corporation is an environment in which the individual men and women who belong to it lose their individuality, or whether the corporation is an environment in which the individual members can achieve their individuality. In other words, *does the corporation absorb persons into its collective identity and actions, or does it encourage persons to flourish and develop as persons within it?*

In western society, however, this ethical challenge to the business corporation has a long history of individualism with which to contend. The influential study "Habits of the Heart" of Robert Bellah and others (1985) well describes the tension within American society between on the one hand the cult of individualism which has come to dominate that society as a whole, and on the other hand underlying aspirations and movements towards community. This phenomenon is not unique to American society, of course, for it springs to a significant extent from what I consider *the systematic and pernicious dualism* introduced by René Descartes (1596-1650) into western thought. In philosophy he began from inside the solitary individual, and attempted to argue logically from there to the existence of other similar individuals in the world. In social and political terms this was expressed most strongly by Thomas Hobbes (1588-1679), who, in the words of John Macmurray, maintained that "the persons who compose society are, by nature, isolated units, afraid of one another, and continuously on the defensive" (Macmurray, 1961).

Macmurray's answer to what he judged the "pervasive dualism of modern thought" was to argue, in his "Persons in Relation" (Macmurray, 1961), that the fundamental human unit is not the individual solitary person, but what he called *"the person-in-relationship"*. In order to develop this idea he distinguished between the concept of "community" as a personal grouping of men and women and the concept of "society" as an impersonal grouping of individuals. And although he does not refer to the German sociologist, Ferdinand Tönnies (1855-1936), in his writings, what Macmurray says is very similar to the distinction made famous by Tönnies between the models, or poles, of *"society" (Gesellschaft)* and *"community" (Gemeinschaft)* (Tönnies, 1957).

In his view, society is an impersonal grouping which is dominated by rationality and efficiency, and which directs all its members in contractual terms as functional means to the end of producing results. Tönnies saw this as occurring typically in the new industrial societies. By contrast, he tended to see the other model, that of "community", as more typical of rural society, and as possessing the qualities of interpersonal interest, affectivity, mutual concern, and the refusal to turn people into means for the purposes of production. This analysis of Tönnies, I suggest, fills in details which are lacking in Macmurray's distinction between "society" and "community" and also gives strength to his conclusion that "to create community is to make friendship the form of all personal relationships".

But now comes the fallacy. I do not think that the next step in approaching ethical responsibilities in and of the corporation is to try to convert it from a society into a community in the sense in which we have been exploring those concepts. Rather the next step is more practical and involves recognising that *the corporation is and should remain a society,* but it should be a society which is *not anti-communitarian or anti-personal.* And the challenge is to find means of ensuring this. In my view the most effective structural way to ensure that corporations are not anti-personal is to recognise and apply the major principle which social philosophy recognises as *the principle of subsidiarity.*

According to this general principle, higher bodies or agents in any society should not undertake the functions of lower bodies, but should let them get on with acting within their own sphere, unless and until they need help *(subsidium)* from above. This is not just the idea of delegation, which is a trickle-down theory of communicating authority and power for more and more detailed purposes. Subsidiarity recognises authority and power at lower levels where they already exist, and respects such authority and power. In other words, and this is my main application to the business corporation, there should be a mutual respect for the role and function of the various individuals or groups at different levels within any society, including the business corporation. The application, then, of the principle of subsidiarity within the corporation recognises that *ethical responsibility is spread throughout the corporation at all levels and in varying degrees,* from the shareholders to the work force. No one can absorb the ethical contribution and responsibility of any fellow member of the corporation.

My next step in considering ethical responsibilities in and of the corporation is to consider how this social principle of subsidiarity also applies to business corporations *within society,* and especially in identifying the ethical agenda of social responsibility for a corporation and all its members. Milton Friedman's view is well known that the sole function of business is to provide returns for the shareholders. Although I do not agree with him, I had already in mind to call this contribution of mine "One cheer for Milton Friedman", because I think he is by implication warning us about a particular danger which we can fall into in identifying the social responsibility of business. That danger is the tendency to *overload business corporations with social expectations, and even "community" expectations,* which are not, strictly speaking, its purpose or *raison d'être.* In other words, I think there is a danger of making business into a surrogate for the satisfaction of personal and social needs which should really be met and satisfied by other agents or groups or individuals in society.

In the United States, business ethics has gone through the phase of corporate good citizenship, and found it useful but not sufficient for identifying the social responsibilities of business. And in his recent book "The Age of Unreason", the management expert, Charles Handy (1989), refers to the *tendency towards corporate welfarism in Britain.* For it has become fashionable in Britain for the government, with its stress on private ownership and on cutting back on public spending, to encourage business to perform social activities and to make contributions to local and national society in terms of what several members of the government last year were calling "good citizenship". This is what I mean by overloading business with social expectations. It is going against the principle of subsidiarity, which would identify the respective and differing roles of all agents in society, including business and government, and would expect them to fulfil their own obligations without passing these off on others.

Does this mean, then, that business has no responsibilities in and to society? I think it is helpful here to learn from the study of *medical ethics,* and to adopt its two basic principles of non-maleficence, or not doing harm, and of beneficence, or actively doing good. The major principle of the medical profession is *primum non nocere,* above all do not harm. And if business were to adopt that *principle of non-maleficence* in all its actions this would already provide a very demanding ethical agenda, in such areas as worker and consumer safety and concern for the environment. After that, when it had satisfied its own particular responsibilities to society, business might then go further, if it wished, and adopt the *principle of beneficence,* or actively doing good, in various social programmes and activities. But this latter should, of course, never be seen as a substitute for the former.

In conclusion, I have explored some fundamental ethical aspects of the corporation by first suggesting that the corporation should be a "community of reflection", and be encouraged to think about its identity and ethical responsibilities. I have argued that the fundamental ethical unit is not the solitary individual, but the person-in-relationship. This does not necessarily mean, however, that corporations have to be "communities" in a strong sense, aiming at meeting all the personal and social needs of all their stakeholders. It does mean that the social principle of subsidiarity can form a structure within the corporation and enable it to identify and to respect the various powers and responsibilities at all levels within that society. Promoting ethics means promoting ethical responsibility at all those levels in the ways appropriate to each. It also means not expecting business to undertake the ethical responsibilities of other agencies in society, including government, but requiring it first of all to concentrate on its own unique contributions in a way which is not harmful to society, and then considering in what other positive ways it can fulfil its role within society.

References

Bellah, R.N. *et al.*: 1985, *Habits of the Heart. Individualism and Commitment in American Life*, New York: Doubleday.

Handy, C.: 1989, *The Age of Unreason*, London: Century Hutchinson.

Macmurray, J.: 1961, *Persons in Relation*, London: Faber.

Tönnies, F.: 1887, *Gemeinschaft und Gesellschaft*, English translation 1957.

PHILOSOPHICAL CONSIDERATIONS OF A TOP MANAGER

Vicente Mortes Alfonso

It is for me, as a professional manager for more than 40 years and as a member of the Catholic church since I was born, an extraordinary positive fact that "morality" and "business" are no longer understood as unconnected or even excluding each other. Such a cultural situation is now starting to be considered past history. Therefore, they are no longer treated independently but together. This does not mean that all companies - nor even most of them - were acting without ethics, but simply that entrepreneurs and business scholars were not thinking enough about the essential moral dimension of the business world. The very fact of many initiatives like the conference on business ethics in Barcelona is the best proof that things are changing and starting to follow the right direction.

In order to have a real and positive impact, it seems to me, however, *necessary to clarify the concepts* we use to study the ethical aspects of business management. Otherwise, we would incur risks such as follows: the ambiguous use of "big words", the confusion of the meaning of the terms used without knowing why, the distance - if not the contradiction - between what is said and what is done, the lack of coherent attitudes because of the absence of inner unity between the diverse aspects of our own existence.

The practical character of ethical knowledge

Faced with the proliferation of recently published books and papers about ethical problems within companies, one is inclined to question whether the moral behaviour level of managers has risen in the same proportion. Because, unlike other knowledge, ethics is directly involved with action. Ethical questions are not only raised for theoretical reasons - such, for example, to satisfy the natural desire for knowledge that by itself enriches the human beings - but, and above all, to better the real concrete behaviour of people.

Ethical discourse is of little use if the persons who belong to the company do not incorporate moral values in their lives. This incorporation is nothing less than incorporating habits which, according to the classics, constitute a "second nature". And it is precisely these ethically correct habits which we call "virtues".

We still do not realise that morality does not consist of abstract recommendations but of concrete requirements whose continous practice will shape the life of human beings. In ethical life, there is a kind of feedback, faster and more powerful than any cybernetic system: when I act ethically, this action has an impact on my own existence and positively reinforces my capacity for acting. In this way, the ethical life can be seen as a process in which one advances or retreats, but never remains at a stand still.

This personal ethical advance or retreat has consequences for those with whom we work, because the company is a community of people capable of perfecting or damaging themselves ethically. Strictly speaking, the only realistic way to promote ethics within the company is through the practice of personal and social virtues. It is excellent for a company to have a code of ethics, and even some have a "creed"! But these solemn statements are of limited effectiveness if they do not reflect the ethical behaviour of the people who belong to it, and especially their managers.

The virtues of the managers are the key to ethics within the company. Of course, the management of an organisation requires technical competence, but ethical competence is much more important. If we remember the distinction of the Romans between auctoritas and potestas, *i. e.* between authority and power, we will notice that the manager of a company will only have authority, if his or her power is based on ethical quality, a straight way of life, that has repercussions on all of his or her decisions.

The essential link between free decision and ethical behaviour

It is almost never in my power to control the fluctuations of the world economy, to influence the dispositions that regulate economic life, or the political measures to "cool" the economy. And I cannot foresee the drought or the abundance of rains. What it *is* in my power to do - and in the power of each one in the company - is to take straight and right steps. We are responsible for what depends on us. And, for that reason, no external circumstances - no matter how extreme - can justify morally perverse behaviour.

When we talk about "corporate culture", we enumerate many aspects of corporate life, but we often forget that the very nucleus of a company lies in its ethical heritage. For what really shapes the essence of a company are the principles which inspire the decisions of managers. The deeper and firmer these principles are, the more stable will the life of the company be, because every one will know on what fundamentals it stands; and furthermore - paradoxically - the more decentralised and the more flexible the management can be, because the strength in these basics will allow it to adapt to accidental circumstances, without running excessive risks.

Therefore, the situation of a company can be qualified as good or bad, ethically speaking, according to the quality of the decisions made in it. And improvements in the ethical quality of the company will depend on the ethical quality of the decision-makers.

There is only one type of ethics

It is not the case that there exists a corporate ethics on the one side and an individual ethics on the other side, as it is often contended. On the contrary, I maintain that there is a unity of ethics which cannot be separated into different types. To me, what is unethical at home, on the road, or in social relations, is also unethical in the office and in the factory, and vice versa. As said Mgr. Escrivá de Balaguer, founder of the Instituto de Estudios Superiores de la Empresa (IESE) and first chancellor of the university of Navarra: "No! We cannot lead a double life. We cannot be like schizophrenics, if we want to be Christians." (*Conversations*, p. 138) This global unity of ethics is founded in the objective and universal character of the moral norms which arise from the nature of man. They are valid norms for all people and it will be wrong to consider them relative for each one of us. To make ethics relative to people and to their circumstances leads inevitably, sooner or later, to immorality.

Even when the human conscience is faced with concrete situation, ethics cannot become relative or subjective. This concrete situation compels one to analyse certain absolute ethical values and to see how to fulfil them in such a situation. The ethical duties are absolute but they are not inflexible and must be adapted to the concrete situation.

As managers we are often confronted by a presumed lack of power in face of demanding duties, whose fulfilment we believe is beyond our own resources. Certainly there are tough and complex circumstances which make ethical behaviour very difficult. It depends on the moral resoluteness and the wisdom of each one of us. But, no matter how difficult the fulfilment of an ethical norm is for a specific situation, the norm does not lose any of its validity. Of course, one cannot say that in matters of business - or on some of its aspects - we are "amoral", as if a certain kind of "selective amorality" were possible. Otherwise, the manager who declared himself or herself amoral, will be saying that he is an incomplete professional because in reality, he or she will be a bad manager. And, I have no doubts that his or her company, sooner or later, will suffer the negative consequences of it.

The unity and universality of ethics demands that our ethical behaviour be directed to all people connected with the company such as managers, employees, clients, colleagues with whom we compete, and so on and so forth. There is no room for a "multitude of ethics", so that - for example - one takes care to watch for truthfulness "within" the company, but is tolerant with lies used in the company's "outside"-relationships. Among other things, and also as an example, the salesman who is allowed to deceive a customer, may well finish up deceiving, at the same time, the sales manager. This is because ethics is indivisible, and therefore any crevices in it will easily destroy it.

My previous reflections might appear hard, but what are really hard are the consequences which come from a lack of ethics. Of course, we should be tolerant with the defects of other people, and even with our own defects. But our own and others' weaknesses are one thing, while confusion is something quite different.

The convergence of natural ethics and religiously inspired ethics

At the risk once more of being accused of "intolerance", I claim that the unity of ethics includes also the conviction that natural ethics and religiously inspired ethics not only are not opposed, but that they come to converge.

Obviously, there are excellent people who lack religious faith and who tend to be ethically irreproachable as far as the dictates of the natural law are concerned. But those who enjoy this faith - and, in particular, the Christian faith - find in their beliefs a confirmation of these natural ethical convictions, valid for all human beings.

The Ten Commandments synthesise and deepen the considerations of natural ethics. And the moral teachings of the Gospel place the ideal of human perfection at a level which could never be reached with the natural forces alone.

The unity of life of the Christian manager - with the greatest respect for the conscience of all other people - demands that he or she looks for this higher wisdom, which has been given as a more powerful fountain of light for the resolution of their ethical perplexities. It seems to me that, within this topic, there are open, very broad perspectives, not only in the theory but also in the practice of management, which should be investigated. But for now I leave this matter simply outlined.

The ethical challenge of the present European situation

After these more philosophical perspectives, I should like to comment on the present European situation which is, to my mind, of historic relevance. For more than a century, capitalism has been compelled to defend itself against accusations of immorality, which have come from socialism inspired by marxism. And, we have to recognise that, in some of its formulations, and also in some of its deeds, classical liberal capitalism has shown, without any doubt, clear and deserved scope for attack. It is also true that, in this ideological confrontation, the reflections of economists and managers emphasised, ever more deeply, the ethical dimension of economic freedom, whilst establishing, at the same time, some qualifications and limits to the market.

We are now facing a new situation, which in itself implies an ethical challenge. I refer to the self-declared ideological bankruptcy of totalitarian socialism, and above all, to the reform process of centralised economies in the Eastern European Block. A phenomenon as complex as "perestroika", with all the implications and concomitances, is difficult to evaluate. However, it is possible to notice that this "turn" towards more liberal economic positions is beginning to leave capitalism without a strong ideological opponent. This, to my mind, could imply a risk, but it also implies a possible hope.

Hope relates to something more difficult to perceive, but much more interesting: the end - or the softening - of the ideological controversy. *This makes it easier for the free market economy to study its own internal problems within a framework which is no longer necessarily ideological, but decisively ethical.* If the Western economies and their agents could prove that they are capable of establishing by themselves their own moral control, they will have made it clear that the impulse which moves the commercial and productive dynamism of these economies has a truly humanistic root. But to achieve this goal, as we well know, it is essential to focus the question upon the being who, as Pope John Paul II so often reminds us, constitutes the origin and the end of economic and managerial activity: the human person.

THE IMPORTANCE OF THE CULTURAL CONTEXT FOR BUSINESS ETHICS: THE ITALIAN EXAMPLE

Mario Unnia

It is not the case that Italy is a country of knaves who know and care nothing about ethics. But for a series of historical reasons, one might well say that Italy is a country with a "low ethical temperature". We operate within a Catholic tradition, first of all. We don't have a strong sense of national identity, nor do we have a strong sense of the state. It is as though we lacked faith in hetero-regulatory mechanisms - such as the law - as well as in any internalised, self-regulating mechanisms, other than those relating to family loyalty. So when Banfield (1976) refers to Italy as a country of *familial amorality* he is quite right. This typically Italian evidence is also a main finding of the research report (ASFOR, 1989) on Italian managers who define many ethical dilemmas in terms of face-to-face problems similar to the familial context. Ours is a country which tends to prefer self-regulatory mechanisms - but then only employs and respects them very partially. Rigour is not the norm with us although our behaviour is much more open and proper than it is often made out to be.

In addition to this cultural feature, those who engage in business ethics have to take into account another Italian particularity which has to do with the business environment - the Italian business community itself. As a self-conscious nucleus of a sector of society, the Italian business community is a very recent, and rather minoritarian social phenomenon. The Italian business world is still divided - organisationally and culturally - into many separate segments: the industrialists, the wholesalers and retailers, the bankers, etc. Moreover, these many separate worlds are in permanent interaction with an Italian professional world which is even more fragmented.

A third characteristic of the Italian situation is the fact - and I cannot emphasise it enough - that in this country, the business community faces two great threats and challenges: the threat and challenge deriving from organised white collar criminality and that deriving from our inefficient and corrupt political system.

Only if we are fully aware of this particular situation, are we able fully to understand the need for business ethics in Italy.

In my view, business ethics is *a logical necessity in as much as it alone is capable of offering social legitimacy to the business world* - thus placing it in a position to converse authoritatively with the political establishment as well as with other, more emergent social actors.

This conviction has grown out of many experiences during the last six years and has been the guiding perspective of our activities since.

A short retrospect

The first significant signs of interest in business ethics in Italy appeared in 1987 - signs coming from within the business world itself. *Before* 1987, only somewhat sporadic activity, which had had a rather limited public impact, had been going on. Certain sectors in the universities, as well as the more theoretically-oriented practitioners, were already well aware of the problem. As a matter of fact, as far back as 1983, PROSPECTA (the research firm which I direct) had organised the first Italian seminar on "Social Responsibility and Business Ethics".

Two years later, in 1985 and in 1986, the association of Catholic businessmen produced two documents on the ethical implications of economic activity, inspired by the recent encyclical "Laborem Exercens" (1981). But in those years, the business world - especially the world of big business - had not yet realised how central the argument was becoming.

Then, in 1987, Cesare Romiti, Fiat's consigliere delegato, gave his extremely influential speech about the ethical implications of business in today's world. Shortly after, the market crash of October 1987 moved the "ethics issue" out of the more limited spheres of the business community to invade the front-lines, front-pages, and vaster sectors of the public opinion.

In 1988, I founded the first issue of the journal entitled "Etica degli Affari", and shortly thereafter, the first two numbers - which I edit - have come off the presses. Our editorial advisory board includes very prominent members of a community which includes both practitioners and academics. Our inspiration is moral, and not explicitly linked to any confessional background. It is obvious that the composition and the ideological orientation of that board have similar features to the formula which the European Business Ethics Network (EBEN) adopts.

In the same year, the first Italian National Conference on Business Ethics took place in Milan, was very well attended, and attracted the interest of universities, corporations, and practitioners. The conference's main outcome has been the creation of the Italian Network. A constitution was drafted and, after lively discussions on the conditions of membership of corporations, the Network's final constitution was approved nearly unanimously admitting individuals, non-profit organisations, and corporations as well: upon the condition that within a given lapse of time they adopt and explicitly communicate a company code of ethics.

How we try to face the challenge for business ethics now

Apart from the more theoretical and foundational work in business ethics for which the journal "Etica degli Affari" provides a forum, we mainly see three important areas of activity: (1) to develop programmes of executive training, (2) to elaborate and introduce codes of ethics in Italian corporations, and (3) to encourage prominent business leaders in their protagonistic role for the promotion of business ethics.

To develop programmes of executive training: If we consider the best-qualified and most prestigious among the independent Italian business schools - such as the Scuola di Direzione Aziendale dell' Università Bocconi in Milano (SDA Bocconi), the Istituto Studi Direzionali in Belgirate, Novara (ISTUD), or the Istituto di Ricerca e Formazione di Direzione Aziendale in Roma (IFAP), we note a certain sensitivity and interest in the topic, but certainly not anything comparable to the seminars or courses held in North American business schools.

The situation is even worse at the Italian universities where there are no ethics programmes on the university agenda at all - neither in economics or sociology departments, nor in the law schools.

In order to change this state of affairs, PROSPECTA and POLITEIA have designed an executive training programme aimed at decision-makers. Not young, middle managers, and not staff professionals either. What we are targeting here are managers between 35 and 45 years of age, empowered by their positions of responsibility to make decisions and allot resources. This course is being offered in Milan as well as in Rome, and is structured as a quite extensive set of full and half-day sessions.

At the same time, efforts are being made to sensitise public opinion and to raise the business community's awareness of the ethics theme. These promotional activities take the form of symposiums, debates, and single, introductory lessons which are inserted in the standard, basic business school curricula and masters programmes.

To elaborate and introduce codes of ethics in Italian companies: At present, very few firms possess specific codes or have in any way institutionalised ethics, and if they do, they are mostly the Italian affiliates of America-based multinationals. This lack of codes is true of large and medium-sized firms, although it is very likely that among the many small companies, some individual entrepreneurs have taken the question to heart.

In my opinion, a process of imitation and emulation must be stimulated. Top executives, groups and managers, and important entrepreneurs who are sensitive to the problem, certainly exist, as do large Italian corporations which are very rightly proud of their own consistently ethical behaviour. The problem is whether or not these inclinations and good intentions can be transformed into a real process of institutionalisation. Ethical codes should be formulated and explicitly communicated internally on all hierarchical levels as well as enhancing the corporate image outside the firm.

To this purpose, the Network will be offering consultancy to any business firms wishing to adopt codes of ethics by illustrating the comparative advantages of existing models or assisting in the design of more individualised ethical tools.

To encourage prominent business leaders in their protagonistic role for the promotion of business ethics: I personally feel that a certain protagonism on the part of prominent business leaders who are sensitive to the theme of ethics would prove to be very influential and greatly accelerate the process of promoting ethics in the corporations. The increasing integration of Italian firms with European and extra-European companies should do the rest, as our corporations will find themselves doing business with firms which are already well on their way to doing their business ethically.

References

ASFOR (Associazione per la formazione alla direzione aziendale): 1989, *Il manager di fronte ai problemi etici. Primo rapporto di ricerca*, Milano: IPSOA Scuola d'Impresa.

Banfield, E.C.: 1976, *Le basi morali di una società arretrata*, Il Mulino.

Etica degli Affari, Rivista di informazione e ricerca su argomenti connessi alla valutazione morale dell'attività economica, Milano 1988 ss.

NOTE ON THE CONTRIBUTORS

José Aguilá is President of IOR Consulting S.A. in Barcelona, Spain, and former President of FEACO (Federation of the European Management Consultancy Associations). He has qualifications in engineering (Barcelona), management (IESE, University of Navarra) and business administration (Harvard University).

François Ailleret is Deputy Director General of Electricité de France. He is a graduate of Ecole Polytechnique and Ecole Nationale des Ponts et des Chaussées. His professional activities include experiences in French technical co-operation (Ivory Coast), in the services of the French Ministère de l'Equipement (Lille, France), and in the management of the Aéroports de Paris and Electricité de France.

Brenda Almond is Reader in Philosophy and Education, and Director of the Social Values Research Centre at the University of Hull, UK. She is joint editor of the Journal of Applied Philosophy and chair of the Society for Applied Philosophy. Her books include *Moral Concerns* (1987) and *The Philosophical Quest* (1990).

Antonio Argandoña is Professor of Economics at IESE, University of Navarra. He received his Doctorate in Economics from the University of Barcelona, Spain, and has been Professor of Economics at the Universities of Barcelona and Málaga. He is a member of the Executive Committee of EBEN. His publications include *Work, economics and ethics* (1987), *Relationships between economics and ethics* (1989), and several books and articles.

John H. Barnett is Associate Professor at the Whittemore School of Business and Economics, University of New Hampshire, USA. His publications include *Strategic Management Concepts and Cases* (1988), *Strategic Management Text and Concepts* (1989), *Cases in Strategic Management* (1989) and numerous articles.

Miquel Bastons is Professor of Philosophy at the University of Navarra and Director of the Research Department of the Permanent Seminar "Enterprise and Humanism" in Pamplona, Spain. He did his doctoral studies in philosophy at the University of Münster, FRG, and at the University of Navarra, Spain, and in economics and business administration at IESE, Barcelona. He published *Knowledge and Freedom. Kantian Theory of the Action* (1989).

Norman E. Bowie is Professor of Corporate Responsibility at the University of Minnesota, USA. He received his Ph.D. from the University of Rochester. He is a member of the advisory boards for ethics projects sponsored by Arthur Anderson and Citicorp and has published numerous books and articles: *Business Ethics* (co-author, second edition), *Ethical Theory and Business* (co-editor, third edition), and other books on professional ethics and political philosophy.

Colin Boyd is Associate Professor of Management at the College of Commerce, University of Saskatchewan, Saskatoon, Canada.

Joanne B. Ciulla is Senior Fellow in the Department of Legal Studies and the Department of Management at The Wharton School of the University of Pennsylvania, Philadelphia, USA. She received her Ph.D. in philosophy from the Temple University. She teaches courses in business ethics and management in the graduate and executive programmes and is currently writing a book on the meaning of work.

Juan Cruz Cruz is Associate Professor of History of the Philosophy in the University of Navarra. He has a Doctorate in Philosophy in the University of Navarra (1967) and did postdoctorate studies in contemporary philosophy in the Federal Republic of Germany (1968, 1970). His research deals with the philosophy of history and the ethics of social phenomena. His books include *Hombre e historia en Vico*, *Existencia y nihilismo*, *Las coordenadas del pensamiento clásico*, *Libertad en el tiempo* and *El sentido del curso histórico*, as well as numerous articles. He is the Secretary of *Anuario Filosófico* of the University of Navarra and Member of the Regional Parliament.

Richard T. De George is University Distinguished Professor of Philosophy and Courtesy Professor of Business Administration at the University of Kansas, Lawrence, USA. He received his Ph.D. in philosophy from Yale University. He holds many editorial positions and is the author of numerous books and articles including: *Ethics, Free Enterprise and Public Policy* (contributing co-editor, 1978), *Nature and Limits of Authority* (1985), *Business Ethics* (third edition 1990). He is presently working on a book *Competing With Integrity in International Business*.

Wisse Dekker is Chairman of the Supervisory Board of N.V. Philips' Gloeilampen-fabrieken (The Netherlands) and Chairman of the European Round Table of Industrialists. He was in charge of numerous high functions of the Philips organisation over more then twenty years in the Far East. He holds honorary doctorates from the University of Strathclyde and from Delft University of Technology. He has been visiting Professor of International Management at Leiden University since 1986. He holds a number of honours.

Philippe de Woot is Professor at the Catholic University of Louvain, Belgium. He has doctorates in law and in economics and holds an honorary doctorate from the University of Bologna. He is a member of the International Academy of Management. His field of research and teaching includes "Strategic Management" and "The 'Raison d'être' of the enterprise".

John Donaldson is a Graduate in Philosophy, Politics and Economics of Oxford University. He is a business writer, researcher and consultant, and chairman of the Centre for Service Management Studies, an independent, non-profit research company in Berkshire, UK. His books include *Key Issues in Business Ethics* (1989), *Pay Differentials* (1985). He is currently writing a book on *European Cases in Business Ethics*. He provides teaching in business ethics to several universities.

Thomas W. Dunfee is Kolodny Professor of Social Responsibility and Professor and Chair of Legal Studies at The Wharton School of the University of Pennsylvania,

Philadelphia. He is currently the President of the American Business Law Association and teaches courses on business ethics and commercial law at The Wharton School. He is the author of numerous books and articles including the widely distributed Wharton report advocating integration of business ethics coverage into MBA programmes. He has consulted for many companies, government agencies and law firms.

Georges Enderle is Privatdozent for Business Ethics at the University of St. Gallen, Switzerland. He holds licentiates in philosophy (Munich) and theology (Lyon), and a doctorate in economics (Fribourg). He is a member of the Executive Committee of EBEN and the author of *Sicherung des Existenzminimums im nationalen und internationalen Kontext - eine wirtschaftsethische Studie* (1987), *Wirtschaftsethik im Werden* (1988), and contributing editor of *Ethik und Wirtschaftswissenschaft* (1985). He has written various articles on business ethics and is presently working on a research project on "Corporate Ethics in the International Context".

Erwin A. Fröhlich is Director of the Institute of Small Business Research affiliated to the University of Economics, Vienna, Austria. He received his doctorate in economics from the University of Economics, Vienna. His books include *Führung kleiner und mittlerer Unternehmer* (1984), *Werte und Typen mittelständischer Unternehmer* (1988; co-author).

Jonathan L. Gorman is Acting Head of the Department of Philosophy and Senior Lecturer in Philosophy at The Queen's University of Belfast, Northern Ireland. He received his Ph.D. in philosophy from the University of Cambridge. He is author of academic books and articles in ethics, philosophy of law, of economics, of politics, and of history.

Marvin J. Karson is Professor of Business Statistics and Professor of Management at the Whittemore School of Business and Economics, The University of New Hampshire, USA. His Ph.D. is in statistics from North Carolina State University. He is the author of *Multivariate Statistical Methods* (1982) and has published in several professional and scholarly journals in both the statistics and applied statistics literature.

Raymond A. Konopka is Professor of Management Control and Accounting at the Instituto de Empresa, Madrid, Spain, and Bond University, Australia. He received his Ph.D. in management control from the University of Navarra (IESE). He is a certified public accountant and chartered accountant. He has published *Deviant Virtue: Corporate Control and Innovative Behaviour* (1989) and various articles in the area of management control and innovative behaviour in corporate organisations.

Francisco López-Frías is Professor of Ethics and Political Philosophy at the University of Barcelona, Spain. He has a doctorate in philosophy. His books include *Principios de Deontología Profesional* (1984), *Etica y Política. En torno al pensamiento de J. Ortega y Gasset* (1985), *Filosofía de Hispanoamérica. Aproximaciones al panorama actual* (1987), *Cincuentenario de la muerte de Unamuno* (1988).

Patrick W. Maclagan is Lecturer at the School of Management in the University of Hull, UK. He had ten years' industrial and commercial experience before entering academic life. He received his diplomas in management studies and administration and his MSc for research in organisational behaviour from the University of Strathclyde. He has written several articles on organisational behaviour, management development and ethics.

Jack Mahoney is a Graduate of Glasgow University as well as being a Jesuit priest. He is Professor of Moral and Social Theology at King's College in the University of London and Professor of Commerce at Gresham College in the City of London. Since 1987 he has been founder director of King's College Business Ethics Research Centre. His recent major publications include *The Making of Moral Theology* (1987) and *Teaching Business Ethics in the USA and Europe* (1990). He writes, lectures, and broadcasts frequently on business ethics.

Domènec Melé is Director of the Business Ethics Department at IESE, Barcelona, Spain. He received his Ph.D. in industrial engineering from the Polytechnic University of Catalonia and his Ph.D. in moral theology from the University of Navarra. He has published numerous articles on business ethics and Christian social ethics, as well as, earlier, on engineering topics.

Sara Morrison is an Executive Director of The General Electric Company p.l.c. (GEC), London, and also a non-Executive Director of the Abbey National p.l.c. She was Chairperson of the National Council for Voluntary Organisations and her roles have included numerous cultural and social councils. She is a member of the Video Appeals Committee, a companion of British Institute of Management and a member of several other public institutions.

Vicente Mortes Alfonso is President of Nestlé España, A.E.P.A., President of La Seda de Barcelona, S.A., and of other corporations. He received his doctorate in engineering from the Escuela Superior de Madrid, Spain, and his diploma in business administration from IESE, University of Navarra. He has been engaged in numerous academic, corporate and cultural activities and holds a number of honours. He has published various articles on issues in business, management, civil engineering, textile and food industry, etc.

Juan Antonio Pérez López is Professor of Organisational Theory at IESE, University of Navarra, Barcelona, where he was the Dean from 1978 to 1984. He has a Doctorate in Business Administration from Harvard University. He teaches Organisational Theory and Theory of the Human Action at IESE and at the Faculty of Philosophy of the University of Navarra. His current research includes a book on *Elements for a Theory of Human Action,* the first volume is currently being published.

John Sheldrake is Principal Lecturer at the City of London Polytechnic. He has studied at Brunel University and at the University of Kent at Canterbury. He has published widely in the fields of labour relations with particular reference to the public sector. He is currently completing a book on *Government Policy and Industrial Relations Since 1890.*

Monique R. Siegel is initiator and organiser of the International Management-Symposium for Women and owner and managing director of MRS Management Related Services AG in Zurich, Switzerland, a management consultant firm specialising in the organisation of symposia, seminars and executive training. She received her Ph.D. from New York University. She was founder of AKAD-FEMINA, the first women's institute of higher learning in Europe, and has published *Frauenkarrieren zwischen Tradition und Innovation* (1989).

Ceferí Soler is Professor of Organisational Behaviour at the Escuela Superior de Administración y Dirección de Empresas (ESADE), Barcelona, Spain. His educational background is in psychology (University of Barcelona) and management (INSEAD). He has published *Ethics in the Leadership. Short-term* (1988) and *The New Role of the Personnel Manager* (1989).

Mario Unnia is Managing Director of Prospecta Srl., Milan, Italy, and Editor of *Etica degli Affari* (Italian journal of business ethics). He graduated in Political Sciences from the University of Turin.

Subject Index

Accounting 50-52, 56
  oriented, corporation 51
Acquired Immune Deficiency Syndrome
  (AIDS) 23
Act, Foreign Corrupt Practices 31
Alienation 50, 51, 53-55, 60, 114
  work 52, 66
Altruism 186, 187
Approach, decision-making 96
  stakeholder 106, 109
Attitude 1, 108, 114, 115
  employees 60
  management 54
  personal conviction 26
Authoritarianism, management 173 176
Authority, manager 176, 244
Awareness of ethical issues, ethics 73, 74

Board of directors, responsibility 136, 139,
  142, 145, 146
Bounded discretion, decision-making 201
  rationality, concept of 198, 199
Bureaucratisation, corporation 44, 58
Business ethics, aspects of 2
  challenge 2, 3
  corporation 243, 244
  debate 1, 3, 28, 69, 151, 152
  definition 13
  dialogue 1,2
  good citizenship 241
  in Italy 247-249
  interdisciplinary approach 5-7
  practical perspective 7
  problem-oriented approach 3-5
  promotion 3
  theoretical perspective 7
  theory-practice relationship 25, 30
Business, relation between ethics and 106
Business strategy, corporation 21, 22, 102, 189
  definition 189

Career advancement, strategy 222
Cartesian rationalism 96
Ceiling, pay rise 74
Choice assumption, self-goal 36
Closed organisation, corporation 44-47
Closed view, human being 99
Code of conduct, corporation 15, 16, 18, 22, 23

Code of ethics, introduction 248, 249
Code of morality 41
Code of practice 73, 74, 75
Collectivism, gang 91
  mob 91
Communication, manager worker 47, 48
Competition, corporation 79, 151-153 passim
Concept of bounded rationality 198, 199
Confidentiality, internal whistle-blowing
  system 136, 137
Consumer manipulation, corporation 13
Contract, labour 6, 119, 120, 122, 124, 125,
  127
Control paradigm, management 49, 50
Control system, management 5, 44, 49, 50-53,
  55-60
Co-operative activity, employees 110, 111,
  151-153
Corporate aim, corporation 12, 13
  culture, corporation 102, 165, 168
  decision-making, corporation 7
    women 153, 165-167
  effectiveness, corporation 4-6, 35, 37, 41, 42,
    65, 66, 67
    women 161
  environment, corporation 52, 53
  ethical policy, corporation 7
  ethics, corporation 19, 20, 23, 26, 102
  performance, corporation 63
  responsibility, corporation 11, 16, 17, 20, 21,
    52, 55, 59, 102, 109, 162
  social responsibility movement, corporation
    101
  strategy, corporation 59
    management 189 190
  value, corporation 27
  whistle-blowing, corporation 6
Corporation, accounting oriented 51
  activities 130
  bureaucratisation 44, 58
  business ethics 243, 244
  business strategy 21, 22, 102, 189
  closed organisation 44-47
  code of conduct 15, 16, 18, 22, 23
  competition 79
  consumer manipulation 13
  corporate aim 12, 13
    culture 102, 165, 168